CASEBOOK SERIES

JANE AUSTEN: *Emma* David Lodge
JANE AUSTEN: *'Northanger Abbey'* & *'Persuasion'* B. C. Southam
JANE AUSTEN: *'Sense and Sensibility'*, *'Pride and Prejudice'* & *'Mansfield Park'*
   B. C. Southam
BECKETT: *Waiting for Godot* Ruby Cohn
WILLIAM BLAKE: *Songs of Innocence and Experience* Margaret Bottrall
CHARLOTTE BRONTË: *'Jane Eyre'* & *'Villette'* Miriam Allott
EMILY BRONTË: *Wuthering Heights* Miriam Allott
BROWNING: *'Men and Women'* & *Other Poems* J. R. Watson
CHAUCER: *Canterbury Tales* J. J. Anderson
COLERIDGE: *'The Ancient Mariner'* & *Other Poems* Alun R. Jones & W. Tydeman
CONRAD: *'Heart of Darkness'*, *'Nostromo'* & *'Under Western Eyes'* C. B. Cox
CONRAD: *The Secret Agent* Ian Watt
DICKENS: *Bleak House* A. E. Dyson
DICKENS: *'Hard Times'*, *'Great Expectations'* & *'Our Mutual Friend'* Norman Page
DICKENS: *'Dombey and Son'* & *'Little Dorrit'* Alan Shelston
DONNE: *Songs and Sonets* Julian Lovelock
GEORGE ELIOT: *Middlemarch* Patrick Swinden
GEORGE ELIOT: *'The Mill on the Floss'* & *'Silas Marner'* R. P. Draper
T. S. ELIOT: *Four Quartets* Bernard Bergonzi
T. S. ELIOT: *'Prufrock'*, *'Gerontion'* & *'Ash Wednesday'* B. C. Southam
T. S. ELIOT: *The Waste Land* C. B. Cox & Arnold P. Hinchliffe
T. S. ELIOT: *Plays* Arnold P. Hinchliffe
HENRY FIELDING: *Tom Jones* Neil Compton
E.M. FORSTER: *A Passage to India* Malcolm Bradbury
WILLIAM GOLDING: *Novels 1954–64* Norman Page
HARDY: *The Tragic Novels* R. P. Draper
HARDY: *Poems* James Gibson & Trevor Johnson
HARDY: *Three Pastoral Novels* R. P. Draper
GERARD MANLEY HOPKINS: *Poems* Margaret Bottrall
HENRY JAMES: *'Washington Square'* & *'The Portrait of a Lady'* Alan Shelton
JONSON: *Volpone* Jonas A. Barish
JONSON: *'Every Man in his Humour'* & *'The Alchemist'* R. V. Holdsworth
JAMES JOYCE: *'Dubliners'* & *'A Portrait of the Artist as a Young Man'* Morris Beja
KEATS: *Odes* G.S. Fraser
KEATS: *Narrative Poems* John Spencer Hill
D.H. LAWRENCE: *Sons and Lovers* Gamini Salgado
D.H. LAWRENCE: *'The Rainbow'* & *'Women in Love'* Colin Clarke
LOWRY: *Under the Volcano* Gordon Bowker
MARLOWE: *Doctor Faustus* John Jump
MARLOWE: *'Tamburlaine the Great'*, *'Edward II'* & *'The Jew of Malta'* J. R. Brown
MARLOWE: *Poems* Arthur Pollard
MAUPASSANT: *In the Hall of Mirrors* T. Harris
MILTON: *Paradise Lost* A. E. Dyson & Julian Lovelock
O'CASEY: *'Juno and the Paycock'*, *'The Plough and the Stars'* & *'The Shadow of a*
   Gunman' Ronald Ayling
EUGENE O'NEILL: *Three Plays* Normand Berlin
JOHN OSBORNE: *Look Back in Anger* John Russell Taylor
PINTER: *'The Birthday Party'* & *Other Plays* Michael Scott
POPE: *The Rape of the Lock* John Dixon Hunt
SHAKESPEARE: *A Midsummer Night's Dream* Antony Price
SHAKESPEARE: *Antony and Cleopatra* John Russell Brown
SHAKESPEARE: *Coriolanus* B. A. Brockman

The Romantic Imagination

A CASEBOOK

EDITED BY

JOHN SPENCER HILL

MACMILLAN

First published 1977 by
THE MACMILLAN PRESS LTD
Houndmills, Basingstoke, Hampshire RG21 2XS
and London
Companies and representatives
throughout the world

ISBN 0–333–21235–5

Printed in Hong Kong

Fifth reprint 1993

CONTENTS

ACKNOWLEDGEMENTS

The editor and publishers wish to thank the following who have kindly given permission for the use of copyright material: J. E. Baker, 'Imagination . . .', from *Shelley's Platonic Answer to a Platonic Attack on Poetry* (1965), by permission of the University of Iowa Press. W. J. Bate, extract from 'Negative Capability', ch. 10 of *John Keats* (1963), by permission of the author and Harvard University Press. C. M. Bowra, extract from *The Romantic Imagination* (1950), by permission of the Oxford University Press. David Lee Clark, extract from *Shelley's Prose, or The Trumpet of a Prophecy* (1954, corrected ed. 1966), by permission of The University of New Mexico Press. Barbara Hardy, article, 'Distinction Without Difference, Coleridge's Fancy and Imagination', in *Essays in Criticism*, 1 (1951), by permission of the author and editors of *Essays in Criticism*. James A. W. Heffernan, extract from *Wordsworth's Theory of Poetry*, © 1969 by Cornell University, reprinted by permission of Cornell University Press. Graham Hough, extract from *The Romantic Poets* (1953, 2nd ed. 1957, reprinted 1970), by permission of the author and Hutchinson Publishing Group Ltd. J. R. de J. Jackson, extract from *Method and Imagination in Coleridge's Criticism* (1969), by permission of Routledge & Kegan Paul Ltd. John Shawcross, extract from Introduction to his edition of *Biographia Literaria* by S. T. Coleridge, 2 vols (1907), by permission of the Oxford University Press. Clarence DeWitt Thorpe, extract from *The Mind of John Keats* (New York: Russell & Russell, 1926, 1964), by permission of the publisher. René Wellek, extract from *A History of Modern Criticism*, by permission of Yale University Press Ltd. Basil Willey, extract from essay on Coleridge in *Nineteenth Century Studies* (1949), by permission of the author and Chatto & Windus Ltd. The publishers have made every effort to trace the copyright-holders but if they have inadvertently overlooked any they will be pleased to make the necessary arrangement at the first opportunity.

GENERAL EDITOR'S PREFACE

The Casebook series, launched in 1968, has become a well-regarded library of critical studies. The central concern of the series remains the 'single-author' volume, but suggestions from the academic community have led to an extension of the original plan, to include occasional volumes on such general themes as literary 'schools' and genres.

Each volume in the central category deals either with one well-known and influential work by an individual author, or with closely related works by one writer. The main section consists of critical readings, mostly modern, collected from books and journals. A selection of reviews and comments by the author's contemporaries is also included, and sometimes comment from the author himself. The Editor's introduction charts the reputation of the work or works from the first appearance to the present time.

Volumes in the 'general themes' category are variable in structure but follow the basic purpose of the series in presenting an integrated selection of readings, with an Introduction which explores the theme and discusses the literary and critical issues involved.

A single volume can represent no more than a small selection of critical opinions. Some critics are excluded for reasons of space, and it is hoped that readers will pursue the suggestions for further reading in the Select Bibliography. Other contributions are severed from their original context, to which some readers may wish to turn. Indeed, if they take a hint from the critics represented here, they certainly will.

A. E. DYSON

INTRODUCTION

In neoclassical literary theory the meaning of the term *Imagination* is determined by its association with the empirical philosophies of Hobbes, Locke, Hume, Hartley and others. In these 'mechanical' systems the human mind is described as being merely the passive recorder of sense impressions (especially those originating in sight); 'images' or replicas of original sense impressions are stored in the memory, whence – in the acts of thinking or reflection – they are recalled and combined with other stored-up 'images' by the faculty of association. William Godwin provides the following succinct statement of empirical epistemology:

The human mind, so far as we are acquainted with it, is nothing else but a faculty of perception. All our knowledge, all our ideas, every thing we possess as intelligent beings, comes from impression. All the minds that exist, set out from absolute ignorance. They received first one impression, then a second. As the impressions became more numerous, and were stored up by the help of memory, and combined by the faculty of association, so the experience increased, and with the experience the knowledge, the wisdom, every thing that distinguishes man from what we understand by a 'clod of the valley'.[1]

In empiricist systems such as this, the Imagination or Fancy (the terms are usually not distinguished) is endowed with a two-fold function. First, it is thought to be a mode of memory, that is, the mental faculty which recalls images from the memory and so represents sense objects not actually present. Hobbes defines Imagination as 'nothing but *decaying sense*' and concludes that 'imagination and memory are but one thing, which for divers considerations has divers names';[2] and Dryden in a similar vein writes that 'the faculty of imagination . . . like a nimble spaniel, beats over and ranges through the field of memory, till it springs the quarry it hunted after. . . . It is some lively or apt description, dressed in such colours of speech, that it sets before your eyes the absent object, as perfectly, and more delightfully than nature.'[3] Second, the Imagination is described as the power by which originally distinct impressions are welded together to form images of things that have no existence in the sense: for example, the image of a horse combined with that of a man yields a hybrid creation known as a centaur. The production of mythological grotesques — chimeras, satyrs and similar hybrids having no precedent in sense experience — was often adduced as an illustration of the way in which Imagination combined distinct sensations in order to fabricate its creations. In these terms, then, the imagination is a *combining* but not a truly *creative* faculty. According to William Duff, the Imagination, 'by its plastic power of inventing new associations of ideas, and of combining them with infinite variety, is enabled to present a creation of its own'.[4] In a similar way, Dugald Stewart limits the Imagination's 'creative' power to its ability 'to make a selection of qualities and of circumstances, from a variety of different objects, and by combining and disposing these to form a new creation of its own'.[5] Perhaps Samuel Johnson best sums up the two functions of the neoclassical Imagination which I have been discussing when he defines Imagination as 'Fancy; the power of forming ideal pictures; the power of representing things absent to one's self or others'.[6]

Whereas neoclassical criticism tended to think of Imagination as a faculty for combining and associating ideas, the Romantic poets and theorists are unanimous in claiming for it a much more exalted position. For them, the Imagination is a truly *creative* faculty; rather than simply rearranging materials fed to it by the senses and the memory, the Imagination is a shaping and ordering power, a 'modifying' power which colours objects of sense with the mind's own light:

> An auxiliar light
> Came from my mind which on the setting sun
> Bestow'd new splendor, the melodious birds,
> The gentle breezes, fountains that ran on,
> Murmuring so sweetly in themselves, obey'd
> A like dominion; and the midnight storm
> Grew darker in the presence of my eye.[7]

Thus a 'perception' – that is, the product resulting from the modified combination of perceiver and thing perceived – is neither a subject (perceiver) nor an object (thing perceived) exclusively, but is the most original union of both.[8] By breaking down the usual connections between things and unifying them into new wholes, the Imagination synthesises disparate elements in order to generate a new reality. It is not, as it was for neoclassical critics, a mechanical power ('aggregative and associative'); it is rather a vital and organic faculty which permits the mind to see beneath the transitory surface of the material world – to see, that is, into the life of things and to perceive the intimate relationship between the perceiving mind and the objects of its contemplation. It is in this 'new and intense faith in the imagination', as Douglas Bush has remarked, that we find 'the common denominator of the greatest poets' of the Romantic period.[9] C. M. Bowra, in *The Romantic Imagination*, the first chapter of which is reprinted in Part Two below, demonstrates that, 'despite significant differences on points of detail', Blake, Coleridge, Wordsworth, Keats and Shelley are to be distinguished from eighteenth-century poets by 'the importance which they attached to the imagination and [by] the special view which they held of it' (p. 87).

*

That Coleridge has been the most influential of the English Romantic critics is virtually an axiom of modern literary criticism. It was not ever thus. Earlier in this century it was fashionable to be condescending toward him, to say that his bequest to posterity consisted in 'a handful of golden poems, an emptiness in the hearts of a few friends, and a will-o'-the-wisp light for bemused thinkers'.[10] Shaking his head sadly over so tragic a waste of talent, the analyst would lament that one so richly endowed as Coleridge should at the same time have been so rudderless. Such a view of his personality reflected adversely on his contributions to literary theory, and the customary scapegoat was the Fancy – Imagination distinction. Irving Babbitt, for instance, complained that Coleridge had never succeeded 'in disengaging his theory of the imagination sufficiently

from the transcendental mist' of German metaphysics; Lascelles
Abercrombie, convinced that 'fancy is nothing but a degree of
imagination', declared that 'the faculty of fancy does not exist: it
is one of Coleridge's chimeras, of which he kept a whole stable';
and even a more sympathetic commentator like John Living-
stone Lowes conceded that 'Fancy and Imagination are not two
powers at all, but one'.[11] F. L. Lucas's curmudgeonly assessment
represents the most extreme position: 'It still seems to me
unnecessary to assume two perfectly distinct "faculties", Fancy
and Imagination. . . . Coleridge's whole theory seems to me an
example of that barren type of classification so dear to those who
believe that if they can invent a few transcendental pigeon-holes,
the Holy Spirit of poetry will descend to nest in them.'[12] Some
recent criticism – savouring much less of *ad hominem*
posteriority – perpetuates the view that the distinction is 'celebrated but useless'. Norman Fruman, for example, argues that
Coleridge's statements on Imagination are best regarded, not as
serious contributions to aesthetic theory, but rather as 'prose
poems celebrating an abstraction'.[13]

The majority of Coleridge's commentators, however, have
defended the critical significance and utility of his theory of
Imagination and have maintained that, despite its fragmentary
nature, it is possible to reconstruct his aesthetic system (at least in
its essentials) from the hints scattered through his writings. The
'standard' explanation of the terms *Fancy* and *Imagination* is that
given by Shawcross in 1907 (see below, Part Two); since that
time, critics have been engaged either in qualifying or in
elaborating the implications of Shawcross's explanation. I. A.
Richards has attempted to make Coleridge's distinction the basis
of a practical aesthetic; and, despite Richards's appropriation of
Coleridge for private ends and despite his desire to jettison the
metaphysical matrix of Coleridge's theory, the attempt is
remarkably successful.[14] In an important paper, W. J. Bate has
demonstrated that Coleridge's conception of Imagination can be
fully understood only when it is set within the framework of his
psychological theory, where Imagination serves as a bridge
between the various faculties of the mind.[15] J. V. Baker has
written an important study of 'the role of the unconscious in

Coleridge's theory of the imagination . . . and the extent to which he admitted association of ideas as fecundating the poetic process'.[16] Other critics have traced the extent and nature of Coleridge's indebtedness to the theories of Imagination of earlier writers — of Plato and Plotinus, for example, and of the Cambridge Platonists; of neoclassical theoreticians like Dryden, Addison and Shaftesbury; of German metaphysicians like Kant, Schelling, Fichte and Tetens. Still other readers have undertaken to apply Coleridge's theory of Imagination to his poetry; see, for example: Robert Penn Warren's essay on 'The Ancient Mariner' (and Humphry House's qualifying response); R. H. Fogle's paper on 'Dejection: An Ode'; Alethea Hayter's remarks on 'Kubla Khan'; and J. D. Boulger's reading of the conversation poems.[17]

Since the variety of approaches to Coleridge's theory of Imagination is truly staggering, it has not been possible to offer a properly *representative* selection of modern criticism in the following pages. Considerations of space and audience have led me to centre the four critical selections on the Fancy – Imagination distinction itself – a distinction which, as J. R. de J. Jackson observes (below, Part Two), 'is the most exhaustively studied passage in all Coleridge's criticism'. The contribution by Shawcross is the classic exposition of Coleridge's debt to Schelling and Kant, and Shawcross also provides what is still the prevailing explanation of the terms *Fancy* and *Imagination* in Coleridge's aesthetic theory. Basil Willey defends the critical utility of the distinction and provides a helpful and straightforward explication of the meaning of the terms. Barbara Hardy sees 'the waste-bin of Fancy' as the scapegoat of Coleridge's aesthetic system and she maintains that the distinction between the two faculties was deliberately exaggerated in order to glorify Imagination at Fancy's expense; Jackson, on the other hand, sets out 'to restore Fancy to the dignity and power with which Coleridge originally endowed it – to present it once again as an integral part of great poetry, and to reject the too common misconception of it as a faculty appropriate to inferior verse only'.

*

Wordsworth, who did not share Coleridge's delight in theory and abstraction, was more concerned with practical demonstration than with descriptive theory: 'it was Mr. Wordsworth's purpose', Coleridge wrote (below, Part One, section I. IV.), 'to consider the influences of fancy and imagination as they are manifested in poetry, and from the different effects to conclude their diversity in kind; while it is my object to investigate the seminal principle, and then from the kind to deduce the degree'. Given Wordsworth's *practical* interest in the Imagination, it is not surprising that of his three most important statements about this faculty two should be in verse (the Simplon Pass and Mount Snowdon episodes in *The Prelude*) and the third a prose preface arguing the distinctions in poetic practice between Fancy and Imagination, and defending the classification of certain of his poems under these headings. It is also not surprising that Wordsworth, a poet rather than a poetic theorist, should have less to say on the Imagination than Coleridge did; it has, therefore, been possible to represent Wordsworth's views more fully than Coleridge's in Part One below.

One important branch of Wordsworth criticism was very firmly established in 1879 by Matthew Arnold, who declared that Wordsworth's philosophy was an impediment to the appreciation of his poetry: 'we must be on our guard against the Wordsworthians, if we want to secure for Wordsworth his due rank as a poet. The Wordsworthians are apt to praise him for the wrong things, and to lay far too much stress upon what they call his philosophy. His poetry is the reality, his philosophy . . . is the illusion. . . . We cannot do him justice until we dismiss his formal philosophy.'[18] Arnold's viewpoint has been reasserted by modern critics like Helen Darbishire and John F. Danby,[19] and F. W. Bateson has gone so far as to say that 'Wordsworth was not primarily a thinker but a feeler' and that 'the determining events of his career and the sources of all that is essential in his poetry were the personal tragedies, the anguished decisions, the half-conscious half-animal terrors and ecstasies, and *not* the discoveries of the intellect'.[20] Attitudes like these quite naturally preclude the possibility of considering Wordsworth's theories of Imagination in any serious way.

There is, however, another branch of Wordsworth criticism which maintains that the poet's 'philosophy' is essential to a proper understanding of his poetry. But there is little agreement among those subscribing to this viewpoint as to the precise nature and relative importance of Wordsworth's 'philosophy'. Even when we restrict discussion to the Wordsworthian Imagination and set other aspects of his philosophy to one side, the variety of critical positions is bewildering. A. C. Bradley, for example, who wishes to stress the mystic and visionary elements of Wordsworth's poetry, declares that 'his poetry is immensely interesting as an imaginative expression of the same mind which, in his day, produced in Germany great philosophies. His poetic experience, his intuitions, his single thoughts, even his large views, correspond in a striking way, sometimes in a startling way, with ideas methodically developed by Kant, Schelling, Hegel, Schopenhauer.'[21] Geoffrey Hartman also stresses the visionary element in Wordsworth; however, defining Imagination as 'consciousness of self raised to apocalyptic pitch', Hartman treats Wordsworth as a would-be visionary poet, a Blake *manqué*, prevented from achieving his aim because he was unable to resolve the opposition between Imagination and Nature by fusing 'self' and the 'principle of things' in unmediated contact.[22] Other commentators have sought to trace the influence of specific writers or schools of thought in Wordsworth's theory of the Imagination: Emile Legouis contends that he is 'a son of Rousseau'; Arthur Beatty stresses his debt to Hartley's associationist psychology; N. P. Stallknecht points to the influence of Jacob Boehme.[23] A number of other examples might be cited.

It is generally agreed, however, that Wordsworth's greatest debt is to Coleridge. Moreover, apart from C. D. Thorpe[24] (who finds a deep and abiding rift between the two theories of Imagination), most modern commentators agree that 'Wordsworth's definition of imagination is substantially the same as that of Coleridge.'[25] 'Basically,' writes J. A. W. Hefferman, 'the two men agree – even though they may not have realized it themselves. The difference between their distinctions [between Imagination and Fancy] is not so much in principle as in perspective and emphasis.'[26] The critics, then, stress that

Wordsworth's definitions of the terms *Fancy* and *Imagination* are essentially identical with Coleridge's, although there are some significant differences in the implications and practical application of these terms. Herbert Read spoke for many when he declared that 'Wordsworth did not, like Coleridge, develop a coherent theory of the imagination; and in so far as his views were systematic (e.g. in the distinction drawn between fancy and imagination), they were derived from Coleridge. What Wordsworth contributed to the discussion (which extends far beyond Coleridge and involves the whole transcendental philosophy developed by Kant, Fichte, Schlegel and Schelling) was a realistic insight into the workings of the mind of the poet.'[27]

As with Coleridge, so also with Wordsworth it is impossible in the space available here to offer a properly representative sample of modern criticism; the two selections reprinted in Part Two provide no more than an introduction to the topic and its problems. René Wellek sees Wordsworth's literary criticism as transitional, looking back to the eighteenth century as well as forward to the nineteenth; he also points out that Wordsworth gives different definitions of the Imagination in different places, and he warns that one cannot justifiably treat poetic statements on Imagination in the same way as one does a passage of analytical prose. The nature and importance of Wordsworth's 'transforming imagination' are discussed in the passage reprinted from J. A. W. Heffernan, who has a good deal more to say about the Wordsworthian imagination than it has been possible to reproduce here; I must content myself with referring the reader to his full account.

*

It is much easier to deal fairly here with Keats and Shelley than with Coleridge and Wordsworth. This is so, not only because Keats and Shelley have less to say about the Imagination than do their two older contemporaries, but also because their views and theories of Imagination have attracted less critical attention from twentieth-century commentators than have those of Coleridge and Wordsworth.

To quote the central passages from Keats's famous letter on the Imagination to Bailey (November 1817), and then – as H. W. Garrod does – to assert that 'it is all of it mere Wordsworthianism',[28] is to distort and to oversimplify what Keats is saying. That Keats owes much to Wordsworth is beyond dispute; but he also is indebted to Coleridge, to Hazlitt, and to others as well. It needs also to be said that what Keats borrows from others he adapts to his own purposes; he stamps all with the seal of his own character and experience. Thus, while his understanding of the poetic Imagination is largely derivative, the elements borrowed from others are synthesised and adapted in such a way that one may legitimately claim that his view is, in a real sense, original. C. L. Finney represents the case more fairly than Garrod when he defines the Keatsian Imagination as 'the faculty by which the negatively capable genius intuits truth'.[29]

In the passage reprinted below from *The Mind of John Keats*, C. D. Thorpe traces Keats's ripening understanding of the poetic Imagination – the development in his thinking from the early escapist statements up to his mature conviction that the creative Imagination is 'a seeing, reconciling, combining force that seizes the old, penetrates beneath its surface, disengages the truth lying slumbering there, and, building afresh, bodies forth anew a reconstructed universe in fair forms of artistic power and beauty'. In the selection reprinted from W. J. Bate's biography of Keats, the discussion centres on the important letters of November – December 1817. Bate discusses the influence of Coleridge, Wordsworth, and (especially) Hazlitt on Keats's maturing aesthetic apprehension, and he examines in detail the place of Imagination in the development of the theory of 'negative capability'.

For Shelley, the Imagination is the most important faculty of the human mind. Unlike the Reason, which is analytic and mechanical, the Imagination is synthetic and organic; moreover, the Imagination works for man's moral good and allows a man to put himself in the place of others. Although all men possess Imagination in some degree, the faculty is pre-eminent in poets. Since Shelley believed Imagination to be 'the great instrument of moral good' and since he defined poetry as 'the expression of the

imagination', it is not difficult to see why he held poetry in such
esteem: poetry is the major instrument in the regeneration of
mankind. W. J. Bate has summarised Shelley's theory of
Imagination and his distinction between Reason and Imagination in the following way:

Reason analyzes; it views things – to use Wordsworth's phrase – 'in
disconnection, dead and spiritless'. . . . The imagination, said Shelley,
thinks in terms of totalities rather than proceeding by artificial analysis;
it grasps the inner activity animating the changing, evolving reality
outside, reacts to the varying crosslights in it, and captures the
qualitative value potential in them. It is in construing this value in
terms of ultimate and universal forms that Shelley reached back to the
Platonic tradition and transcendentalized his romantic, organic theory
of nature. Hence the remark that poetry tries to reveal 'the image [the
organic concreteness] of life expressed in its eternal truth', and that
poets, in disclosing this reality, are the ultimate teachers and 'unacknowledged legislators of the world'. To this aim, Shelley subjoined
another classical tenet: in conveying an awareness of reality in its full
value and meaning, poetry is formative and moral in the highest sense.
And Shelley gave this tenet a characteristically romantic phrasing by
putting it in terms of 'sympathy', though the spirit of what he said is
essentially classical. The 'great secret of morals is love' – it is a 'going
out of one's own nature', a sympathetic identification with others. Now
the 'imagination' is the means by which we do this; and poetry enlarges
the range and scope of the imagination, gives it knowledge and
experience, sharpens its delicacy and readiness to react, and in general
strengthens and exercises this fundamental 'instrument of moral
good'.[30]

Each of the four selections from Shelleyan criticism that are
reprinted in Part Two deals specifically with Shelley's *Defence of
Poetry*. M. T. Solve examines the place of the Imagination in
Shelley's psychology generally; Graham Hough treats Imagination in the course of his discussion of 'Shelley's beliefs about
the nature and functions of poetry' as these are revealed in the
Defence of Poetry. J. E. Baker stresses the Platonism of Shelley's
view of Imagination, and D. L. Clark shuns considerations of
influence and debt in order to emphasise the immediate (and
continuing) sociological significance of Shelley's theory.

I greatly regret that limited space has made it necessary to exclude Blake and Hazlitt. I have tried to remedy these omissions in part by including in the Bibliography a section on each of these two figures; in addition, Blake is discussed at some length in the chapter reprinted from C. M. Bowra's *The Romantic Imagination*, and I have put several of Hazlitt's more important pronouncements on the 'sympathetic imagination' in the notes to Keats's letter to Richard Woodhouse (see below, Part One, section 4. iv.).

The task of selecting modern critical essays has been formidable. I am only too well aware of the many fine papers which it has been necessary to omit; some of these are listed in the Bibliography. In general, my choice of critical essays and passages to be reprinted has been governed by the needs of the undergraduate students for whom this work is primarily intended. For this reason, specialist and highly technical studies have been omitted.

Finally, it should be said that my exclusion of Victorian critics and poetic theorists has been intentional. As critics, the Victorians do little to illuminate what the Romantics meant by Imagination (and Fancy). As theorists in their own right, their claims to our attention here are no stronger. 'Post-romantic theories of imagination and fancy are almost entirely derivative', writes A. H. Warren, Jr, 'and have little or nothing to add to the discoveries of Wordsworth and Coleridge. . . . G. H. Lewes in *The Principles of Success in Literature* (1865) reduced the Imagination to the mere image-making faculty, and E. S. Dallas in the *Poetics* makes an abortive attempt to define imagination in terms of the unconscious activity of the mind. For the rest, criticism merely elaborates on the earlier formulations, introducing minor variations of which the contention that fancy is only a lower degree of imagination is perhaps the most worthy of record.'[31] Those who wish to pursue the post-Romantic imagination might begin with Warren's book, or with chapter 5 ('The Myth of Nature and the Victorian Compromise of the Imagination')[32] of R. A. Forsyth's *The Lost Pattern* (1976), or with E. D. H. Johnson's *The Alien Vision of Victorian Poetry: Sources of the Poetic Imagination in Tennyson, Browning, and Arnold* (1952).

NOTES

1. Godwin, *Enquiry Concerning Political Justice* (1793) I v.
2. Thomas Hobbes, *Leviathan* (1651) I ii.
3. John Dryden, Preface to *Annus Mirabilis* (1667).
4. Duff, *Essay on Original Genius* (1767) quoted in M. H. Abrams, *The Mirror and the Lamp* (1953) p. 362, note 21.
5. Stewart, *Elements of the Philosophy of the Human Mind* (1792) quoted in Abrams, *The Mirror and the Lamp*, p. 162.
6. Johnson, *A Dictionary of the English Language* (1755) s.v. Imagination.
7. Wordsworth, *The Prelude* (1805) II 387–93.
8. I have adapted (and narrowed the scope of) a sentence from Coleridge's *Biographia Literaria*: see below, Part One, section I. VI., thesis VIII.
9. Bush, *English Poetry: The Main Currents from Chaucer to the Present* (1952) p. 112.
10. E. K. Chambers, *Samuel Taylor Coleridge: A Biographical Study* (1938) p. 331.
11. Babbitt, 'The Problem of the Imagination: Coleridge', *On Being Creative and Other Essays* (1932) p. 129; Abercrombie, *The Idea of Great Poetry* (1925) p. 58; Lowes, *The Road to Xanadu* (1927) p. 103.
12. Lucas, *The Decline and Fall of the Romantic Ideal* (1937) pp. 176, 180.
13. Fruman, *Coleridge, The Damaged Archangel* (1972) p. 189.
14. Richards, *Coleridge on Imagination*. (See Bibliography.)
15. Bate, 'Coleridge on the Function of Art'. (See Bibliography.)
16. Baker, *The Sacred River*, p. 4. (See Bibliography.)
17. For Warren and House, see Bibliography. Fogle, 'The Dejection of Coleridge's Ode', *Journal of English Literary History*, XVII (1950) 71–7; Hayter, *Opium and the Romantic Imagination* (1968) pp. 214–24; Boulger, 'Imagination and Speculation in Coleridge's Conversation Poems', *Journal of English and Germanic Philology*, LXIV (1965) 691–711.
18. Arnold, *Essays in Criticism: Second Series* (1888).
19. Darbishire, *The Poet Wordsworth* (1950); Danby, *The Simple Wordsworth* (1960).
20. Bateson, *Wordsworth: A Reinterpretation*, 2nd ed. (1956) p. 40.
21. Bradley, *Oxford Lectures on Poetry* (1961) pp. 129–30. The original lecture was delivered in 1903.
22. Hartman, *Wordsworth's Poetry 1787–1814* (1964) pp. 17, 124, 211, 233.

23. Legouis, *The Early Life of William Wordsworth* (1921) pp. 54–67; Beatty, *William Wordsworth: His Doctrine and Art in Their Historical Relations* (1922) pp. 137–69; Stallknecht, *Strange Seas of Thought* (1966) pp. 23–4, 37–40, 87–8, 204–6.

24. Thorpe, 'The Imagination: Coleridge *versus* Wordsworth', *Philological Quarterly*, XVIII (1939) 1–18.

25. A. E. Powell, *The Romantic Theory of Poetry* (1926; reissued 1962) p. 145.

26. Heffernan, *Wordsworth's Theory of Poetry: The Transforming Imagination* (1969) p. 189.

27. Read, *Wordsworth* (1930; repr. 1968) pp. 186–7.

28. Garrod, *Keats* (1926; 2nd ed. 1939) p. 38. For the letter to Bailey, see below, Part One, section 4. II.

29. Finney, *The Evolution of Keats's Poetry*, 2 vols (1936; reissued 1963) vol. I, p. 243.

30. Bate, *Criticism: The Major Texts* (1952) p. 428.

31. Warren, *English Poetic Theory 1825–1865* (1950) pp. 19–20.

32. This chapter first appeared (with the same title) as an article in *A Journal of English Literary History*, XXXI (1964) 213–40.

PART ONE

Extracts from the Poets Correspondence and Comment: Coleridge, Wordsworth, Keats and Shelley

1. SAMUEL TAYLOR COLERIDGE

1. AN EARLY VIEW OF FANCY AND IMAGINATION

It has struck [me] with great force lately, that the Psalms afford a most compleat answer to those, who state the Jehovah of the Jews, as a personal & national God – & the Jews, as differing from the Greeks, only in calling the minor Gods, Cherubim & Seraphim – & confining the word God to their Jupiter. It must occur to every Reader that the Greeks in their religious poems address always the Numina Loci,[1] the Genii, the Dryads, the Naiads, &c &c – All natural Objects were *dead* – mere hollow Statues – but there was a Godkin or Goddessling *included* in each – In the Hebrew Poetry you find nothing of this poor Stuff – as poor in genuine Imagination, as it is mean in Intellect – / At best, it is but Fancy, or the aggregating Faculty of the mind – not *Imagination*, or the *modifying*, and *co-adunating* Faculty. This the Hebrew Poets appear to me to have possessed beyond all others – & next to them the English. In the Hebrew Poets each Thing has a Life of it's own, & yet they are all one Life. In God they move & live, & *have* their Being – not *had*, as the cold System of Newtonian Theology represents/but *have*.

SOURCE: extract from letter to William Sotheby, 10 September 1802; in *Collected Letters of Samuel Taylor Coleridge*, ed. E. L. Griggs, 6 vols (London and New York, 1956–71) vol. II, pp. 865–6.

NOTE

1. *Numina Loci*: 'Spirits of the place'. A *numen* is 'the power or spirit dwelling in each natural object – a tree, a fountain, the earth – and also in each man, controlling the phenomena of nature and the actions of man' (P. Harvey, *Oxford Companion to Classical Literature*, s.v. Numen).

A *genius* (plural: *genii*) was the indwelling spirit or *numen* of Man; *dryads* were the indwelling spirits of trees, and *naiads* were those of springs, rivers and lakes.

II. WORDSWORTH AND IMAGINATION

Wordsworth is a Poet, a most original Poet – he no more resembles Milton than Milton resembles Shakespere – no more resembles Shakespere than Shakespere resembles Milton – he is himself: and I dare affirm that he will hereafter be admitted as the first & greatest philosophical Poet – the only man who has effected a compleat and constant synthesis of Thought & Feeling and combined them with Poetic Forms, with the music of pleasurable passion and with Imagination or the *modifying* Power in that highest sense of the word in which I have ventured to oppose it to Fancy, or the *aggregating* power – in that sense in which it is a dim Analogue of Creation, not all that we can *believe* but all that we can *conceive* of creation.

SOURCE: extract from letter to Richard Sharp, 15 January 1804; in *Collected Letters*, ed. Griggs, vol. II, p. 1034.

III. SHAKESPEARE AND IMAGINATION: LECTURE NOTES

. . . we have shewn that he [Shakespeare] possessed Fancy, considered as the faculty of bringing together &c &c. – 'Full gently now she' &c/[1] Still mounting, we find undoubted proof in his mind of Imagination or the power by which one image or feeling is made to modify many others, & by a sort of *fusion to force many into one* – that which after shewed itself in such might & energy in Lear, where the deep anguish of a Father spreads the feeling of Ingratitude & Cruelty over the very Elements of Heaven –. Various are the workings of this greatest faculty of the human mind – both passionate & tranquil – in its tranquil & purely pleasurable operation it acts chiefly by producing out of many things, as it would have appeared in the description of an ordinary mind, described slowly & in unimpassioned succession, a oneness/even as Nature, the greatest of Poets, acts upon us when we open our eyes upon an extended prospect – Thus the flight of Adonis from the enamoured Goddess in the dusk of the Evening –

> Look! how a bright star shooteth from the Sky,
> So glides he in the night from Venus' Eye –.[2]

How many Images & feelings are here brought together without effort & without discord – the beauty of Adonis – the rapidity of his flight – the yearning yet hopelessness of the enamoured gazer – and a shadowy ideal character thrown over the whole – /or it acts by impressing the stamp of humanity, of human feeling, over inanimate objects – The Pines shorn by the Sea wind & seen in twilight/[3]
Then

> Lo! here the gentle Lark – [4]

and lastly, which belongs only to a great poet, the power of so carrying on the Eye of the Reader as to make him almost lose the consciousness of words – to make him *see* every thing – & this without exciting any painful or laborious attention, without any *anatomy* of description, (a fault not uncommon in descriptive poetry) but with the sweetness & easy movement of nature –

SOURCE: extract from Coleridge's Notebooks, probably January 1808; in *The Notebooks of Samuel Taylor Coleridge*, ed. K. Coburn (London, 1962–) vol. III, entry 3290.

NOTES

1. Shakespeare's 'Venus and Adonis', l. 361. In the Notebook entry immediately preceding the present one, Coleridge wrote: 'Fancy, or the aggregative Power . . . Full gently now &c – the bringing together Images dissimilar in the main by some one point or more of Likeness –'. His argument is that the images in the stanza as a whole (ll. 361–6) provide an instance of Fancy.

2. 'Venus and Adonis', ll. 815–16.
3. This image of pine trees is elaborated in ch. 15 of *Biographia Literaria*: cf. Shawcross edition, vol. II, p. 17.
4. 'Venus and Adonis', l. 853.

IV. FANCY AND IMAGINATION DESYNONYMISED

This excellence, [1] which in all Mr. Wordsworth's writings is more or less predominant, and which constitutes the character of his mind, I no sooner felt, than I sought to understand. Repeated meditations led me first to suspect, (and a more intimate analysis of the human faculties, their appropriate marks, functions, and effects matured my conjecture into full conviction,) that fancy and imagination were two distinct and widely different faculties, instead of being, according to the general belief, either two names with one meaning, or, at furthest, the lower and higher degree of one and the same power. It is not, I own, easy to conceive a more opposite translation of the Greek *Phantasia* than the Latin *Imaginatio*;[2] but it is equally true that in all societies there exists an instinct of growth, a certain collective, unconscious good sense working progressively to desynonymize those words originally of the same meaning, which the conflux of dialects had supplied to the more homogeneous languages, as the Greek and German: and which the same cause, joined with accidents of translation from original works of different countries, occasion in mixt languages like our own. The first and most important point to be proved is, that two conceptions perfectly distinct are confused under one and the same word, and (this done) to appropriate that word exclusively to one meaning, and the synonyme (should there be one) to the other. But if (as will be often the case in the arts and sciences) no synonyme exists, we must either invent or borrow a word. In the present instance the appropriation has already begun, and been legitimated in the derivative adjective: Milton had a highly *imaginative*, Cowley a very *fanciful* mind. If therefore I should succeed in establishing the actual existences of two faculties generally different, the nomenclature would be at once determined. To the faculty by which I had characterized Milton, we should confine the term *imagination*; while the other would be contra-distinguished as *fancy*. Now were it once fully ascertained, that this division is no less grounded in nature, than that of delirium from mania,[3] or Otway's

> Lutes, lobsters, seas of milk, and ships of amber,[4]

from Shakespear's

> What! have his daughters brought him to this pass?[5]

or from the preceding apostrophe to the elements;[6] the theory of the fine arts, and of poetry in particular, could not, I thought, but derive some additional and important light. It would in its immediate effects furnish a torch of guidance to the philosophical critic; and ultimately to the poet himself. In energetic minds, truth soon changes by domestication into power; and from directing in the discrimination and appraisal of the product, becomes influencive in the production. To admire on principle, is the only way to imitate without loss of originality.

It has been already hinted, that metaphysics and psychology have long been my hobby-horse. But to have a hobby-horse, and to be vain of it, are so commonly found together, that they pass almost for the same. I trust therefore, that there will be more good humour than contempt, in the smile with which the reader chastises my self-complacency, if I confess myself uncertain, whether the satisfaction from the perception of a truth new to myself may not have been rendered more poignant by the conceit, that it would be equally so to the public. There was a time, certainly, in which I took some little credit to myself, in the belief that I had been the first of my countrymen, who had pointed out the diverse meaning of which the two terms were capable, and analyzed the faculties to which they should be appropriated. Mr. W. Taylor's recent volume[7] of synonymes I have not yet seen; but his specification of the terms in question has been clearly shown to be both insufficient and erroneous by Mr. Wordsworth in the Preface added to the late collection of his 'Lyrical Ballads and other poems.' The explanation which Mr. Wordsworth has himself given will be found to differ from mine, chiefly perhaps, as our objects are different. It could scarcely indeed happen otherwise, from the advantage I have enjoyed of frequent conversation with him on a subject to which a poem of his own first directed my attention, and my conclusions concern- ing which, he had made more lucid to myself by many happy instances drawn from the operation of natural objects on the mind. But it was Mr. Wordsworth's purpose to consider the influences of fancy and imagination as they are manifested in poetry, and from the different effects to conclude their diversity in kind; while it is my object to investigate the seminal principle, and then from the kind to deduce the degree. My friend has drawn a masterly sketch of the branches with their *poetic* fruitage. I wish to add the trunk, and even the roots as far as they lift themselves above ground, and are visible to the naked eye of our common consciousness.

SOURCE: extract from *Biographia Literaria* (1817), ed. J. Shawcross, chapter 4; (revised edition, Oxford, 1954) vol. I, pp. 60–4 (hereinafter referred to as Shawcross edition).

NOTES

1. The poetic *excellence* referred to is that of producing 'the strongest impressions of novelty', while at the same time rescuing 'the most admitted truths from the impotence caused by the very circumstance of their universal admission'.

2. *Phantasia*: 'a making visible, displaying; a display, parade (Latin, *ostentatio*); *in philosophic usage* = the power of the mind, by which it places objects before itself, presentative power'. (Liddell and Scott, *Greek – English Lexicon*.) *Imaginatio*: a mental image, e.g. *libidinum imaginationes in somno*, '*mental images* of desires in sleep'.

3. See this section, extract XII.

4. Thomas Otway, *Venice Preserv'd* (1682) vi 369: 'Lutes, laurels, seas of milk and ships of amber'. The misquotation here is probably to be accounted for as an unconscious conflation of Otway's line with an image from Butler's *Hudibras*, which Coleridge frequently used as an instance of Fancy: see this section, extract XII.

5. *King Lear*, III iv 63.

6. Ibid., III ii I ff.

7. W. Taylor, *British Synonymes Discriminated* (1813). For Wordsworth's use of Taylor's book, see below, section 3. VI.

V. THE IMAGINATIVE FACULTY: ACTIVE AND PASSIVE

Let us consider what we do when we leap. We first resist the gravitating power by an act purely voluntary, and then by another act, voluntary in part, we yield to it in order to light on the spot, which we had previously proposed to ourselves. Now let a man watch his mind while he is composing; or, to take a still more common case, while he is trying to recollect a name; and he will find the process completely analogous. Most of my readers will have observed a small water-insect on the surface of rivulets, which throws a cinque-spotted shadow fringed with prismatic colours on the sunny bottom of the brook; and will have noticed, how the little animal *wins* its way up against the stream, by alternate pulses of active and passive motion, now resisting the current, and now yielding to it in order to gather strength and a momentary *fulcrum* for a further propulsion. This is no unapt emblem of the mind's self-experience in the act of thinking. There are evidently two powers at work, which relatively to each other are active and passive; and this is not possible without an intermediate faculty, which is at once both active and passive. (In philosophical language, we must denominate this intermediate faculty in all its degrees and determinations, the IMAGINATION. But, in common language, and especially on the subject of poetry, we appropriate the name to a superior degree of the faculty, joined to a superior voluntary controul over it.)

SOURCE: *Biographia Literaria*, chapter 7; Shawcross edition, vol. I, pp. 85–6.

VI. PHILOSOPHIC PREPARATIONS FOR THE FANCY – IMAGINATION DISTINCTION

Thesis VI:

. . . the SUM or I AM, which I shall hereafter indiscriminately express by the words spirit, self, and self-consciousness. In this, and in this alone, object and subject, being and knowing are identical, each involving, and supposing the other. In other words, it is a subject which becomes a subject by the act of constructing itself objectively to itself; but which never is an object except for itself, and only so far as by the very same act it becomes a subject. It may be described therefore as a perpetual self-duplication of one and the same power into object and subject, which presuppose each other, and can only exist as antitheses.

SCHOLIUM. If a man be asked how he *knows* that he is? he can only answer, sum quia sum. But if (the absoluteness of this certainty having been admitted) he be again asked, how he, the individual person, came to be, then in relation to the ground of his *existence*, not to the ground of his *knowledge* of that existence, he might reply, sum quia Deus est, or still more philosophically, sum quia in Deo sum.[1]

But if we elevate our conception to the absolute self, the great eternal I AM, then the principle of being, and of knowledge, of idea, and of reality; the ground of existence, and the ground of the knowledge of existence, are absolutely identical, Sum quia sum;[2] I am, because I affirm myself to be; I affirm myself to be, because I am.

Thesis VII.

If then I know myself only through myself, it is contradictory to require any other predicate of self, but that of self-consciousness. Only in the self-consciousness of a spirit is there the required identity of object and of representation; for herein consists the essence of a spirit, that it is self-representative. If therefore this be the one only immediate truth, in the certainty of which the reality of our collective knowledge is grounded, it must follow that the spirit in all the objects which it views, views only itself. If this could be proved, the immediate reality of all intuitive knowledge would be assured. It has been shown, that a spirit is that, which is its own object, yet not originally an object, but an absolute subject for which all, itself included, may become an object. It must therefore be an ACT; for every object is, as an *object*, dead, fixed, incapable in itself of any action, and necessarily finite. Again the spirit (originally the identity, of object and subject) must in some sense dissolve this identity, in order to be conscious of it: fit alter et idem.[3] But this implies an act, and it follows therefore that intelligence or self-consciousness is impossible, except by and in a will. The self-conscious spirit therefore is a will; and freedom must be assumed as a *ground* of philosophy, and can never be deduced from it.

Thesis VIII.
Whatever in its origin is objective, is likewise as such necessarily finite. Therefore, since the spirit is not originally an object, and as the subject exists in antithesis to an object, the spirit cannot originally be finite. But neither can it be a subject without becoming an object, and, as it is originally the identity of both, it can be conceived neither as infinite nor finite exclusively, but as the most original union of both. In the existence, in the reconciling, and the recurrence of this contradiction consists the process and mystery of production and life.

Thesis IX.
This principium commune essendi et cognoscendi,[4] as subsisting in a WILL, or primary ACT of self-duplication, is the mediate or indirect principle of every science; but it is the immediate and direct principle of the ultimate science alone, i.e. of transcendental philosophy alone. For it must be remembered, that all these Theses refer solely to one of the two Polar Sciences, namely, to that which commences with, and rigidly confines itself within, the subjective, leaving the objective (as far as it is exclusively objective) to natural philosophy, which is its opposite pole. In its very idea therefore as a systematic knowledge of our collective KNOWING, (scientia scientiæ)[5] it involves the necessity of some one highest principle of knowing, as at once the source and accompanying form in all particular acts of intellect and perception. This, it has been shown, can be found only in the act and evolution of self-consciousness. We are not investigating an absolute principium essendi; for then, I admit, many valid objections might be started against our theory; but an absolute

principium cognoscendi. The result of both the sciences, or their equatorial point, would be the principle of a total and undivided philosophy, as, for prudential reasons, I have chosen to anticipate in the Scholium to Thesis VI and the note subjoined. In other words, philosophy would pass into religion, and religion become inclusive of philosophy. We begin with the I KNOW MYSELF, in order to end with the absolute I AM. We proceed from the SELF, in order to lose and find all self in God.

SOURCE: *Biographia Literaria*, chapter 12; Shawcross edition, vol. I, pp. 183–6.

NOTES

1. *sum quia sum*: 'I am because I am' ('am' = 'exist'); *sum quia Deus est*: 'I am because God is'; *sum quia in Deo sum*: 'I am because I am in God'.

2. 'It is most worthy of notice, that in the first revelation of himself, not confined to individuals; indeed in the very first revelation of his absolute being, Jehovah at the same time revealed the fundamental truth of all philosophy, which must either commence with the absolute, or have no fixed commencement; that is, cease to be philosophy. I cannot but express my regret, that in the equivocal use of the word *that*, for *in that*, or *because*, our admirable version [i.e., the Authorised Version (1611) of the Bible] has rendered the passage [Exodus 3:14] susceptible of degraded interpretation in the mind of common readers or hearers, as if it were a mere reproof to an impertinent question, I am what I am, which might be equally affirmed of himself by any existent being.' *Coleridge's note*.

3. *fit alter et idem*: 'become other and the same'.

4. *principium . . . cognoscendi*: 'general principle of being and knowing'.

5. *scientia scientiæ*: 'science of knowledge', i.e. epistemology.

VII. COLERIDGE ON WORDSWORTH'S 1815 PREFACE

I shall now proceed to the nature and genesis of the imagination; but I must first take leave to notice, that after a more accurate perusal of Mr. Wordsworth's remarks on the imagination, in the preface to the new edition of his poems, I find that my conclusions are not so consistent with his as, I confess, I had taken for granted.[1] In an article contributed by me to Mr. Southey's Omniana, on the soul and its organs of sense, are the following sentences. 'These (the human faculties) I would arrange under the different senses and powers: as the eye, the ear, the touch, &c.; the imitative power, voluntary and automatic; the imagination, or shaping and modifying power; the fancy, or the aggregative and associative power; the understanding, or the regulative, substantiating and realizing power; the speculative reason, vis theoretica et scientifica,[2] or the power by which we produce or aim to produce unity, necessity, and universality in all our knowledge by means of principles a priori;[3] the will, or practical reason; the faculty of choice (*Germanice*, Willkür) and (distinct both from the moral will and the choice,) the *sensation* of volition, which I have found reason to include under the head of single and double touch.' To this, as far as it relates to the subject in question, namely the words (*the aggregative and associative power*) Mr. Wordsworth's 'only objection is that the definition is too general. To aggregate and to associate, to evoke and to combine, belong as well to the imagination as to the fancy.' I reply, that if, by the power of evoking and combining, Mr. Wordsworth means the same as, and no more than, I meant by the aggregative and associative, I continue to deny, that it belongs at all to the imagination; and I am disposed to conjecture, that he has mistaken the co-presence of fancy with imagination for the operation of the latter singly. A man may work with two different tools at the same moment; each has its share in the work, but the work effected by each is distinct and different. But it will probably appear in the next Chapter,[4] that deeming it necessary to go back much further than Mr. Wordsworth's subject required or permitted, I have attached a meaning to both fancy and imagination, which he had not in view, at least while he was writing that preface.

SOURCE: extract from *Biographia Literaria*, chapter 12; Shawcross edition, vol. I, pp. 193–4.

NOTES

1. See above, extract IV., and also below, section 3. V.–VI.

2. *vis theoretica et scientifica*: 'a power for speculation and knowledge'.

3. 'This phrase, *a priori*, is in common, most grossly misunderstood, and an absurdity burdened on it, which it does not deserve. By knowledge, *a priori*, we do not mean, that we can know anything previously to experience, which would be a contradiction in terms; but that having once known it by occasion of experience (that is, something acting upon us from without) we then know, that it must have pre-existed, or the experience itself would have been impossible. By experience only I know, that I have eyes; but then my reason convinces me, that I must have had eyes in order to [have] had the experience.' *Coleridge's note.*

4. Ch. 13. The reference is to the Fancy – Imagination distinction, quoted immediately following.

VIII. THE FAMOUS FANCY – IMAGINATION DISTINCTION

The IMAGINATION then, I consider either as primary, or secondary. The primary IMAGINATION I hold to be the living Power and prime Agent of all human Perception, and as a repetition in the finite mind of the eternal act of creation in the infinite I AM. The secondary Imagination I consider as an echo of the former, co-existing with the conscious will, yet still as identical with the primary in the *kind* of its agency, and differing only in *degree*, and in the *mode* of its operation. It dissolves, diffuses, dissipates, in order to re-create; or where this process is rendered impossible, yet still at all events it struggles to idealize and to unify. It is essentially *vital*, even as all objects (*as* objects) are essentially fixed and dead.

FANCY, on the contrary, has no other counters to play with, but fixities and definites. The Fancy is indeed no other than a mode of Memory emancipated from the order of time and space; while it is blended with, and modified by that empirical phenomenon of the will, which we express by the word CHOICE. But equally with the ordinary memory the Fancy must receive all its materials ready made from the law of association.

SOURCE: extract from *Biographia Literaria*, chapter 13; Shawcross edition, vol. I, p. 202.

IX. IMAGINATION AND THE RECONCILIATION OF OPPOSITES

My own conclusions on the nature of poetry, in the strictest use of the word, have been in part anticipated in the preceding disquisition on the fancy and imagination.[1] What is poetry? is so nearly the same question with, what is a poet? that the answer to the one is involved in the solution of the other. For it is a distinction resulting from the poetic genius itself, which sustains and modifies the images, thoughts, and emotions of the poet's own mind.

The poet, described in *ideal* perfection, brings the whole soul of man into activity, with the subordination of its faculties to each other, according to their relative worth and dignity.[2] He diffuses a tone and spirit of unity, that blends, and (as it were) *fuses*, each into each, by that synthetic and magical power to which we have exclusively appropriated the name of imagination. This power, first put in action by the will and understanding, and retained under their irremissive, though gentle and unnoticed, controul (*laxis effertur habenis*)[3] reveals itself in the balance or reconciliation of opposite or discordant qualities:[4] of sameness, with difference; of the general, with the concrete; the idea, with the image; the individual, with the representative; the sense of novelty and freshness, with old and familiar objects; a more than usual state of emotion, with more than usual order; judgement ever awake and steady self-possession, with enthusiasm and feeling profound or vehement; and while it blends and harmonizes the natural and the artificial, still subordinates art to nature; the manner to the matter; and our admiration of the poet to our sympathy with the poetry. 'Doubtless', as Sir John Davies observes of the soul[5] (and his words may with slight alteration be applied, and even more appropriately, to the poetic IMAGINATION)

> Doubtless this could not be, but that she turns
> Bodies to spirit by sublimation strange,

As fire converts to fire the things it burns,
    As we our food into our nature change.

From their gross matter she abstracts their forms,
    And draws a kind of quintessence from things;
Which to her proper nature she transforms,
    To bear them light on her celestial wings.

Thus does she, when from individual states
    She doth abstract the universal kinds;
Which then re-clothed in divers names and fates
    Steal access through our senses to our minds.

Finally, GOOD SENSE is the BODY of poetic genius, FANCY its
DRAPERY, MOTION its LIFE, and IMAGINATION the SOUL that is
everywhere, and in each; and forms all into one graceful and
intelligent whole.

SOURCE: extract from *Biographia Literaria*, chapter 14;
Shawcross edition, vol. II, pp. 12−13.

NOTES

1. Refers to the Fancy – Imagination distinction in *Biographia
Literaria*, ch. 13; see preceding extract.
2. See above, extract VII.
3. *laxis effertur habenis*: 'transported with loose reins'. (Variant of
Virgil, *Georgics*, II 364.)
4. For the reconciliation of opposites in practice, see 'Kubla Khan',
ll. 31−6.
5. Davies, 'Nosce Teipsum' (1599) Part IV. Coleridge's 'slight
alteration' is in the last stanza quoted above, where the last two lines in
the original poem read:

Which bodyless and immaterial are,
And can be only lodged within our minds.

X. IMAGINATION AND SCRIPTURAL HISTORY

And in nothing is Scriptural history more strongly contrasted with the histories of highest note in the present age than in its freedom from the hollowness of abstractions. While the latter present a shadow-fight of Things and Quantities, the former gives us the history of Men, and balances the important influence of individual Minds with the previous state of the national morals and manners, in which, as constituting a specific susceptibility, it presents to us the true cause both of the Influence itself, and of the Weal or Woe that were its Consequents. How should it be otherwise? The histories and political economy of the present and preceding century partake in the general contagion of its mechanic philosophy, and are the *product* of an unenlivened generalizing Understanding. In the Scriptures they are the living *educts* of the Imagination; of that reconciling and mediatory power, which incorporating the Reason in Images of the Sense, and organizing (as it were) the flux of the Senses by the permanence and self-circling energies of the Reason, gives birth to a system of symbols, harmonious in themselves, and consubstantial with the truths, of which they are the *conductors*. These are the Wheels which Ezekiel beheld, when the hand of the Lord was upon him, and he saw visions of God as he sate among the captives by the river of Chebar. *Whithersoever the Spirit was to go, the wheels went, and thither was their spirit to go: for the spirit of the living creature was in the wheels also.*[1] The truths and the symbols that represent them move in conjunction and form the living chariot that bears up (for *us*) the throne of the Divine Humanity. Hence, by a derivative, indeed, but not a divided, influence, and though in a secondary yet in more than a metaphorical sense, the Sacred Book is worthily intitled *the* WORD OF GOD. Hence too, its contents present to us the stream of time continuous as Life and a symbol of Eternity, inasmuch as the Past and the Future are virtually contained in the Present. According therefore to our relative position on its banks the Sacred History becomes prophetic, the Sacred Prophecies historical, while the power and substance of both inhere in its Laws, its Promises, and its Comminations. In the Scriptures therefore both Facts and Persons must of necessity have a two-fold significance, a past and a future, a temporary and a perpetual, a particular and a universal application. They must be at once Portraits and Ideals.

Eheu! paupertina philosophia in paupertinam religionem ducit:[2] – A hunger-bitten and idea-less philosophy naturally produces a starveling and comfortless religion. It is among the miseries of the present age that it recognizes no medium between *Literal* and *Metaphorical*. Faith is either to be buried in the dead letter, or its name and honours usurped by a counterfeit product of the mechanical understanding, which in the blindness of self-complacency confounds SYMBOLS with ALLEGORIES. Now an Allegory is but a translation of abstract notions into a picture-language which is itself nothing but an abstraction of objects of the senses; the principle being more worthless even than its phantom proxy, both alike unsubstantial, and the former shapeless to boot. On the other hand a Symbol (ὁ ἔστιν ἀεί ταυτηγόρικον)[3] is characterized by a translucence of the Special in the Individual or of the Universal in the General. Above all by the translucence of the Eternal through and in the Temporal. It always partakes of the Reality which it renders intelligible; and while it enunciates the whole, abides itself as a living part in that Unity, of which it is the representative. The other are but empty echoes which the fancy arbitrarily associates with apparitions of matter, less beautiful but not less shadowy than the sloping orchard or hill-side pasture-field seen in the transparent lake below. Alas! for the flocks that are to be led forth to such pastures! *'It shall even be as when the hungry dreameth, and behold! he eateth; but he waketh and his soul is empty: or as when the thirsty dreameth, and behold he drinketh; but he awaketh and is faint!'*[4]

SOURCE: extract from *The Statesman's Manual* (1816); in *The Collected Works of Samuel Taylor Coleridge*, ed. K. Coburn (London, 1967–) vol. VI, pp. 28–31.

NOTES

1. Ezekiel 1:20, *variatim*.
2. *Eheu! paupertina . . . ducit*: 'Alas! an impoverished philosophy leads to an impoverished religion'.

3. ὁ ἔστιν ἀεί ταντηγόρικον: 'which is always tautegorical'. The word *tautegorical* is Coleridge's coinage, and he himself explicates the neologism in his *Aids to Reflection* (1825): 'The base of Symbols and symbolical expressions; the nature of which [is] always tautegorical (i.e. expressing the same subject but with a difference) in contra-distinction from metaphors and similitudes, that are always allegorical (i.e. expressing a different subject but with a resemblance).'

4. Isaiah 29:8, *variatim*.

XI. IMAGINATION IN RELATION TO REASON AND UNDERSTANDING

Reason and Religion differ only as a two-fold application of the same power. But if we are obliged to distinguish, we must *ideally* separate. In this sense I affirm, that Reason is the knowledge of the laws of the WHOLE considered as ONE: and as such it is contradistinguished from the Understanding, which concerns itself exclusively with the quantities, qualities, and relations of *particulars* in time and space. The UNDERSTANDING, therefore, is the science of phenomena, and their subsumption under distinct kinds and sorts, (*genus* and *species*.) Its functions supply the rules and constitute the possibility of EXPERIENCE; but remain mere logical *forms*, except as far as *materials* are given by the senses or sensations. The REASON, on the other hand, is the science of the *universal*, having the ideas of ONENESS and ALLNESS as its two elements or primary factors. In the language of the old schools,

$$\text{Unity} + \text{Omnëity} = \text{Totality.}$$

The Reason first manifests itself in man by the *tendency* to the comprehension of all as one. We can neither rest in an infinite that is not at the same time a whole nor in a whole that is not infinite. Hence the natural Man is always in a state either of resistance or of captivity to the understanding and the fancy, which cannot represent totality without limit: and he either loses the ONE in striving after the INFINITE, (i.e. Atheism with or without polytheism) or the INFINITE in the striving after the ONE, (i.e. anthropomorphic monotheism.) . . .

Of this latter faculty [i.e. the Understanding] considered in and of itself the peripatetic aphorism, nihil in intellectu quod non prius in sensu,[1] is strictly true, as well as the legal maxim, de rebus non apparentibus et non existentibus eadem est ratio.[2] The eye is not more inappropriate to sound, than the *mere* understanding to the modes and laws of spiritual existence. In this sense I have used the term; and in this sense I assert that 'the understanding or experiential faculty, unirradiated by the reason and the spirit, has no appropriate object but the material world in relation to our worldly interests. The far-sighted prudence of man, and the more narrow but at the same time far less fallible cunning of the fox, are both no other than a nobler *substitute for salt, in order* that the hog may not putrefy before its destined hour.' FRIEND, p. 80.

It must not, however be overlooked, that this insulation of the understanding is our own act and deed. The man of healthful and undivided intellect uses his understanding in this state of abstraction only as a tool or organ: even as the arithmetician uses numbers, that is, as the means not the end of knowledge. Our Shakespear in agreement both with truth and the philosophy of his age names it '*discourse* of reason,'[3] as an instrumental faculty *belonging* to reason: and Milton opposes the discursive to the intuitive, as the lower to the higher,

Differing but in degree, in *kind* the same![4]

Of the *discursive* understanding, which forms for itself general notions and terms of classification for the purpose of comparing and arranging phaenomena, the Characteristic is Clearness without Depth. It contemplates the unity of things in their *limits* only, and is consequently a knowledge of superficies without substance. So much so indeed, that it entangles itself in contradictions in the very effort of comprehending the *idea* of substance. The completing power which unites clearness with depth, the plenitude of the sense with the comprehensibility of the understanding, is the IMAGINATION, impregnated with which the understanding itself becomes intuitive, and a living power. The REASON, (not the abstract reason, not the reason as a mere *organ* of science, or as the faculty of scientific principles and schemes a priori; but reason) as the integral *spirit* of the regenerated man, reason substantiated and vital, 'one only, yet manifold, overseeing all, and going through all understanding; the breath of the power of God, and a pure influence from the glory of the Almighty; which remaining in itself regenerateth all other powers, and in all ages entering into holy souls maketh them friends of God and prophets;' (Wisdom of Solomon, c. vii.)[5] the REASON without being either the SENSE, the UNDERSTANDING or the IMAGINATION contains all three within itself, even as the mind contains its thoughts, and is present in and through them all; or as the expression pervades the different features of an intelligent countenance. Each individual must bear witness of it to his own mind, even as he describes light and life: and with the silence of light it describes itself, and dwells in *us* only as far as we dwell in *it*. It cannot in strict language be called a faculty, much less a personal property, of any human mind! He, with whom it is present, can as little appropriate it, whether totally or by partition, as he can claim ownership in the breathing air or make an inclosure in the cope of heaven.

The object of the preceding discourse was to recommend the Bible, as the end and center of our reading and meditation. . . .

SOURCE: extracts from *The Statesman's Manual*, Appendix C; in *Collected Works*, ed. Coburn, vol. VI, pp. 59–60, 67–70.

NOTES

1. *nihil in intellectu . . . sensu*: 'there is nothing in the mind that is not first in the senses'.

2. *de rebus . . . ratio*: 'the rule is the same both for things which do not appear and those which do not exist'.

3. *Hamlet*, I ii 150.

4. *Paradise Lost*, v 490, *variatim*.

5. A pastiche of verses 22–7. The Wisdom of Solomon is to be found in the Apocrypha.

XII. FANCY — IMAGINATION AND DELIRIUM — MANIA

You may conceive the difference in kind between the Fancy and
the Imagination in this way, that if the check of the senses and the
reason were withdrawn, the first would become delirium, and the
last mania. The Fancy brings together images which have no
connexion natural or moral, but are yoked together by the poet
by means of some accidental coincidence; as in the well-known
passage in *Hudibras*:

> The sun had long since in the lap
> Of Thetis taken out his nap,
> And like a lobster boyl'd, the morn
> From black to red began to turn.[1]

The Imagination modifies images, and gives unity to variety; it
sees all things in one, *il piu nell' uno*.[2] There is the epic
imagination, the perfection of which is in Milton; and the
dramatic, of which Shakespeare is the absolute master. The first
gives unity by throwing back into the distance; as after the
magnificent approach of the Messiah to battle, the poet, by one
touch from himself —

> . . . far off their coming shone —

makes the whole one image.[3] And so at the conclusion of the
description of the appearance of the entranced angels, in which
every sort of image from all the regions of earth and air is
introduced to diversify and illustrate, the reader is brought back
to the single image by:

> He call'd so loud, that all the hollow deep
> Of Hell resounded.[4]

The dramatic imagination does not throw back, but brings close;
it stamps all nature with one, and that its own, meaning, as in
Lear throughout.[5]

SOURCE: *Table Talk*, entry for 23 June 1834; in *The Table
Talk and Omniana of Samuel Taylor Coleridge*, ed. H. N.
Coleridge (Oxford, 1917).

NOTES

1. Butler, *Hudibras*, II ii 29–32.
2. *il piu nell' uno*: 'the many in the one'.
3. The description of Christ in his battle-chariot moving to en-counter the rebellious Satan is in *Paradise Lost*, VI 749–79.
4. *Paradise Lost*, I 314–15.
5. See also above, extract iv., where Fancy – Imagination are likened to delirium – mania, and where *Lear* is discussed.

2. IMAGINATION AND THE *LYRICAL BALLADS*

I. THE COLERIDGEAN VIEW

During the first year [1797] that Mr. Wordsworth and I were neighbours,[1] our conversations turned frequently on the two cardinal points of poetry, the power of exciting the sympathy of the reader by a faithful adherence to the truth of nature, and the power of giving the interest of novelty by the modifying colours of imagination. The sudden charm, which accidents of light and shade, which moon-light or sun-set diffused over a known and familiar landscape, appeared to represent the practicability of combining both. These are the poetry of nature. The thought suggested itself (to which of us I do not recollect) that a series of poems might be composed of two sorts. In the one, the incidents and agents were to be, in part at least, supernatural; and the excellence aimed at was to consist in the interesting of the affections by the dramatic truth of such emotions, as would naturally accompany such situations, supposing them real. And real in *this* sense they have been to every human being who, from whatever source of delusion, has at any time believed himself under supernatural agency. For the second class, subjects were to be chosen from ordinary life; the characters and incidents were to be such, as will be found in every village and its vicinity, where there is a meditative and feeling mind to seek after them, or to notice them, when they present themselves.

In this idea originated the plan of the 'Lyrical Ballads'; in which it was agreed, that my endeavours should be directed to persons and characters supernatural, or at least romantic; yet so as to transfer from our inward nature a human interest and a semblance of truth sufficient to procure for these shadows of imagination that willing suspension of disbelief for the moment, which constitutes poetic faith. Mr. Wordsworth, on the other hand, was to propose to himself as his object, to give the charm of novelty to things of every day, and to excite a feeling analogous to the supernatural, by awakening the mind's attention from the lethargy of custom, and directing it to the loveliness and the wonders of the world before us; an inexhaustible treasure, but for which, in consequence of the film of familiarity and selfish solicitude we have eyes, yet see not, ears that hear not, and hearts that neither feel nor understand.

SOURCE: extract from *Biographia Literaria*, chapter 14; Shawcross edition, vol. II, pp. 5–6.

NOTE

1. In 1797 Coleridge was living at Nether Stowey, in Somerset, and the Wordsworths at Alfoxden, some three miles away.

II. THE WORDSWORTHIAN VIEW

The principal object, then, proposed in these Poems was to choose incidents and situations from common life, and to relate or describe them, throughout, as far as was possible in a selection of language really used by men, and, at the same time, to throw over them a certain colouring of imagination, whereby ordinary things should be presented to the mind in an unusual aspect; and, further, and above all, to make these incidents and situations interesting by tracing in them, truly though not ostentatiously, the primary laws of our nature: chiefly, as far as regards the manner in which we associate ideas in a state of excitement.

SOURCE: extract from Preface to *Lyrical Ballads* (1850); in *The Prose Works of William Wordsworth*, ed. W. J. B. Owen and J. W. Smyser (Oxford, 1974) vol. I, pp. 123, 125.

3. WILLIAM WORDSWORTH

I. EPIPHANY AT THE SIMPLON PASS

[While touring Europe with Robert Jones in the summer of 1790, Wordsworth crossed through the Simplon Pass in the Swiss Alps. In the passage from *The Prelude* quoted here, lines 525–48 are prompted by the recollection of that moment when their guide (the peasant in the poem) informed them *'that we had cross'd the Alps'*, and lines 549–72 describe the ensuing descent into the Pass.]

> Imagination! lifting up itself
> Before the eye and progress of my Song
> Like an unfather'd vapour; here that Power,
> In all the might of its endowments, came
> Athwart me; I was lost as in a cloud,
> Halted, without a struggle to break through.
> And now recovering, to my Soul I say
> I recognize thy glory; in such strength
> Of usurpation, in such visitings
> Of awful promise, when the light of sense
> Goes out in flashes that have shewn to us
> The invisible world, doth Greatness make abode,
> There harbours whether we be young or old.
> Our destiny, our nature, and our home
> Is with infinitude, and only there;

With hope it is, hope that can never die,
Effort, and expectation, and desire,
And something evermore about to be.
The mind beneath such banners militant
Thinks not of spoils or trophies, nor of aught
That may attest its prowess, blest in thoughts
That are their own perfection and reward,
Strong in itself, and in the access of joy
Which hides it like the overflowing Nile.[1]

The dull and heavy slackening that ensued
Upon those tidings by the Peasant given
Was soon dislodg'd; downwards we hurried fast,
And enter'd with the road which we had miss'd
Into a narrow chasm; the brook and road
Were fellow-travellers in this gloomy Pass,
And with them did we journey several hours
At a slow step. The immeasurable height
Of woods decaying, never to be decay'd,
The stationary blasts of water-falls,
And every where along the hollow rent
Winds thwarting winds, bewilder'd and forlorn,
The torrents shooting from the clear blue sky,
The rocks that mutter'd close upon our ears,
Black drizzling crags that spake by the way-side
As if a voice were in them, the sick sight
And giddy prospect of the raving stream,
The unfetter'd clouds, and region of the Heavens,
Tumult and peace, the darkness and the light
Were all like workings of one mind, the features
Of the same face, blossoms upon one tree,
Characters of the great Apocalypse,
The types and symbols of Eternity,
Of first and last, and midst, and without end.

SOURCE: extract from *The Prelude, or Growth of a Poet's Mind*
(text of 1805) VI 525–72; E. de Selincourt's revised edition
(Oxford, 1960) pp. 99–100.

NOTE

1. In the revised version (Oxford, 1960) of his edition of the 1805 *Prelude*, E. de Selincourt writes of lines 525–48: 'No passage illustrates better than this at once Wordsworth's relation with the sensationist, empirical philosophy of the eighteenth century and the manner in which he transcends and spiritualizes it. All intellectual and spiritual growth comes from the reaction of the senses, chiefly of eye and ear, to the external world, which is "exquisitely fitted to the mind", but the highest vision is superinduced upon this in a state of ecstasy, in which the light of sense goes out and the soul feels its kinship with that which is beyond sense. Cf. *Lines composed . . . above Tintern Abbey*, 35–49. And this great spiritual experience comes generally not immediately after the sense experience which has inspired it, but perhaps years later, when the original emotion, recollected in tranquillity, is rekindled' (p. 278). To these remarks I would only add that the 'theory' of lines 525–48 is translated into a concrete example in lines 549–72, for the recollected experience of the Simplon Pass becomes an illustrative emblem of the imagination at work.

II. THE ASCENT OF MOUNT SNOWDON

[In the summer of 1791, having visited Salisbury Plain and Tintern Abbey, Wordsworth and Robert Jones extended their walking tour into northern Wales, where they decided to climb Snowdon. It was dark when they 'Rouz'd up the Shepherd, who by ancient right / Of Office is the Stranger's usual guide'; and the three of them set off in darkness, hoping to have gained the summit in time to see the sunrise from the mountain's peak.]

> . . . With forehead bent
> Earthward, as if in opposition set
> Against an enemy, I panted up
> With eager pace, and no less eager thoughts.
> Thus might we wear perhaps an hour away,
> Ascending at loose distance each from each,
> And I, as chanced, the foremost of the Band;
> When at my feet the ground appear'd to brighten,
> And with a step or two seem'd brighter still;

Nor had I time to ask the cause of this,
For instantly a Light upon the turf
Fell like a flash: I look'd about, and lo!
The Moon stood naked in the Heavens, at height
Immense above my head, and on the shore
I found myself of a huge sea of mist,
Which, meek and silent, rested at my feet:
A hundred hills their dusky backs upheaved
All over this still Ocean, and beyond,
Far, far beyond, the vapours shot themselves,
In headlands, tongues, and promontory shapes,
Into the Sea, the real Sea, that seem'd
To dwindle, and give up its majesty,
Usurp'd upon as far as sight could reach.
Meanwhile, the Moon look'd down upon this shew
In single glory, and we stood, the mist
Touching our very feet; and from the shore
At distance not the third part of a mile
Was a blue chasm; a fracture in the vapour,
A deep and gloomy breathing-place through which
Mounted the roar of waters, torrents, streams
Innumerable, roaring with one voice.
The universal spectacle throughout
Was shaped for admiration and delight,
Grand in itself alone, but in that breach
Through which the homeless voice of waters rose,
That dark deep thoroughfare had Nature lodg'd
The Soul, the Imagination of the whole.

    A meditation rose in me that night
Upon the lonely Mountain when the scene
Had pass'd away, and it appear'd to me
The perfect image of a mighty Mind,
Of one that feeds upon infinity,
That is exalted by an underpresence,
The sense of God, or whatsoe'er is dim
Or vast in its own being, above all
One function of such mind had Nature there

Exhibited by putting forth, and that
With circumstance most awful and sublime,
That domination which she oftentimes
Exerts upon the outward face of things,
So moulds them, and endues, abstracts, combines,
Or by abrupt and unhabitual influence
Doth make one object so impress itself
Upon all others, and pervade them so
That even the grossest minds must see and hear
And cannot chuse but feel. The Power which these
Acknowledge when thus moved, which Nature thus
Thrusts forth upon the senses, is the express
Resemblance, in the fulness of its strength
Made visible, a genuine Counterpart
And Brother of the glorious faculty
Which higher minds bear with them as their own.
That is the very spirit in which they deal
With all the objects of the universe;
They from their native selves can send abroad
Like transformations, for themselves create
A like existence, and, whene'er it is
Created for them, catch it by an instinct;
Them the enduring and the transient both
Serve to exalt; they build up greatest things
From least suggestions, ever on the watch,
Willing to work and to be wrought upon,
They need not extraordinary calls
To rouze them, in a world of life they live,
By sensible impressions not enthrall'd,
But quicken'd, rouz'd, and made thereby more fit
To hold communion with the invisible world.
Such minds are truly from the Deity,
For they are Powers; and hence the highest bliss
That can be known is theirs, the consciousness
Of whom they are habitually infused
Through every image, and through every thought,
And all impressions; hence religion, faith,
And endless occupation for the soul

Whether discursive or intuitive;[1]
Hence sovereignty within and peace at will,
Emotion which best foresight need not fear,
Most worthy then of trust when most intense.
Hence chearfulness in every act of life,
Hence truth in moral judgements and delight
That fails not in the external universe.

SOURCE: extract from *The Prelude* (text of 1805) XIII
29–119; de Selincourt edition, pp. 229–32.

NOTE

1. In *Paradise Lost* (v 487ff.), Raphael tells Adam that *reason* is either
'Discursive, or intuitive', and explains that discursive reason is
appropriate to men, while intuitive reason is proper to angels. In *The
Prelude*, XIII 168–70, Wordsworth observes that *Imagination*

Is but another name for absolute strength
And clearest insight, amplitude of mind,
And reason in her most exalted mood.

III. IMAGINATION AND 'THE WHITE DOE OF RYLSTONE':
TWO STATEMENTS

(i)

I . . . told Lamb that I did not think the Poem[1] could ever be
popular first because there was nothing in it to excite curiosity,
and next, because the main catastrophe was not a material but an
intellectual one; I said to him further that it could not be popular
because some of the principal objects and agents, such as the
Banner and the Doe, produced their influences and effects not by
powers naturally inherent in them, but such as they were endued
with by the Imagination of the human minds on whom they
operated: further, that the principle of action in all the characters, as in the Old Man, and his Sons, and Francis, when he has

the prophetic vision of the overthrow of his family, and the fate of his sister, and takes leave of her as he does, was throughout imaginative; and that all action (save the main traditionary tragedy), i.e. all the action proceeding from the will of the chief agents, was fine-spun and inobtrusive, consonant in this to the principle from which it flowed, and in harmony with the shadowy influence of the Doe, by whom the poem is introduced, and in whom it ends. It suffices that everything tends to account for the weekly pilgrimage of the Doe, which is made interesting by its connection with a human being, a Woman, who is intended to be honoured and loved for what she *endures*, and the manner in which she endures it; accomplishing a conquest over her own sorrows (which is the true subject of the Poem) by means, partly, of the native strength of her character, and partly by the persons and things with whom and which she is connected; and finally, after having exhibited the 'fortitude of patience and heroic martyrdom',[2] ascending to pure etherial spirituality, and for-warded in that ascent of love by communion with a creature not of her own species, but spotless, beautiful, innocent and loving, in that temper of earthly love to which alone she can conform, without violation to the majesty of her losses, or degradation from those heights of heavenly serenity to which she has been raised.

(ii)

Of the White Doe I have little to say, but that I hope it will be acceptable to the intelligent, for whom alone it is written. It starts from a high point of imagination, and comes round through various wanderings of that faculty to a still higher; nothing less than the Apotheosis of the Animal, who gives the first of the two titles to the Poem.[3] And as the Poem thus begins and ends with pure and lofty Imagination, every motive and impulse that actuates the persons introduced is from the same source, a kindred spirit pervades, and is intended to harmonize, the whole. Throughout, objects (the Banner, for instance) derive their influence not from properties inherent in them, not from what they are actually in themselves, but from such as are bestowed upon them by the minds of those who are conversant with or affected by those objects. Thus the Poetry, if there be any in the work, proceeds whence it ought to do, from the soul of Man, communicating its creative energies to the images of the external world.

> SOURCES: (i) extract from letter to Coleridge, 19 April 1808; in *The Letters of William and Dorothy Wordsworth*, ed. E. de Selincourt (Oxford, 1937) vol. I, pp. 197–8. (ii) extract from letter to Francis Wrangham, 18 January 1816; in ibid., vol. II, pp. 704–5.

NOTES

1. Although composed in 1807–8, 'The White Doe' was not published until 1815.
2. *Paradise Lost*, IX 31–2.
3. The full title of the poem is 'The White Doe of Rylstone, or The Fate of the Nortons'.

IV. THE REPLY TO 'MATHETES'

[In December 1809 Coleridge published in *The Friend* a letter on the moral problems of adolescence; the contribution was signed simply 'Mathetes' (i.e. 'a learner'). The author was John Wilson. Wordsworth's unsigned reply was published in *The Friend* in two parts: 14 December 1809, and 4 January 1810.]

Range against each other as Advocates, oppose as Combatants, two several Intellects, each strenuously asserting doctrines which he sincerely believes; but the one contending for the worth and beauty of that garment which the other has outgrown and cast away. Mark the superiority, the ease, the dignity, on the side of the more advanced Mind;[1] how he overlooks his Subject, commands it from centre to circumference; and hath the same thorough knowledge of the tenets which his Adversary, with impetuous zeal, but in confusion also and thrown off his guard at every turn of the argument, is labouring to maintain! If it be a question of the fine Arts (Poetry for instance) the riper mind not only sees that his Opponent is deceived; but, what is of far more importance, sees *how* he is deceived. The imagination stands before him with all its imperfections laid open; as duped by shews, enslaved by words, corrupted by mistaken delicacy and false refinement, – as not having even attended with care to the reports of the senses, and therefore deficient grossly in the rudiments of her own power. He has noted how, as a supposed necessary condition, the Understanding sleeps in order that the Fancy may dream. Studied in the history of Society, and versed in the secret laws of thought, he can pass regularly through all the gradations, can pierce infallibly all the windings which false taste through ages has pursued, – from the very time when first, through inexperience, heedlessness, or affectation, she took her departure from the side of Truth, her original parent.

SOURCE: extract from a contribution to *The Friend*, 4 January 1810; in *Prose Works*, ed. Owen and Smyser, vol. II, pp. 21–2.

NOTE

1. The argument of the passage as a whole is that moral discipline is necessary for accurate criticism; the 'more advanced Mind', therefore, is the mind that is morally disciplined by the search for truth, whereas the mind of the hypothetical 'Opponent' is not at all well developed morally.

V. A SONNET ON IMAGINATION

'Weak is the will of Man, his judgment blind;
Remembrance persecutes, and Hope betrays;
Heavy is woe; – and joy, for human-kind,
A mournful thing, so transient is the blaze!'
Thus might *he* paint our lot of mortal days
Who wants the glorious faculty assigned
To elevate the more-than-reasoning Mind,
And colour life's dark cloud with orient rays.

Imagination is that sacred power,
Imagination lofty and refined:
'Tis hers to pluck the amaranthine flower
Of Faith, and round the sufferer's temples bind
Wreaths that endure affliction's heaviest shower,
And do not shrink from sorrow's keenest wind.

SOURCE: *Poems* (1815); in *The Poetical Works of Wordsworth*,
ed. T. Hutchinson and E. de Selincourt (Oxford, 1904;
second edition 1936) p. 206.

VI. FANCY AND IMAGINATION

[In the 1815 edition of his poems, Wordsworth undertook to
classify his poems according to subject-matter and the
psychology of literary creation. Hence the poems were grouped
under 'appropriate' subtitles: 'Naming of Places', 'Old Age',
'Fancy', 'Imagination', and so on. It is clear that the main
purpose of the Preface (from which the following extract is taken)
is to attempt to define 'the words Fancy and Imagination, as
employed in the classification of the . . . Poems' in the 1815
volume.]

Let us now come to the consideration of the words Fancy and
Imagination, as employed in the classification of the following
Poems. 'A man', says an intelligent author, 'has imagination in
proportion as he can distinctly copy in idea the impressions of
sense: it is the faculty which *images* within the mind the
**phenomena of sensation. A man has fancy in proportion as he
can call up, connect or associate, at pleasure, those internal**
images (φαντάζειν is to cause to appear) so as to complete ideal
representations of absent objects. Imagination is the power of
depicting, and fancy of evoking and combining. The imagination
is formed by patient observation; the fancy by a voluntary
activity in shifting the scenery of the mind. The more accurate
the imagination, the more safely may a painter, or a poet,
undertake a delineation, or a description, without the presence of
the objects to be characterized. The more versatile the fancy, the

more original and striking will be the decorations produced.' – *British Synonyms discriminated, by W. Taylor.*[1]

Is not this as if a man should undertake to supply an account of a building, and be so intent upon what he had discovered of the foundation, as to conclude his task without once looking up at the superstructure? Here, as in other instances throughout the volume, the judicious Author's mind is enthralled by Etymology; he takes up the original word as his guide and escort, and too often does not perceive how soon he becomes its prisoner, without liberty to tread in any path but that to which it confines him. It is not easy to find out how imagination, thus explained, differs from distinct remembrance of images; or fancy from quick and vivid recollection of them: each is nothing more than a mode of memory.[2] If the two words bear the above meaning, and no other, what term is left to designate that faculty of which the Poet is 'all compact;'[3] he whose eye glances from earth to heaven, whose spiritual attributes body forth what his pen is prompt in turning to shape; or what is left to characterise Fancy, as insinuating herself into the heart of objects with creative activity? – Imagination, in the sense of the word as giving title to a class of the following Poems, has no reference to images that are merely a faithful copy, existing in the mind, of absent external objects; but is a word of higher import, denoting operations of the mind upon those objects, and processes of creation or of composition, governed by certain fixed laws. I proceed to illustrate my meaning by instances. A parrot *hangs* from the wires of his cage by his beak or by his claws; or a monkey from the bough of a tree by his paws or his tail. Each creature does so literally and actually. In the first Eclogue of Virgil, the shepherd, thinking of the time when he is to take leave of his farm, thus addresses his goats: –

> Non ego vos posthac viridi projectus in antro
> Dumosa *pendere* procul de rupe videbo.[4]

> half way down
> *Hangs* one who gathers samphire,[5]

is the well-known expression of Shakspeare, delineating an ordinary image upon the cliffs of Dover. In these two instances is a slight exertion of the faculty which I denominate imagination, in the use of one word: neither the goats nor the samphire-gatherer do literally hang, as does the parrot or the monkey; but, presenting to the senses something of such an appearance, the mind in its activity, for its own gratification, contemplates them as hanging.

> As when far off at sea a fleet descried
> *Hangs* in the clouds, by equinoctial winds
> Close sailing from Bengala, or the isles
> Of Ternate or Tidore, whence merchants bring
> Their spicy drugs; they on the trading flood
> Through the wide Ethiopian to the Cape
> Ply, stemming nightly toward the Pole: so seemed
> Far off the flying Fiend.[6]

Here is the full strength of the imagination involved in the word *hangs*, and exerted upon the whole image: First, the fleet, an aggregate of many ships, is represented as one mighty person, whose track, we know and feel, is upon the waters; but, taking advantage of its appearance to the senses, the Poet dares to represent it as *hanging in the clouds*, both for the gratification of the mind in contemplating the image itself, and in reference to the motion and appearance of the sublime object to which it is compared.

From impressions of sight we will pass to those of sound; which, as they must necessarily be of a less definite character, shall be selected from these volumes:

> Over his own sweet voice the Stock-dove *broods*;[7]

of the same bird,

> His voice was *buried* among trees,
> Yet to be come at by the breeze;

> O, Cuckoo! shall I call thee *Bird,*
> Or but a wandering *Voice?*[8]

The stock-dove is said to *coo*, a sound well imitating the note of the bird; but, by the intervention of the metaphor *broods*, the affections are called in by the imagination to assist in marking the manner in which the bird reiterates and prolongs her soft note, as if herself delighting to listen to it, and participating of a still and quiet satisfaction, like that which may be supposed inseparable from the continuous process of incubation. 'His voice was buried among trees', a metaphor expressing the love of *seclusion* by which this Bird is marked; and characterising its note as not partaking of the shrill and the piercing, and therefore more easily deadened by the intervening shade; yet a note so peculiar and withal so pleasing, that the breeze, gifted with that love of the sound which the Poet feels, penetrates the shades in which it is entombed, and conveys it to the ear of the listener.

> Shall I call thee Bird,
> Or but a wandering Voice?

This concise interrogation characterises the seeming ubiquity of the voice of the cuckoo, and dispossesses the creature almost of a corporeal existence; the Imagination being tempted to this exertion of her power by a consciousness in the memory that the cuckoo is almost perpetually heard throughout the season of spring, but seldom becomes an object of sight.

Thus far of images independent of each other, and immediately endowed by the mind with properties that do not inhere in them, upon an incitement from properties and qualities the existence of which is inherent and obvious. These processes of imagination are carried on either by conferring additional properties upon an object, or abstracting from it some of those which it actually possesses, and thus enabling it to re-act upon the mind which hath performed the process, like a new existence.

I pass from the Imagination acting upon an individual image to a consideration of the same faculty employed upon images in a conjunction by which they modify each other. The Reader has already had a fine instance before him in the passage quoted from Virgil, where the apparently perilous situation of the goat, hanging upon the shaggy precipice, is contrasted with that of the shepherd contemplating it from the seclusion of the cavern in which he lies stretched at ease and in security. Take these images separately, and how unaffecting the picture compared with that produced by their being thus connected with, and opposed to, each other!

> As a huge stone is sometimes seen to lie
> Couched on the bald top of an eminence,
> Wonder to all who do the same espy
> By what means it could thither come, and whence,
> So that it seems a thing endued with sense, .
> Like a sea-beast crawled forth, which on a shelf
> Of rock or sand reposeth, there to sun himself.
>
> Such seemed this Man; not all alive or dead
> Nor all asleep, in his extreme old age. . . .
>
> Motionless as a cloud the old Man stood,
> That heareth not the loud winds when they call,
> And moveth altogether if it move at all.[9]

In these images, the conferring, the abstracting, and the modifying powers of the Imagination, immediately and mediately acting, are all brought into conjunction. The stone is endowed with something of the power of life to approximate the sea-beast; and the sea-beast stripped of some of its vital qualities to assimilate it to the stone; which intermediate image is thus treated for the purpose of bringing the original image, that of the stone, to a nearer resemblance to the figure and condition of the aged Man; who is divested of so much of the indications of life and motion as to bring him to the point where the two objects unite and coalesce in just comparison. After what has been said, the image of the cloud need not be commented upon.

Thus far of an endowing or modifying power: but the Imagination also shapes and *creates*; and how? By innumerable processes; and in none does it more delight than in that of consolidating numbers into unity, and dissolving and separating unity into number, – alternations proceeding from, and governed by, a sublime consciousness of the soul in her own mighty and almost divine powers. Recur to the passage already cited from Milton. When the compact Fleet, as one Person, has been introduced 'Sailing from Bengala,' 'They,' *i.e.* the 'merchants,' representing the fleet resolved into a multitude of ships, 'ply' their voyage towards the extremities of the earth: 'So,' (referring to the word 'As' in the commencement) 'seemed the flying Fiend;' the image of his Person acting to recombine the multitude of ships into one body, – the point from which the comparison set out. 'So seemed,' and to whom seemed? To the heavenly Muse who dictates the poem, to the eye of the Poet's mind, and to that of the Reader, present at one moment in the wide Ethiopian, and the next in the solitudes, then first broken in upon, of the infernal regions!

> Modo me Thebis, modo ponit Athenis.[10]

Hear again this mighty Poet, – speaking of the Messiah going forth to expel from heaven the rebellious angels,

> Attended by ten thousand thousand Saints
> He onward came: far off His coming shone, – [11]

the retinue of Saints, and the person of the Messiah himself, lost almost and merged in the splendour of that indefinite abstraction 'His coming!'

As I do not mean here to treat this subject further than to throw some light upon the present Volumes, and especially upon one division of them, I shall spare myself and the Reader the trouble of considering the Imagination as it deals with thoughts and sentiments, as it regulates the composition of characters, and determines the course of actions: I will not consider it (more than I have already done by implication) as that power which, in the language of one of my most esteemed Friends, 'draws all things to one; which makes things animate or inanimate, beings with their attributes, subjects with their accessaries, take one colour and serve to one effect'.[12] The grand storehouses of enthusiastic and meditative Imagination, of poetical, as contradistinguished from human and dramatic Imagination, are the prophetic and lyrical parts of the Holy Scriptures, and the works of Milton; to which I cannot forbear to add those of Spenser. I select these writers in preference to those of ancient Greece and Rome, because the anthropomorphitism of the Pagan religion subjected the minds of the greatest poets in those countries too much to the bondage of definite form; from which the Hebrews were preserved by their abhorrence of idolatry.[13] This abhorrence was almost as strong in our great epic Poet, both from circumstances of his life, and from the constitution of his mind. However imbued the surface might be with classical literature, he was a Hebrew in soul; and all things tended in him towards the sublime. Spenser, of a gentler nature, maintained his freedom by aid of his allegorical spirit, at one time inciting him to create persons out of abstractions; and, at another, by a superior effort of genius, to give the universality and permanence of abstractions to his human beings, by means of attributes and emblems that belong to the highest moral truths and the purest sensations, — of which his character Una is a glorious example. Of the human and dramatic Imagination the works of Shakspeare are an inexhaustible source.

> I tax not you, ye Elements, with unkindness,
> I never gave you kingdoms, call'd you Daughters![14]

And if, bearing in mind the many Poets distinguished by this prime quality, whose names I omit to mention; yet justified by recollection of the insults which the ignorant, the incapable, and the presumptuous, have heaped upon these and my other writings, I may be permitted to anticipate the judgment of posterity upon myself, I shall declare (censurable, I grant, if the notoriety of the fact above stated does not justify me) that I have given in these unfavourable times, evidence of exertions of this faculty upon its worthiest objects, the external universe, the moral and religious sentiments of Man, his natural affections, and his acquired passions; which have the same ennobling tendency as the productions of men, in this kind, worthy to be holden in undying remembrance.

To the mode in which Fancy has already been characterised as the power of evoking and combining, or, as my friend Mr. Coleridge has styled it, 'the aggregative and associative power', my objection is only that the definition is too general.[15] To aggregate and to associate, to evoke and to combine, belong as well to the Imagination as to the Fancy; but either the materials evoked and combined are different; or they are brought together under a different law, and for a different purpose. Fancy does not require that the materials which she makes use of should be susceptible of change in their constitution, from her touch; and, where they admit of modification, it is enough for her purpose if it be slight, limited, and evanescent. Directly the reverse of these, are the desires and demands of the Imagination. She recoils from every thing but the plastic, the pliant, and the indefinite. She leaves it to Fancy to describe Queen Mab as coming,

> In shape no bigger than an agate-stone
> On the fore-finger of an alderman.[16]

Having to speak of stature, she does not tell you that her gigantic Angel was as tall as Pompey's Pillar; much less that he was twelve cubits, or twelve hundred cubits high; or that his dimensions equalled those of Teneriffe or Atlas; — because these, and if they were a million times as high it would be the same, are bounded: The expression is, 'His stature reached the sky!' the illimitable firmament! — When the Imagination frames a comparison, if it does not strike on the first presentation, a sense of the truth of the likeness, from the moment that it is perceived, grows — and continues to grow — upon the mind; the resemblance depending less upon outline of form and feature, than upon expression and effect; less upon casual and outstanding, than upon inherent and internal, properties: moreover, the images invariably modify each other. — The law under which the processes of Fancy are carried on is as capricious as the accidents of things, and the effects are surprising, playful, ludicrous, amusing, tender, or pathetic, as the objects happen to be appositely produced or

fortunately combined. Fancy depends upon the rapidity and
profusion with which she scatters her thoughts and images;
trusting that their number, and the felicity with which they are
linked together, will make amends for the want of individual
value: or she prides herself upon the curious subtilty and the
successful elaboration with which she can detect their lurking
affinities. If she can win you over to her purpose, and impart to
you her feelings, she cares not how unstable or transitory may be
her influence, knowing that it will not be out of her power to
resume it upon an apt occasion. But the Imagination is conscious
of an indestructible dominion; – the Soul may fall away from it,
not being able to sustain its grandeur; but, if once felt and
acknowledged, by no act of any other faculty of the mind can it be
relaxed, impaired, or diminished. – Fancy is given to quicken
and to beguile the temporal part of our nature, Imagination to
incite and to support the eternal. – Yet is it not the less true that
Fancy, as she is an active, is also, under her own laws and in her
own spirit, a creative faculty. In what manner Fancy ambitiously
aims at a rivalship with Imagination, and Imagination stoops to
work with the materials of Fancy, might be illustrated from the
compositions of all eloquent writers, whether in prose or verse;
and chiefly from those of our own Country. Scarcely a page of the
impassioned parts of Bishop Taylor's Works can be opened that
shall not afford examples. – Referring the Reader to those
inestimable volumes, I will content myself with placing a conceit
(ascribed to Lord Chesterfield) in contrast with a passage from
the Paradise Lost: –

> The dews of the evening most carefully shun,
> They are the tears of the sky for the loss of the sun.[17]

After the transgression of Adam, Milton, with other appearances
of sympathising Nature, thus marks the immediate consequence,

> Sky lowered, and, muttering thunder, some sad drops
> Wept at completion of the mortal sin.[18]

The associating link is the same in each instance: Dew and rain, not distinguishable from the liquid substance of tears, are employed as indications of sorrow. A flash of surprise is the effect in the former case; a flash of surprise, and nothing more; for the nature of things does not sustain the combination. In the latter, the effects from the act, of which there is this immediate consequence and visible sign, are so momentous, that the mind acknowledges the justice and reasonableness of the sympathy in nature so manifested; and the sky weeps drops of water as if with human eyes, as 'Earth had before trembled from her entrails, and Nature given a second groan.'[19]

SOURCE: extract from the Preface to *Poems* (1815); in *Prose Works*, ed. Owen and Smyser, vol. III, pp. 30–7.

NOTES

1. For Coleridge's comment, see above, section I. IV.

2. The dependence of Fancy and Imagination on the memory is a commonplace of empirical philosophy and of the eighteenth-century aesthetic systems based on that philosophy. Coleridge, for instance, in an *early* letter (9 Mar 1798) addressed to John Wicksteed wrote: 'People in general are not sufficiently aware how often the imagination creeps in and counterfeits the memory — perhaps to a certain degree it does always blend with our supposed recollections.' Moving toward a more exalted view of the imagination, Coleridge argues that this faculty *modifies* our memories, instead of being (as the empirical philosopher would maintain) dependent on the memory for all its materials.

3. See *A Midsummer Night's Dream*, v i 7ff.

4. Virgil, *Eclogue I*, 75–6. Translation: 'Never again, shall I, stretched out in some green glen, see you far away, *hanging* on the rocky hillside covered with thorny brambles.'

5. *King Lear*, IV vi 15–16.

6. *Paradise Lost*, II 636–43.

7. 'Resolution and Independence', 5.

8. 'O Nightingale', 13–14; 'To the Cuckoo', 3–4.

9. 'Resolution and Independence', 57–65, 75–7.

10. Horace, *Epistles*, II i 213. Translation: 'Sets me down now in Thebes, now in Athens'.

11. *Paradise Lost*, VI 767–8.

12. 'Charles Lamb upon the genius of Hogarth.' *Wordsworth's note.*

13. Cf. Coleridge's letter to Sotheby: above, section 1. I.

14. *King Lear*, III ii 16–17.

15. See above, section 1. VII.

16. *Romeo and Juliet*, I iv 56–7.

17. 'Advice to a Lady in Autumn', in *The Life of the Late Earl of Chesterfield* (1774) ii 248–9.

18. *Paradise Lost*, IX 1002–3.

19. Ibid., 1000–1.

VII. 'PETER BELL' AND THE IMAGINATION

The Poem of 'Peter Bell', as the Prologue will show, was composed under a belief that the Imagination not only does not require for its exercise the intervention of supernatural agency, but that, though such agency be excluded, the faculty may be called forth as imperiously and for kindred results of pleasure, by incidents, within the compass of poetic probability, in the humblest departments of daily life.

> SOURCE: extract from note to Robert Southey, 7 April 1819; in *The Poetical Works of William Wordsworth*, ed. T. Hutchinson (Oxford, 1933) p. 236.

VIII. RELIGION AND IMAGINATION

All religions owe their origin or acceptation to the wish of the human heart to supply in another state of existence the deficiencies of this, and to carry still nearer to perfection whatever we admire in our present condition; so that there must be many modes of expression, arising out of this coincidence, or rather identity of feeling, common to all Mythologies; and under this observation I should shelter the phrase from your censure; but I may be wrong in the particular case, though certainly not in the general principle. This leads to a remark in your last, 'that you are disgusted with all books that treat of religion'. I am afraid it is a bad sign in me, that I have little relish for any other — even in poetry it is the imaginative only, viz., that which is conversant [with], or turns upon infinity, that powerfully affects me, — perhaps I ought to explain: I mean to say that, unless in those passages where things are lost in each other, and limits vanish, and aspirations are raised, I read with something too much like indifference — but all great poets are in this view powerful Religionists, and therefore among many literary pleasures lost, I have not yet to lament over that of verse as departed.

SOURCE: extract from letter to Walter Savage Landor, 21 January 1824; in *Letters*, ed. de Selincourt, vol. I, pp. 134–5.

4. JOHN KEATS

I. AN EARLY STATEMENT

. . . the high Idea I have of poetical fame makes me think I see it towering to high above me. At any rate I have no right to talk until Endymion is finished — it will be a test, a trial of my Powers of Imagination and chiefly of my invention which is a rare thing indeed — by which I must make 4000 Lines of one bare circumstance and fill them with Poetry; and when I consider that this is a great task, and that when done it will take me but a dozen paces towards the Temple of Fame — it makes me say — God forbid that I should be without such a task! I have heard Hunt say and [I] may be asked — why endeavour after a long Poem? To which I should answer — Do not the Lovers of Poetry like to have a little Region to wander in where they may pick and choose, and in which the images are so numerous that many are forgotten and found new in a second Reading: which may be food for a Week's stroll in the summer? Do not they like this better than what they can read through before Mrs Williams comes down stairs? a Morning work at most. Besides a long Poem is a test of Invention which I take to be the Polar Star of Poetry, as Fancy is the Sails, and Imagination the Rudder. Did our great Poets ever write short Pieces? I mean in the shape of Tales − This same invention seems indeed of late Years to have been forgotten as a Poetical excellence.

> SOURCE: extract from letter to Benjamin Bailey, 8 October 1817; in *The Letters of John Keats*, ed. M. B. Forman, 4th. edition (Oxford, 1952) p. 52.

II. 'THE IMAGINATION MAY BE COMPARED TO ADAM'S DREAM'

I am certain of nothing but of the holiness of the Heart's affections and the truth of Imagination − What the imagination seizes as Beauty must be truth − whether it existed before or not − for I have the same Idea of all our Passions as of Love [:]they are all in their sublime, creative of essential Beauty. In a Word, you may know my favorite Speculation by my first Book[1] and the little song[2] I sent in my last − which is a representation from the fancy of the probable mode of operating in these Matters. The Imagination may be compared to Adam's dream − he awoke and found it truth.[3] I am the more zealous in this affair, because I have never yet been able to perceive how any thing can be known for truth by consequitive reasoning[4] − and yet it must be. Can it be that even the greatest Philosopher ever arrived at his goal without putting aside numerous objections. However it may be, O for a Life of Sensations rather than of Thoughts! It is 'a Vision in the form of Youth' a Shadow of reality to come − and this consideration has further convinced me for it has come as auxiliary to another favorite Speculation of mine, that we shall enjoy ourselves here after by having what we call happiness on Earth repeated in a finer tone and so repeated. And yet such a fate can only befall those who delight in Sensation rather than hunger as you do after Truth. Adam's dream will do here and seems to be a conviction that Imagination and its empyreal reflection is the same as human Life and its Spiritual repetition. But as I was saying – the simple imaginative Mind may have its rewards in the repeti[ti]on of its own silent Working coming continually on the Spirit with a fine Suddenness – to compare great things with small – have you never by being Surprised with an old Melody – in a delicious place – by a delicious voice, fe[l]t over again your very Speculations and Surmises at the time it first operated on your Soul – do you not remember forming to yourself the singer's face more beautiful than it was possible and yet with the elevation of the Moment you did not think so – even then you were mounted on the Wings of Imagination so high – that the Prototype must be here after – that delicious face you will see. What a time! I am continually running away from the subject – sure this cannot be exactly the case with a complex Mind – one that is imaginative and at the same time careful of its fruits – who would exist partly on Sensation partly on thought – to whom it is necessary that years should bring the philosophic Mind – such an one I consider your's and therefore it is necessary to your eternal Happiness that you not only drink this old Wine of Heaven, which I shall call the redigestion of our most ethereal Musings on Earth; but also increase in knowledge and know all things.

SOURCE: extract from letter to Benjamin Bailey, 22 November 1817; in *Letters*, ed. Forman, pp. 67–8.

NOTES

1. Keats's *Poems* (1817).
2. The song beginning 'O Sorrow / Why dost borrow. . . .'
3. *Paradise Lost*, VIII 460–90.
4. Cf. Keats's later remark to J. H. Reynolds that 'axioms in philosophy are not axioms until they are proved upon our pulses' (3 May 1818), and also the following statements in letters to his brother George: 'I can never feel certain of any truth but from a clear perception of its Beauty' (Dec 1818); 'Nothing ever becomes real till it is experienced – Even a Proverb is no proverb to you till your Life has illustrated it' (Mar 1819).

III. 'NEGATIVE CAPABILITY'

I had not a dispute but a disquisition with Dilke, on various subjects; several things dovetailed in my mind, and at once it struck me what quality went to form a Man of Achievement especially in Literature and which Shakespeare possessed so enormously – I mean *Negative Capability*, that is when man is capable of being in uncertainties, Mysteries, doubts, without any irritable reaching after fact and reason – Coleridge, for instance, would let go by a fine isolated verisimilitude caught from the Penetralium of mystery, from being incapable of remaining Content with half knowledge. This pursued through Volumes would perhaps take us no further than this, that with a great poet the sense of Beauty overcomes every other consideration, or rather obliterates all consideration.

SOURCE: extract from letter to George and Thomas Keats, 21 December 1817; in *Letters*, ed. Forman, p. 71.

IV. THE POETICAL CHARACTER AND HAZLITT'S 'SYMPATHETIC IMAGINATION'

[Keats ends a letter (10 January 1818) to Haydon, the painter, with the words: 'I am convinced that there are three things to rejoice at in this Age – The Excursion, Your Pictures, and Hazlitt's depth of Taste.' Conspicuous among Keats's debts to Hazlitt is his adoption of the concept of the 'sympathetic imagination'. 'Poetry', Hazlitt asserts in his essay 'On Poetry in General' (1818), 'is the language of the imagination and the passions.' His understanding of the term *imagination* is clarified in 'The Same Subject Continued' (the second part of the essay 'On Genius and Common Sense', in *Table Talk*, 1821–2):

Imagination is, more properly, the power of carrying on a given feeling into other situations, which must be done best according to the hold which the feeling itself has taken of the mind. In new and unknown combinations, the impression must act by sympathy, and not by rule; but there can be no sympathy, where there is no passion, no original interest. The personal interest may in some cases oppress and circumscribe the imaginative faculty, as in the instance of Rousseau: but in general the strength and consistency of the imagination will be in proportion to the strength and depth of feeling. . . .

The Notes at the end of this extract from Keats elucidate this definition of Hazlitt's.]

As to the poetical Character itself (I mean that sort of which, if I am any thing, I am a Member; that sort distinguished from the Wordsworthian or egotistical sublime;[1] which is a thing per se and stands alone) it is not itself – it has no self – it is every thing and nothing[2] – It has no character – it enjoys light and shade; it lives in gusto,[3] be it foul or fair, high or low, rich or poor, mean or elevated – It has as much delight in conceiving an Iago as an Imogen.[4] What shocks the virtuous philosopher, delights the camelion Poet.[5] It does no harm from its relish of the dark side of things any more than from its taste for the bright one; because they both end in speculation. A Poet is the most unpoetical of any thing in existence; because he has no Identity – he is continually in for – and filling some other Body – The Sun, the Moon, the Sea and Men and Women who are creatures of impulse are poetical and have about them an unchangeable attribute – the poet has none; no identity – he is certainly the most unpoetical of all God's Creatures. If then he has no self, and if I am a Poet, where is the Wonder that I should say I would write no more? Might I not at that very instant have been cogitating on the Characters of Saturn and Ops?[6] It is a wretched thing to confess; but is a very fact that not one word I ever utter can be taken for granted as an opinion growing out of my identical nature – how can it, when I have no nature? When I am in a room with People if I ever am free from speculating on creations of my own brain, then not myself goes home to myself: but the identity of every one in the room begins so to press upon me that I am in a very little time an[ni]hilated – not only among Men; it would be the same in a Nursery of children.[7]

SOURCE: extract from letter to Richard Woodhouse, 22 October 1818; in *Letters*, ed. Forman, pp. 226–7.

NOTES

1. In 'On the Character of Rousseau' (1816), Hazlitt argues that both Rousseau and Wordsworth 'create an interest out of nothing, or rather out of their own feelings; both weave numberless recollections into one sentiment; both wind their own being round whatever object occurs to them. . . . Mr. Wordsworth would persuade you that the most insignificant objects are interesting in themselves, because he is interested in them.' In 'The Same Subject Continued', his tone is more acerbic still: 'He [Wordsworth] is the greatest, that is, the most original poet of the present day, only because he is the greatest egotist. . . . Whatever does not relate exclusively and wholly to himself, is foreign to his views. He contemplates a whole-length figure of himself, he looks along the unbroken line of his personal identity. He thrusts aside all other objects, all other interests with scorn and impatience, that he may repose on his own being, that he may dig out the treasures of thought contained in it, that he may unfold the precious stores of a mind forever brooding over itself. His genius is the effect of his individual character. He stamps that character, that deep individual interest, on whatever he meets. The object is nothing but as it furnishes food for internal meditation, for old association. If there had been no other being in the universe, Mr. Wordsworth's poetry would have been just what it is.'

2. In 'On Shakespeare and Milton', Hazlitt writes: 'The striking peculiarity of Shakespeare's mind was its generic quality, its power of communication with all other minds − so that it contained a universe of thought and feeling within itself, and had no one peculiar bias, or exclusive excellence more than another. He was just like any other man, but that he was like all other men. He was the least of an egotist that it was possible to be. He was nothing in himself; but he was all that others were, or that they could become. . . . He was like the genius of humanity, changing places with all of us at pleasure, and playing with our purposes as with his own. He turned the globe round for his amusement, and surveyed the generations of men. . . . He had only to think of anything in order to become that thing, with all the circumstances belonging to it.'

3. 'Gusto in art is power or passion defining any object', Hazlitt writes in 'On Gusto' (1816). ' . . . Claude's landscapes, perfect as they are, want gusto. . . . They do not interpret one sense by another; they do not distinguish the character of different objects as we are taught,

and can only be taught, to distinguish them by their effect on the different senses. That is, his eye wanted imagination: it did not strongly sympathise with his other faculties. He saw the atmosphere, but he did not feel it. . . . His trees are perfectly beautiful, but quite immovable; they have a look of enchantment. In short, his landscapes are unequalled imitations of nature, released from its subjection to the elements, as if all objects were become a delightful fairy vision, and the eye had rarefied and refined away the other senses.'

4. 'That which, perhaps, more than anything else distinguishes the dramatic productions of Shakespeare from all others, is this wonderful truth and individuality of conception. Each of his characters is as much itself, and as absolutely independent of the rest, as well as of the author, as if they were living persons, not fictions of the mind. The poet may be said, for the time, to identify himself with the character he wishes to represent, and to pass from one to another, like the same soul successively animating different bodies. By an art like that of the ventriloquist, he throws his imagination out of himself, and makes every word appear to proceed from the mouth of the person in whose name it is given. His plays alone are properly expressions of the passions, not descriptions of them.' – Hazlitt, 'On Shakespeare and Milton' (1818).

5. Cf. Hazlitt's description of Shakespeare in 'The Same Subject Continued': 'His genius consisted in the faculty of transforming himself at will into whatever he chose: his originality was the power of seeing every object from the exact point of view in which others would see it. He was the Proteus of human intellect. Genius in ordinary is a more obstinate and less versatile thing. . . . It [ordinary genius] is just the reverse of the cameleon; for it does not borrow, but lends its colour to all about it: or like the glow-worm, discloses a little circle of gorgeous light in the twilight of obscurity, in the night of intellect, that surrounds it.'

6. Saturn and Ops are figures in *Hyperion*, which Keats was composing in late 1818.

7. Writing to Benjamin Bailey (22 Nov 1817), Keats had said: 'nothing startles me beyond the Moment. The setting Sun will always set me to rights – or if a Sparrow come before my Window I take part in its existince and pick about the Gravel.'

V. THE SYMPATHETIC IMAGINATION IN ACTION

Notwithstanding your Happiness and your recommendation I hope I shall never marry. . . . The roaring of the wind is my wife and the Stars through the window pane are my Children. The mighty abstract Idea I have of Beauty in all things stifles the more divided and minute domestic happiness – an amiable wife and sweet Children I contemplate as a part of that Beauty – but I must have a thousand of those beautiful particles to fill up my heart. I feel more and more every day, as my imagination strengthens, that I do not live in this world alone but in a thousand worlds. No sooner am I alone than shapes of epic greatness are stationed around me, and serve my Spirit the office which is equivalent to a King's body guard – then 'Tragedy with scepter'd pall, comes sweeping by'.[1] According to my state of mind I am with Achilles shouting in the Trenches, or with Theocritus in the Vales of Sicily.

SOURCE: extract from letter to George and Georgiana Keats, October 1818; in *Letters*, ed. Forman, pp. 239–40.

NOTE

1. Milton, 'Il Penseroso', 97–8.

5. PERCY BYSSHE SHELLEY

I. MAN IS AN IMAGINATIVE BEING

Most of the errors of philosophers have arisen from considering the human being in a point of view too detailed and circumscribed. He is not a moral, and an intellectual, – but also, and pre-eminently, an imaginative being. His own mind is his law; his own mind is all things to him. If we would arrive at a knowledge which should be serviceable from the practical conclusions to which it leads, we ought to consider the mind of man and the universe as the great whole on which to exercise our speculations.

SOURCE: extract from *Speculations on Metaphysics*, IV (c. 1812–15); in *The Complete Works of Percy Bysshe Shelley*, ed. R. Ingpen and W. E. Peck (London, 1965) vol. VII, p. 65.

II. MORALS AND IMAGINATION

If a child observes without emotion its nurse or its mother suffering acute pain, it is attributable rather to ignorance than insensibility. So soon as the accents and gestures significant of pain are referred to the feelings which they express, they awaken in the mind of the beholder a desire that they should cease. Pain is thus apprehended to be evil for its own sake. . . . The inhabitant of a highly civilised community will more acutely sympathise with the sufferings and enjoyments of others, than the inhabitant of a society of a less degree of civilisation. He who shall have cultivated his intellectual powers by familiarity with the finest specimens of poetry and philosophy, will usually [sympathise more] than one engaged in the less refined functions of manual labour.

The imagination thus acquires by exercise a habit as it were of perceiving and abhorring evil, however remote from the immediate sphere of sensations with which that individual mind is conversant. Imagination or mind employed in prophetically [imaging forth] its objects is that faculty of human nature on which every gradation of its progress, nay, every, the minutest change depends. Pain or pleasure, if subtly analysed, will be found to consist entirely in prospect. The only distinction between the selfish man, and the virtuous man, is that the imagination of the former is confined within a narrow limit, whilst that of the latter embraces a comprehensive circumference. In this sense, wisdom and virtue may be said to be inseparable, and criteria of each other. Selfishness is thus the offspring of ignorance and mistake; it is the portion of unreflecting infancy, and savage solitude, or of those whom toil or evil occupations have [blunted and rendered torpid;] disinterested benevolence is the product of a cultivated imagination,

and has an intimate connexion with all the arts which add
ornament, or dignity, or power, or stability to the social state of
man. Virtue is thus entirely a refinement of civilised life; a
creation of the human mind or rather a combination which it has
made, according to elementary rules contained within itself, of
the feelings suggested by the relations established between man
and man.

SOURCE: extract from *Speculations on Morals*, I; in *Complete
Works*, ed. Ingpen and Peck, vol. VII, pp. 75–6.

III. IMAGINATION AND PLATONIC LOVE

Let it not be imagined that because the Greeks were deprived of
its legitimate object,[1] they were incapable of sentimental love;
and that this passion is the mere child of chivalry and the
literature of modern times. This object, or its archetype, forever
exists in the mind, which selects among those who resemble it,
that which most resembles it; and instinctively fills up the
interstices of the imperfect image, in the same manner as the
imagination moulds and completes the shapes in clouds, or in the
fire, into resemblances of whatever form, animal, building, &c.,
happens to be present to it.[2]

SOURCE: extract from *A Discourse on the Manners of the
Ancients Relative to the Subject of Love* (1818); in *Complete Works*,
ed. Ingpen and Peck, vol. VII, p. 228.

NOTES

1. The 'legitimate object' of love is woman. The classical Greek
devotion to homosexual passion, however, made heterosexual re-
lationships seem less important; Greek women, says Shelley, 'possessed,
except with extraordinary exceptions, the habits and the qualities of
slaves'.

2. After quoting this sentence, J. A. Notopoulos comments: 'Shelley
is restating here Plato's theory of ideas and their relation to particulars
as set forth in *Symposium*, 210–211; the archetype is grasped by the mind

alone, whereas the particulars in the world of time and space are imperfect images of this intellectual archetype. Thus far Shelley is in harmony with Plato; however, he interpolates an element which changes the Platonic complexion of the passage. Shelley makes poetic imagination play an integrating role between the particular and its Platonic archetype, whereas Plato stresses reason and makes the archetype not a mental concept but a transcendental, objective essence' — *The Platonism of Shelley* (1949), p. 335.

IV. REASON AND IMAGINATION: TWO FRAGMENTS AND A
FINISHED STATEMENT

(i)

In one mode of considering these two classes of action of the human mind which are called reason and imagination, the former may be considered as mind employed upon the relations borne by one thought to another, however produced, and imagination as mind combining the elements of thought itself. It has been termed the power of association; and on an accurate anatomy of the functions of the mind, it would be difficult to assign any other origin to the mass of what we perceive and know than this power. Association is, however, rather a law according to which this power is exerted than the power itself; in the same manner as gravitation is a passive expression of the reciprocal tendency of heavy bodies towards their respective centres. Were these bodies conscious of such a tendency, the name which they would assign to that consciousness would express the cause of gravitation; and it were a vain inquiry as to what might be the cause of that cause. Association bears the same relation to imagination as a mode to a source of action: when we look upon shapes in the fire or the clouds and imagine to ourselves the resemblance of familiar objects, we do no more than seize the relation of certain points of visible objects, and fill up, blend together. . . [MS. breaks off thus.]

(ii)

The imagination is a faculty not less imperial and essential to the happiness and dignity of the human being, than the reason.

(iii)

According to one mode of regarding those two classes of mental action, which are called reason and imagination, the former may be considered as mind contemplating the relations borne by one thought to another, however produced; and the latter, as mind acting upon those thoughts so as to colour them with its own light, and composing from them, as from elements, other thoughts, each containing within itself the principle of its own integrity. The one is the $τὸ\ ποιεῖν$,[1] or the principle of synthesis, and has for its objects those forms which are common to universal nature and existence itself; the other is the $τo\ λογίζειν$,[2] or principle of analysis, and its action regards the relations of things, simply as relations; considering thoughts, not in their integral unity, but as the algebraical representations which conduct to certain general results. Reason is the enumeration of quantities already known; imagination is the perception of the value of those quantities, both separately and as a whole. Reason respects differences, and imagination the similitudes of things. Reason is to imagination as the instrument to the agent, as the body to the spirit, as the shadow to the substance.

SOURCE: two undated fragments and an extract from *A Defence of Poetry* (1821); in *Complete Works*, ed. Ingpen and Peck, vol. VII, pp. 107, 109.

NOTES

The undated fragments, sections (i) and (ii), almost certainly are part of an early draft of *A Defence of Poetry*. They are reprinted here unabridged.

1. $τὸ\ ποιεῖν$: 'the maker, the creator'. See Sidney's *Apologie for Poetrie* (1595): 'The Greekes named him 'Poet,' which name, hath as the most excellent, gone through other languages; it commeth of this word *Poiein*, which is to make: wherein I know not whether by luck or wisedome, we Englishmen have met with the Greekes in calling him a Maker.'

2. $τὸ\ λογίζειν$: 'the calculator, that which reckons or computes'.

V. IMAGINATION AND THE SUPREMACY OF POETRY

Language, colour, form, and religious and civil habits of action, are all the instruments and materials of poetry; they may be called poetry by that figure of speech which considers the effect as a synonyme of the cause. But poetry in a more restricted sense expresses those arrangements of language, and especially metrical language, which are created by that imperial faculty, whose throne is curtained within the invisible nature of man. And this springs from the nature itself of language, which is a more direct representation of the actions and passions of our internal being, and is susceptible of more various and delicate combinations, than colour, form, or motion, and is more plastic and obedient to the control of that faculty of which it is the creation. For language is arbitrarily produced by the imagination, and has relation to thoughts alone; but all other materials, instruments, and conditions of art, have relations among each other, which limit and interpose between conception and expression.[1] The former is as a mirror which reflects, the latter as a cloud which enfeebles, the light of which both are mediums of communication. Hence the fame of sculptors, painters, and musicians, although the intrinsic powers of the great masters of these arts may yield in no degree to that of those who have employed language as the hieroglyphic of their thoughts, has never equalled that of poets in the restricted sense of the term; as two performers of equal skill will produce unequal effects from a guitar and a harp. The fame of legislators and founders of religions, so long as their institutions last, alone seem to exceed that of poets in the restricted sense. . . .

SOURCE: extract from *A Defence of Poetry*; in *Complete Works*, ed. Ingpen and Peck, vol. VII, p. 113.

NOTE

1. D. H. Reiman glosses this difficult passage by observing that, for Shelley, 'poetry and the other products of the imagination (scientific thought, political theory) compete for the imaginative energy of the

human mind'; thus, attempting to justify poetry 'as the most useful expression of the imagination', he began 'by saying that language, the arbitrary product of the imagination, can give expression to it more directly and faithfully than can materials produced by nature (the sculptor's stone, the scientist's chemicals, the economist's crops and people)'–Reiman, *Percy Bysshe Shelley* (1969: paperback 1976), pp. 122–3.

VI. IMAGINATION AS THE GREAT INSTRUMENT OF MORAL GOOD

Poetry acts in another and diviner manner. It awakens and enlarges the mind itself by rendering it the receptacle of a thousand unapprehended combinations of thought. Poetry lifts the veil from the hidden beauty of the world, and makes familiar objects be as if they were not familiar; it reproduces all that it represents, and the impersonations clothed in its Elysian light stand thenceforward in the minds of those who have once contemplated them, as memorials of that gentle and exalted content which extends itself over all thoughts and actions with which it coexists. The great secret of morals is love; or a going out of our own nature, and an identification of ourselves with the beautiful which exists in thought, action, or person, not our own. A man, to be greatly good, must imagine intensely and comprehensively; he must put himself in the place of another and of many others; the pains and pleasures of his species must become his own. The great instrument of moral good is the imagination;[1] and poetry administers to the effect by acting upon the cause. Poetry enlarges the circumference of the imagination by replenishing it with thoughts of ever new delight, which have the power of attracting and assimilating to their own nature all other thoughts, and which form new intervals and interstices whose void for ever craves fresh food. Poetry strengthens that faculty which is the organ of the moral nature of man, in the same manner as exercise strengthens a limb.

SOURCE: extract from *A Defence of Poetry*; in *Complete Works*, ed. Ingpen and Peck, vol. VII, pp. 117–18.

NOTE

1. Compare the following sentence from Shelley's preface to *The Cenci* (1819): 'Imagination is as the immortal God which should assume flesh for the redemption of mortal passion.'

PART TWO

Modern Critical Studies

C. M. Bowra

THE ROMANTIC IMAGINATION (1950)

If we wish to distinguish a single characteristic which differentiates the English Romantics from the poets of the eighteenth century, it is to be found in the importance which they attached to the imagination and in the special view which they held of it. On this, despite significant differences on points of detail, Blake, Coleridge, Wordsworth, Shelley, and Keats agree, and for each it sustains a deeply considered theory of poetry. In the eighteenth century imagination was not a cardinal point in poetical theory. For Pope and Johnson, as for Dryden before them, it has little importance, and when they mention it, it has a limited significance. They approve of fancy, provided that it is controlled by what they call 'judgement', and they admire the apt use of images, by which they mean little more than visual impressions and metaphors. But for them what matters most in poetry is its truth to the emotions, or, as they prefer to say, sentiment. They wish to speak in general terms for the common experience of men, not to indulge personal whims in creating new worlds. For them the poet is more an interpreter than a creator, more concerned with showing the attractions of what we already know than with expeditions into the unfamiliar and the unseen. They are less interested in the mysteries of life than in its familiar appearance, and they think that their task is to display this with as much charm and truth as they can command. But for the Romantics imagination is fundamental, because they think that without it poetry is impossible.

This belief in the imagination was part of the contemporary belief in the individual self. The poets were conscious of a wonderful capacity to create imaginary worlds, and they could not believe that this was idle or false. On the contrary, they thought that to curb it was to deny something vitally necessary to their whole being. They thought that it was just this which made them poets, and that in their exercise of it they could do far better than other poets who sacrificed it to caution and common sense. They saw that the power of poetry is strongest when the creative impulse works untrammelled, and they knew that in their own case this happened when they shaped fleeting visions into concrete forms and pursued wild thoughts until they captured and mastered them. Just as in politics men turned their minds from the existing order to vast prospects of a reformed humanity, so in the arts they abandoned the conventional plan of existence for private adventures which had an inspiring glory. As in the Renaissance poets suddenly found the huge possibilities of the human self and expressed them in a bold and far-flung art, which is certainly much more than an imitation of life, so the Romantics, brought to a fuller consciousness of their own powers, felt a similar need to exert these powers in fashioning new worlds of the mind.

The Romantic emphasis on the imagination was strengthened by considerations which are both religious and metaphysical. For a century English philosophy had been dominated by the theories of Locke. He assumed that in perception the mind is wholly passive, a mere recorder of impressions from without, 'a lazy looker-on on an external world'. His system was well suited to an age of scientific speculation which found its representative voice in Newton. The mechanistic explanation which both philosophers and scientists gave of the world meant that scanty respect was paid to the human self and especially to its more instinctive, though not less powerful, convictions. Thus both Locke and Newton found a place for God in their universes, the former on the ground that 'the works of nature in every part of them sufficiently evidence a deity',[1] and the latter on the principle that the great machine of the world implies a mechanic. But this was not at all what the Romantics demanded from religion. For them it was a question less of reason than of feeling, less of argument than of experience, and they complained that these mechanistic explanations were a denial of their innermost convictions. So too with poetry. Locke had views on poetry, as he had on most human activities, but no very high regard for it. For him it is a matter of 'wit', and the task of wit is to combine ideas and 'thereby to make up pleasant pictures and agreeable visions in the fancy'.[2] Wit, in his view, is quite irresponsible and not troubled with truth or reality. The Romantics rejected with contumely a theory which robbed their work of its essential connection with life.

Locke is the target both of Blake and of Coleridge, to whom he represents a deadly heresy on the nature of existence. They are concerned with more than discrediting his special views on God and poetry: they are hostile to his whole system which supports those views, and, even worse, robs the human self of importance. They reject his conception of the universe and replace it by their own systems, which deserve the name of 'idealist' because mind is their central point and governing factor. But because they are poets, they insist that the most vital activity of the mind is the imagination. Since for them it is the very source of spiritual energy, they cannot but believe that it is divine, and that, when they exercise it, they in some way partake of the activity of God. Blake says proudly and prophetically:

This world of Imagination is the world of Eternity; it is the divine bosom into which we shall all go after the death of the Vegetated body. This World of Imagination is Infinite and Eternal, whereas the world of Generation, or Vegetation, is Finite and Temporal. There Exist in that Eternal World the Permanent Realities of Every Thing which we see reflected in this Vegetable Glass of Nature. All Things are comprehended in their Eternal Forms in the divine body of the Saviour, the True Vine of Eternity, The Human Imagination.[3]

For Blake the imagination is nothing less than God as He operates in the human soul. It follows that any act of creation performed by the imagination is divine and that in the imagination man's spiritual nature is fully and finally realized. Coleridge does not speak with so apocalyptic a certainty, but his conclusion is not very different from Blake's: 'The primary IMAGINATION I hold to be the living Power and prime Agent of all human Perception, and as a repetition in the finite mind of the eternal act of creation in the infinite I AM.'[4] It is true that he regards poetry as a product of the secondary imagination, but since this differs only in degree from the primary, it remains clear that for Coleridge the imagination is of first importance because it partakes of the creative activity of God.

This is a tremendous claim, and it is not confined to Blake and Coleridge. It was to some degree held by Wordsworth and Shelley and Keats. Each was confident not only that the imagination was his most precious possession but that it was somehow concerned with a supernatural order. Never before had quite such a claim been made, and from it Romantic poetry derives much that is most magical in it. The danger of so bold an assumption is that the poet may be so absorbed in his own private universe and in the exploration of its remoter corners that he may be unable to convey his essential experience to other men and fail to convert them to his special creed. The Romantics certainly created worlds of their own, but they succeeded in persuading others that these were not absurd or merely fanciful. Indeed, in this respect they were closer to earth and the common man than some of their German contemporaries. They have not the respect for unsatisfied longing as an end in itself or the belief in hallucination and magic which play so large a part in the mind of Brentano, nor have they that nihilistic delight in being detached from life, of which Novalis writes to Caroline Schlegel: 'I know that imagination is most attracted by what is most immoral, most animal; but I also know how like a dream all imagination is, how it loves night, meaninglessness, and solitude.'[5] This was not what the English Romantics thought. They believed that the imagination stands in some essential relation to truth and reality, and they were at pains to make their poetry pay attention to them.

In doing this they encountered an old difficulty. If a man gives free play to his imagination, what assurance is there that what he says is in any sense true? Can it tell us anything that we do not know, or is it so removed from ordinary life as to be an escape from it? The question had been answered in one sense by Locke when he dealt so cavalierly with poetic wit, and a similar answer was given by Blake's revolutionary friend, Tom Paine, in his *Age of Reason*: 'I had some turn, and I believe some talent for poetry; but this I rather repressed than encouraged as leading too much into the field of imagination.' This is a point of view, and it is not new. It is based on the assumption that the creations of the imagination are mere fantasies and, as such, divorced from life. The problem had troubled the Elizabethans, and Shakespeare shows acquaintance with it when he makes Theseus say:

> The poet's eye, in a fine frenzy rolling,
> Doth glance from heaven to earth, from earth to heaven;
> And, as imagination bodies forth
> The forms of things unknown, the poet's pen
> Turns them to shapes, and gives to airy nothing
> A local habitation and a name.[6]

This would have won the approval of an Italian philosopher like Pico della Mirandola, who thought that the imagination is almost a diseased faculty, and would certainly have welcomed Theseus' association of the poet with the lunatic and the lover. Even those who did not venture so far as this thought that the creations of the imagination have little to do with actual life and provide no more than an agreeable escape from it. This was Bacon's view in *The Advancement of Learning:* 'The imagination, being not tied to the laws of matter, may at pleasure join that which nature hath severed and sever that which nature hath joined, and so make unlawful matches and divorces of things.' Bacon regards this as a harmless and not unpleasant activity, but not more. Though the Elizabethans excelled almost all other ages in the creation of imaginary worlds, their gravest thinkers made no great claim for them and were on the whole content that they should do no more than give a respite from the cares of ordinary life.

Such a position is plainly unsatisfactory for poets who believe that the imagination is a divine faculty concerned with the central issues of being. Indeed, it must be difficult for almost any poet to think that what he creates is imaginary in the derogatory sense which Bacon and his like give to the word. Poets usually believe that their creations are somehow concerned with reality, and this belief sustains them in their work. Their approach is indeed not that of the analytical mind, but it is none the less penetrating. They assume that poetry deals in some sense with truth, though this truth may be different from that of science or philosophy. That Shakespeare understood the question is clear from what Hippolyta says in answer to Theseus' discourse on the imagination:

> But all the story of the night told over,
> And all their minds transfigur'd so together,
> More witnesseth than fancy's images,
> And grows to something of great constancy,
> But, howsoever, strange and admirable.[7]

Hippolyta has sense enough to see that a poet's inventions are not an 'airy nothing' but stand in some relation to reality. In this she presents a view which is in opposition to that of the Platonist Pico but which has some affinity with that of Guarino, who says that the statements of poetry are true not literally but symbolically.[8] For Hippolyta the creations of the imagination are related to living experience and reflect some kind of reality.

The Romantics face this issue squarely and boldly. So far from thinking that the imagination deals with the non-existent, they insist that it reveals an important kind of truth. They believe that when it is at work it sees things to which the ordinary intelligence is blind and that it is intimately connected with a special insight or perception or intuition. Indeed, imagination and insight are in fact inseparable and form for all practical purposes a single faculty. Insight both awakes the imagination to work and is in turn sharpened by it when it is at work. This is the assumption on which the Romantics wrote poetry. It means that, when their creative gifts are engaged, they are inspired by their sense of the mystery of things to probe it with a peculiar insight and to shape their discoveries into imaginative forms. Nor is this process difficult to understand. Most of us, when we use our imaginations, are in the first place stirred by some alluring puzzle which calls for a solution, and in the second place enabled by our own creations in the mind to see much that was before dark or unintelligible. As our fancies take coherent shape, we see more clearly what has puzzled and perplexed us. This is what the Romantics do. They combine imagination and truth because their creations are inspired and controlled by a peculiar insight. Coleridge makes the point conclusively when he praises Wordsworth:

It was the union of deep feeling with profound thought; the fine balance of truth in observing, with the imaginative faculty in modifying the objects observed; and above all the original gift of spreading the tone, the *atmosphere*, and with it the depth and height of the ideal world around forms, incidents, and situations, of which, for the common view, custom had bedimmed all the lustre, had dried up the sparkle and the dew drops.[9]

So long as the imagination works in this way, it cannot fairly be accused of being an escape from life or of being no more than an agreeable relaxation.

The perception which works so closely with the imagination is not of the kind in which Locke believed, and the Romantics took pains to dispel any misunderstanding on the point. Since what mattered to them was an insight into the nature of things, they rejected Locke's limitation of perception to physical objects, because it robbed the mind of its most essential function, which is at the same time to perceive and to create. On this Blake speaks with prophetic scorn: 'Mental Things are alone Real; what is call'd Corporeal, Nobody Knows of its Dwelling Place: it is in Fallacy, and its Existence an Imposture. Where is the Existence Out of Mind or Thought? Where is it but in the Mind of a Fool?'[10] Coleridge came to a similar conclusion for not very different reasons: 'If the mind be not *passive*, if it be indeed made in God's image, and that, too, in the sublimest sense, the *Image of the Creator*, there is ground for the suspicion that any system built on the passiveness of the mind must be false as a system.'[11]

When they rejected the sensationalist view of an external world, Blake and Coleridge prepared the way to restoring the supremacy of the spirit which had been denied by Locke but was at this time being propounded by German metaphysicians. Blake knew nothing of them, and his conclusions arose from his own visionary outlook, which could not believe that matter is in any sense as real as spirit. Coleridge had read Kant and Schelling and found in them much to support his views, but those views were derived less from them than from his own instinctive conviction that the world of spirit is the only reality. Because he was first a poet and only secondly a metaphysician, his conception of a universe of spirit came from his intense sense of an inner life and from his belief that the imagination, working with intuition, is more likely than the analytical reason to make discoveries on matters which really concern us.

In rejecting Locke's and Newton's explanations of the visible world, the Romantics obeyed an inner call to explore more fully the world of spirit. In different ways each of them believed in an order of things which is not that which we see and know, and this was the goal of their passionate search. They wished to penetrate to an abiding reality, to explore its mysteries, and by this to understand more clearly what life means and what it is worth. They were convinced that, though visible things are the instruments by which we find this reality, they are not everything and have indeed little significance unless they are related to some embracing and sustaining power. Nor is it hard to see what this means. Most of us feel that a physical universe is not enough and demand some scheme which will explain why our beliefs and convictions are valid and why in an apparently mechanistic order we have scales of values for which no mechanism can account. Locke and Newton explain what the sensible world is, but not what it is worth. Indeed, in explaining mental judge-ments by physical processes they destroy their validity, since the only assurance for the truth of our judgements is the existence of an objective truth which cannot be determined by a causal, subjective process. Such systems embody a spirit of negation, because in trying to explain our belief in the good or the holy or the beautiful they succeed only in explaining it away. That is why Blake dismissed atomic physicists and their like as men who try in vain to destroy the divine light which alone gives meaning to life, and proclaimed that in its presence their theories cease to count:

> The Atoms of Democritus
> And Newton's Particles of light
> Are sands upon the Red sea shore,
> Where Israel's tents do shine so bright.[12]

The Romantics were concerned with the things of the spirit and hoped that through imagination and inspired insight they could both understand them and present them in compelling poetry.

It was this search for an unseen world that awoke the inspiration of the Romantics and made poets of them. The power of their work comes partly from the driving force of their desire to grasp these ultimate truths, partly from their exaltation when they thought that they had found them. Unlike their German contemporaries, who were content with the thrills of *Sehnsucht*, or longing, and did not care much what the *Jenseits*, or 'beyond', might be, so long as it was sufficiently mysterious, the English Romantics pursued their lines of imaginative enquiry until they found answers which satisfied them. Their aim was to convey the mystery of things through individual manifestations and thereby to show what it means. They appeal not to the logical mind but to the complete self, to the whole range of intellectual faculties, senses, and emotions. Only individual presentations of imaginative experience can do this. In them we see examples of what cannot be expressed directly in words and can be conveyed only by hint and suggestion. The powers which Wordsworth saw in nature or Shelley in love are so enormous that we begin to understand them only when they are manifested in single, concrete examples. Then, through the single cases, we apprehend something of what the poet has seen in vision. The essence of the Romantic imagination is that it fashions shapes which display these unseen forces at work, and there is no other way to display them, since they resist analysis and description and cannot be presented except in particular instances.

The apprehension of these spiritual issues is quite different from the scientific understanding of natural laws or the philosophical grasp of general truths. Such laws and truths are properly stated in abstract words, but spiritual powers must be introduced through particular examples, because only then do we see them in their true individuality. Indeed, only when the divine light of the imagination is on them do we begin to understand their significance and their appeal. That is why Blake is so stern on the view that art deals with general truths. He has none of Samuel Johnson's respect for the 'grandeur of generality', and would disagree violently with him when he says, 'nothing can please many and please long, but just representation of general nature'. Blake thought quite otherwise:

To Generalize is to be an Idiot. To Particularize is the Alone Distinction of Merit. General Knowledges are those Knowledges that Idiots possess.[13]

What is General Nature? is there Such a Thing? what is General Knowledge? is there such a Thing? Strictly Speaking All Knowledge is Particular.[14]

Blake believed this because he lived in the imagination. He knew that nothing had full significance for him unless it appeared in a particular form. And with this the Romantics in general agreed. Their art aimed at presenting as forcibly as possible the moments of vision which give to even the vastest issues the coherence and simplicity of single events. Even in 'Kubla Khan', which keeps so many qualities of the dream in which it was born, there is a highly individual presentation of a remote and mysterious experience, which is in fact the central experience of all creation in its Dionysiac delight and its enraptured ordering of many elements into an entrancing pattern. Coleridge may not have been fully conscious of what he was doing when he wrote it, but the experience which he portrays is of the creative mood in its purest moments, when boundless possibilities seem to open before it. No wonder he felt that, if he could only realize all the potentialities of such a moment, he would be like one who has supped with the gods:

> And all should cry, Beware! Beware!
> His flashing eyes, his floating hair!
> Weave a circle round him thrice,
> And close your eyes with holy dread,
> For he on honey-dew hath fed,
> And drunk the milk of Paradise.

It was in such experience, remote and strange and beyond the senses, that the Romantics sought for poetry, and they saw that the only way to convey it to others was in particular instances and examples.

The invisible powers which sustain the universe work through and in the visible world. Only by what we see and hear and touch can we be brought into relation with them. Every poet has to work with the world of the senses, but for the Romantics it was the instrument which set their visionary powers in action. It affected them at times in such a way that they seemed to be carried beyond it into a transcendental order of things, but this would never have happened if they had not looked on the world around them with attentive and loving eyes. One of the advantages which they gained by their deliverance from abstractions and general truths was a freedom to use their senses and to look on nature without conventional prepossessions. More than this, they were all gifted with a high degree of physical sensibility and sometimes so enthralled by what they saw that it entirely dominated their being. This is obviously true of Wordsworth and of Keats, who brought back to poetry a keenness of eye and of ear which it had hardly known since Shakespeare. But it is no less true of Blake and Coleridge and Shelley. The careful, observing eye which made Blake a cunning craftsman in line and colour was at work in his poetry. It is true that he was seldom content with mere description of what he saw, but, when he used description for an ulterior purpose to convey some vast mystery, his words are exact and vivid and make his symbols shine brightly before the eye. Though Coleridge found some of his finest inspiration in dreams and trances, he gave to their details a singular brilliance of outline and character. Though Shelley lived among soaring ideas and impalpable abstractions, he was fully at home in the visible world, if only because it was a mirror of eternity and worthy of attention for that reason. There are perhaps poets who live entirely in dreams and hardly notice the familiar scene, but the Romantics are not of their number. Indeed, their strength comes largely from the way in which they throw a new and magic light on the common face of nature and lure us to look for some explanation for the irresistible attraction which it exerts. In nature all the Romantic poets found their initial inspiration. It was not everything to them, but they would have been nothing without it; for through it they found those exalting moments when they passed from sight to vision and pierced, as they thought, to the secrets of the universe.

Though all the Romantic poets believed in an ulterior reality and based their poetry on it, they found it in different ways and made different uses of it. They varied in the degree of importance which they attached to the visible world and in their interpretation of it. At one extreme is Blake, who held that the imagination is a divine power and that everything real comes from it. It operates with a given material, which is nature, but Blake believed that a time would come when nature will disappear and the spirit be free to create without it. While it is there, man takes his symbols from it and uses them to interpret the unseen. Blake's true home was in vision, in what he saw when he gave full liberty to his creative imagination and transformed sense-data through it. For him the imagination uncovers the reality masked by visible things. The familiar world gives hints which must be taken and pursued and developed:

> To see a World in a Grain of Sand
> And a Heaven in a Wild Flower,
> Hold Infinity in the palm of your hand
> And Eternity in an hour.[15]

Through visible things Blake reached that transcendent state which he called 'eternity' and felt free to create new and living worlds. He was not a mystic striving darkly and laboriously towards God, but a visionary who could say of himself:

> I am in God's presence night and day,
> And he never turns his face away.[16]

Of all the Romantics, Blake is the most rigorous in his conception of the imagination. He could confidently say, 'One Power alone makes a Poet: Imagination, The Divine Vision',[17] because for him the imagination creates reality, and this reality is the divine activity of the self in its unimpeded energy. His attention is turned towards an ideal, spiritual world, which with all other selves who obey the imagination he helps to build.

Though Blake had a keen eye for the visible world, his special concern was with the invisible. For him every living thing was a symbol of everlasting powers, and it was these which he wished to grasp and to understand. Since he was a painter with a remarkably pictorial habit of mind, he described the invisible in the language of the visible, and no doubt he really saw it with his inner vision. But what he saw was not, so to speak, an alternative to the given world, but a spiritual order to which the language of physical sight can be applied only in metaphor. What concerned him most deeply and drew out his strongest powers was the sense of a spiritual reality at work in all living things. For him even the commonest event might be fraught with lessons and meanings. How much he found can be seen from his 'Auguries of Innocence', where in epigrammatic, oracular couplets he displays his sense of the intimate relations which exist in reality and bind the worlds of sight and of spirit in a single whole. His words look simple enough, but every word needs attention, as when he proclaims:

> A Robin Red breast in a Cage
> Puts all Heaven in a Rage.

Blake's robin redbreast is itself a spiritual thing, not merely a visible bird, but the powers which such a bird embodies and symbolizes, the free spirit which delights in song and in all that song implies. Such a spirit must not be repressed, and any repression of it is a sin against the divine life of the universe. Blake was a visionary who believed that ordinary things are unsubstantial in themselves and yet rich as symbols of greater realities. He was so at home in the spirit that he was not troubled by the apparent solidity of matter. He saw something else: a world of eternal values and living spirits.

Keats had a more passionate love than Blake for the visible world and has too often been treated as a man who lived for sensuous impressions, but he resembled Blake in his conviction that ultimate reality is to be found only in the imagination. What it meant to him can be seen from some lines in 'Sleep and Poetry' in which he asks why the imagination has lost its old power and scope:

> Is there so small a range
> In the present strength of manhood, that the high
> Imagination cannot freely fly
> As she was wont of old? prepare her steeds,
> Paw up against the light, and do strange deeds
> Upon the clouds? Has she not shown us all?
> From the clear space of ether, to the small
> Breath of new buds unfolding? From the meaning
> Of Jove's large eye-brow, to the tender greening
> Of April meadows?

Keats was still a very young man when he wrote this, and perhaps his words are not so precise as we might like. But it is clear that he saw the imagination as a power which both creates and reveals, or rather reveals through creating. Keats accepted the works of the imagination not merely as existing in their own right, but as having a relation to ultimate reality through the light which they shed on it. This idea he pursued with hard thought until he saw exactly what it meant, and made it his own because it answered a need in his creative being.

Through the imagination Keats sought an absolute reality to which a door was opened by his appreciation of beauty through the senses. When the objects of sense laid their spell upon him, he was so stirred and exalted that he felt himself transported to another world and believed that he could almost grasp the universe as a whole. Sight and touch and smell awoke his imagination to a sphere of being in which he saw vast issues and was at home with them. Through beauty he felt that he came into the presence of the ultimately real. The more intensely a beautiful object affected him, the more convinced he was that he had passed beyond it to something else. In *Endymion* he says that happiness raises our minds to a 'fellowship with essence' and leaves us 'alchemized and free of space':

Feel we these things? that moment we have stept
Into a sort of oneness, and our state
Is like a fleeting spirit's. But there are
Richer entanglements, enthralments far
More self-destroying, leading by degrees
To the chief intensity.[18]

The beauty of visible things carried Keats into ecstasy, and this was the goal of his desires, since it explained the extraordinary hold which objects of sense had on him and justified his wish to pass beyond them to something permanent and universal. Keats' notion of this reality was narrower than Blake's, and he speaks specifically as a poet, whereas Blake included in the imagination all activities which create or increase life. Moreover, while Blake's imagination is active, Keats suggests that his is largely passive and that his need is to feel the 'chief intensity'. But he is close to Blake in the claims which he makes for the imagination as something absorbing and exalting which opens the way to an unseen spiritual order.

Coleridge, too, gave much thought to the imagination and devoted to it some distinguished chapters of his *Biographia Literaria*. With him it is not always easy to disentangle theories which he formed in later life from the assumptions upon which he acted almost instinctively before his creative faculties began to fail. At times he seems to be still too aware of the sensationalist philosophy of his youth. From it he inherits a conception of a world of facts, an 'inanimate cold world', in which 'objects, *as* objects, are essentially fixed and dead'. But as a poet he transcended this idea, or turned it to an unexpected conclusion. Just because the external world is like this, the poet's task is to transform it by the imagination. Just as 'accidents of light and shade' may transmute 'a known and familiar landscape',[19] so this dead world may be brought to life by the imagination. Coleridge justified this by a bold paradox: 'Dare I add that genius must act of the feeling that body is but a striving to become mind – that is mind in its essence.'[20] What really counted with him was his own deep trust in the imagination as something which gives a shape to life. What this meant to him in practice can be seen from the lines

in 'Dejection' in which he explains that nature lives only in us
and that it is we who create all that matters in her:

> Ah! from the soul itself must issue forth
> A light, a glory, a fair luminous cloud
> Enveloping the Earth —
> And from the soul itself must there be sent
> A sweet and potent voice, of its own birth,
> Of all sweet sounds the life and element!

Coleridge does not go so far as Blake in the claims which he makes
for the imagination. He is still a little hampered by the presence
of an external world and feels that in some way he must conform
to it. But when his creative genius is at work, it brushes these
hesitations aside and fashions reality from a shapeless, un-
differentiated 'given'. In the end he believes that meaning is
found for existence through the exercise of a creative activity
which is akin to that of God.

Coleridge advanced no very definite view of the ultimate
reality which poetry explores. If we may judge by 'Kubla Khan',
he seems to have felt, at least in some moods, that the mere act of
creation is itself transcendental and that we need ask for nothing
more. But perhaps the evidence of 'Kubla Khan' should not be
pressed too far. Indeed, if we turn to 'The Ancient Mariner' and
'Christabel', it seems clear that Coleridge thought that the task of
poetry is to convey the mystery of life. The ambiguous nature of
both poems, with their suggestion of an intermediate state
between dreaming and waking, between living people and
unearthly spirits, gives an idea of the kind of subject which stirred
Coleridge's genius to its boldest flights. Whatever he might think
as a philosopher, as a poet he was fascinated by the notion of
unearthly powers at work in the world, and it was their influence
which he sought to catch. Of course, he did not intend to be taken
literally, but we cannot help feeling that his imaginative
conception of reality was of something behind human actions
which is more vivid than the familiar world because of its sharper
contrasts of good and evil and the more purposeful way in which
it moves. This conception was developed only in poetry, and even

then only in two or three poems. Coleridge seems to have been forced to it by a troubled and yet exciting apprehension that life is ruled by powers which cannot be fully understood. The result is a poetry more mysterious than that of any other Romantic, and yet, because it is based on primary human emotions, singularly poignant and intimate.

Wordsworth certainly agreed with Coleridge in much that he said about the imagination, especially in the distinction between it and fancy. For him the imagination was the most important gift that a poet can have, and his arrangement of his own poems shows what he meant by it. The section which he calls 'Poems of the Imagination' contains poems in which he united creative power and a special, visionary insight. He agreed with Coleridge that this activity resembles that of God. It is the divine capacity of the child who fashions his own little worlds:

> For feeling has to him imparted power
> That through the growing faculties of sense
> Doth like an agent of the one great Mind
> Create, creator and receiver both,
> Working but in alliance with the works
> Which it beholds.[21]

The poet keeps this faculty even in maturity, and through it he is what he is. But Wordsworth was fully aware that mere creation is not enough, that it must be accompanied by a special insight. So he explains that the imagination

> Is but another name for absolute power
> And clearest insight, amplitude of mind,
> And Reason in her most exalted mood.[22]

Wordsworth did not go so far as the other Romantics in relegating reason to an inferior position. He preferred to give a new dignity to the word and to insist that inspired insight is itself rational.

Wordsworth differs from Coleridge in his conception of the external world. He accepts its independent existence and insists

that the imagination must in some sense conform to it. Once
again he sees the issue illustrated by childhood:

> A plastic power
> Abode with me; a forming hand, at times
> Rebellious, acting in a devious mood;
> A local spirit of his own, at war
> With general tendency, but, for the most,
> Subservient strictly to external things
> With which it communed.[23]

For Wordsworth the imagination must be subservient to the
external world, because that world is not dead but living and has
its own soul, which is, at least in the life that we know, distinct
from the soul of man. Man's task is to enter into communion with
this soul, and indeed he can hardly avoid doing so, since from
birth onward his life is continuously shaped by nature, which
penetrates his being and influences his thoughts. Wordsworth
believed that he helped to bring this soul of nature closer to man,
that he could show

> by words
> Which speak of nothing more than what we are[24]

how exquisitely the external world is fitted to the individual
mind, and the individual mind to the external world. This, it
must be admitted, was not to Blake's taste, and he commented:
'You shall not bring me down to believe such fitting and fitted.'[25]
But for Wordsworth this was right. Nature was the source of his
inspiration, and he could not deny to it an existence at least as
powerful as man's. But since nature lifted him out of himself, he
sought for a higher state in which its soul and the soul of man
should be united in a single harmony. Sometimes he felt that this
happened and that through vision he attained an understanding
of the oneness of things.

Though Shelley's mind moved in a way unlike that of his
fellow Romantics, he was no less attached to the imagination and
gave to it no less a place in his theory of poetry. He understood the

creative nature of his work and shows what he thought of it when in *Prometheus Unbound* a Spirit sings of the poet:

> He will watch from dawn to gloom
> The lake-reflected sun illume
> The yellow bees in the ivy-bloom,
> Nor heed nor see, what things they be;
> But from these create he can
> Forms more real than living man,
> Nurslings of immortality!

Shelley saw that though the poet may hardly notice the visible world, he none the less uses it as material to create independent beings which have a superior degree of reality. Nor did he stop at this. He saw that reason must somehow be related to the imagination, and he decided, in contradistinction to Wordsworth, that its special task is simply to analyse the given and to act as an instrument for the imagination, which uses its conclusions to create a synthetic and harmonious whole. He calls poetry 'the expression of the Imagination', because in it diverse things are brought together in harmony instead of being separated through analysis. In this he resembles such thinkers as Bacon and Locke, but his conclusion is quite different from theirs, since he insists that the imagination is man's highest faculty and through it he realizes his noblest powers.

In his *Defence of Poetry* Shelley controverted the old disparaging view of the imagination by claiming that the poet has a special kind of knowledge:

He not only beholds intensely the present as it is, and discovers those laws according to which present things ought to be ordered, but he beholds the future in the present, and his thoughts are the germs of the flower and the fruit of latest time. . . . A poet participates in the eternal, the infinite, and the one.[26]

For Shelley the poet is also a seer, gifted with a peculiar insight into the nature of reality. And this reality is a timeless, unchanging, complete order, of which the familiar world is but a broken reflection. Shelley took Plato's theory of knowledge and applied it to beauty. For him the Ideal Forms are a basis not so much of knowing as of that exalted insight which is ours in the presence of beautiful things. The poet's task is to uncover this absolute real in its visible examples and to interpret them through it. It is spiritual in the sense that it includes all the higher faculties of man and gives meaning to his transient sensations. Shelley tried to grasp the whole of things in its essential unity, to show what is real and what is merely phenomenal, and by doing this to display how the phenomenal depends on the real. For him the ultimate reality is the eternal mind, and this holds the universe together:

> This Whole
> Of suns, and worlds, and men, and beasts, and flowers,
> With all the silent or tempestuous workings
> By which they have been, are, or cease to be,
> Is but a vision; — all that it inherits
> Are motes of a sick eye, bubbles and dreams;
> Thought is its cradle, and its grave, nor less
> The future and the past are idle shadows
> Of thought's eternal flight — they have no being:
> Nought is but that which feels itself to be.[27]

In thought and feeling, in consciousness and spirit, Shelley found reality and gave his answer to Prospero's nihilism. He believed that the task of the imagination is to create shapes by which this reality can be revealed.

The great Romantics, then, agreed that their task was to find through the imagination some transcendental order which explains the world of appearances and accounts not merely for the existence of visible things but for the effect which they have on us, for the sudden, unpredictable beating of the heart in the presence of beauty, for the conviction that what then moves us cannot be a cheat or an illusion, but must derive its authority from the power which moves the universe. For them this reality could not but be spiritual, and they provide an independent illustration of Hegel's doctrine that nothing is real but spirit. In so far as they made sweeping statements about the oneness of things, they were metaphysicians, but, unlike professional metaphysicians, they trusted not in logic but in insight, not in the analytical reason but in the delighted, inspired soul which in its full nature transcends both the mind and the emotions. They were, too, in their own way, religious, in their sense of the holiness of reality and the awe which they felt in its presence. But, so far as their central beliefs were concerned, they were not orthodox. Blake's religion denied the existence of God apart from men; Shelley liked to proclaim that he was an atheist; Keats was uncertain how far to accept the doctrines of Christianity. Though later both Coleridge and Wordsworth conformed almost with enthusiasm, in their most creative days their poetry was founded on a different faith. The Romantic movement was a prodigious attempt to discover the world of spirit through the unaided efforts of the solitary soul. It was a special manifestation of that belief in the worth of the individual which philosophers and politicians had recently preached to the world.

This bold expedition into the unknown, conducted with a scrupulous sincerity and a passionate faith, was very far from being an emotional self-indulgence. Each of these poets was convinced that he could discover something very important and that he possessed in poetry a key denied to other men. To this task they were prepared to devote themselves, and in different ways they paid heavily for it, in happiness, in self-confidence, in the very strength of their creative powers. They were not content to dream their own dreams and to fashion comforting illusions. They insisted that their creations must be real, not in the narrow sense that anything of which we can think has some sort of existence, but in the wide sense that they are examples and embodiments of eternal things which cannot be presented otherwise than in individual instances. Because the Romantics were poets, they set forth their visions with the wealth that poetry alone can give, in the concrete, individual form which makes the universal vivid and significant to the finite mind. They refused to accept the ideas of other men on trust or to sacrifice imagination to argument. As Blake says of Los,

I must Create a System or be enslav'd by another Man's.
I will not Reason and Compare: my business is to Create.[28]

The Romantics knew that their business was to create, and
through creation to enlighten the whole sentient and conscious
self of man, to wake his imagination to the reality which lies
behind or in familiar things, to rouse him from the deadening
routine of custom to a consciousness of immeasurable distances
and unfathomable depths, to make him see that mere reason is
not enough and that what he needs is inspired intuition. They
take a wider view both of man and of poetry than was taken by
their staid and rational predecessors of the eighteenth century,
because they believed that it is the whole spiritual nature of man
that counts, and to this they made their challenge and their
appeal.

SOURCE: chapter 1 of *The Romantic Imagination* (1950;
reprinted 1961) pp. 1–24.

NOTES

1. John Locke, *The Reasonableness of Christianity* (1695); in *Works*,
12th ed. (1824) vol. VI, p. 135.

2. John Locke, *An Essay Concerning Human Understanding* (1690); in
Works, vol. II, ii, p. 3.

3. *A Vision of the Last Judgement*; in *Poetry and Prose of William Blake*,
ed. Geoffrey Keynes, 4th ed. (London: The Nonesuch Press, 1939) p.
639.

4. Coleridge, *Biographia Literaria*, ed. Shawcross, vol. I, p. 202. Cf.
Coleridge's review of poems of Drake and Halleck in the *Southern Literary
Messenger*, Apr 1836: 'Imagination is possibly in man a lesser degree of
the creative power of God.'

5. Novalis (Friedrich von Hardenberg), letter of 27 Feb 1799, in
Gesämmelte Werke, ed. Carl Seelig (Zürich, 1945) vol. V, p. 274.

6. Shakespeare, *A Midsummer Night's Dream*, v i 12–17.

7. Ibid., v i 23–7.

8. W. H. Woodward, *Vittorino da Feltre* (Florence, 1923) p. 175.

9. Coleridge, *Biographia Literaria*, ed. Shawcross, vol. I, p. 59.

10. Blake, *A Vision of the Last Judgement*; in *Poetry and Prose*, p. 651.

11. *Letters of Samuel Taylor Coleridge*, ed. Ernest Hartley Coleridge, 2 vols (London, 1895) vol. I, p. 352.

12. Blake, Fragment; in *Poetry and Prose*, p. 107.

13. Blake, Marginalia to Sir Joshua Reynolds's *Discourses*; in *Poetry and Prose*, p. 777.

14. Ibid., p. 788.

15. Blake, 'Auguries of Innocence'; in *Poetry and Prose*, p. 118.

16. Blake, Fragment; in *Poetry and Prose*, p. 128.

17. Blake, Annotations to Wordsworth's Poems; in *Poetry and Prose*, p. 821.

18. Keats, *Endymion*, I 795–800.

19. Coleridge, *Biographia Literaria*, ed. Shawcross, vol. II, p. 5.

20. *Letters of S. T. Coleridge*, vol. II, p. 450.

21. Wordsworth, *The Prelude*, II 255–60.

22. Ibid., XIV 190–2.

23. Ibid., II 362–9.

24. Wordsworth, *The Recluse*, 71–2.

25. Blake, Annotations to *The Excursion*; in *Poetry and Prose*, p. 823.

26. *A Defence of Poetry*; in *Prose Works of Percy Bysshe Shelley*, ed. Harry Buxton Forman, 4 vols (London, 1880) vol. III, p. 104.

27. *Hellas*, 776–85.

28. Blake, *Jerusalem*; in *Poetry and Prose*, p. 442.

J. Shawcross

'COLERIDGE'S "FANCY" AND "IMAGINATION"'(1907)

The large verbal borrowings from Schelling in the course of the 'deduction of the imagination' suggest that when he began to write he had accepted Schelling's account of the faculty, or at least found his own conclusions happily expressed therein. Of these excerpts by far the greater number are taken from the *Transcendental Idealism* (1804); it is, therefore, the account of the imagination presented in this work which concerns us here.

Now to the imagination Schelling daringly assigns a function of high, indeed of the highest, dignity and importance. It is proclaimed as the organ of truth, and of truth not as the artist only, but as the philosopher apprehends it. And the quality, which makes it thus their common instrument, is the power of reconciling opposites in virtue of their inner unity; of discovering the ground of harmony between apparent contradictories. Such a reconciliation is demanded by transcendental philosophy. For the task of this philosophy is to discover *in consciousness itself* an explanation of the apparent contradiction involved in the fact, that the self or subject is conceived as both active and passive as regards the object, as both determining it and determined by it. Such a solution can take only one form: the recognition, namely, that these apparently opposed and unrelated activities are really but a twofold aspect of the same activity, that the power which determines is also the power which is determined. As the transcendental philosopher starts from the fact of consciousness, it is in consciousness itself that he must discover the original and prototype of this activity. And this he finds in the act of pure self-consciousness, in which the subject becomes its own object, and subject and object are therefore identical. Now from its very nature the apprehension of this pure self-consciousness, or pure activity returning upon itself, cannot be other than immediate and intuitive. Moreover, as reflecting the ultimate ground of all knowledge, it is productive and an act of the same power, whereby that ultimate principle is reflected objectively in the work of art. In either case the reflective or productive power is the imagination.

But the imagination, in this its highest potency, is itself identical in kind, though not in degree, with that very activity which it contemplates and reflects. For the original act whereby pure intelligence (the Absolute or Urselbst, as Schelling calls it) objectifies and limits itself in order to contemplate itself in its limitation, is an act of imagination, and indeed the primary act, an act which is subsequently repeated in the experience of every individual mind, in becoming conscious of an external world. This degree of imagination is common to all thinking beings. But as we rise in the scale of self-knowledge, the faculty reaches a higher intensity and is confined proportionately in extent, till in its highest power it pertains only to a chosen few. In the ordinary consciousness, imagination renders possible the distinction of self from a world of objects; in the philosopher it is the power of contemplating inwardly the ground of this distinction, and so overcoming it; and in the artist of giving to the reconciling principle an outward and objective expression. Hence the superiority of art to all other modes of the revelation of truth.

Philosophy starts with an infinite division of two opposed activities; but the same division is at the root of every aesthetic production, and is completely resolved by every individual representation of art. What is then that marvellous faculty by which, according to the assertion of the philosopher, an infinite contradiction is resolved in the productive intuition? . . . That productive faculty is the same which enables art to compass the impossible, to resolve an infinite contradiction in a finite product. It is the poetic faculty, which in its first power is the original intuition, and contrariwise, it is only the productive intuition reasserting itself in the highest power, that we call the poetic faculty. It is one and the same power which is active in both, the sole power whereby we are able to think and comprehend what is contradictory – namely, the imagination.[1]

In attributing to the imagination the function in consciousness of reconciling opposites and so underlying all acts of knowledge, Schelling is but developing the conception of Kant, according to which the faculty mediates between the understanding and the senses. But to Kant this reconciling power implied no community of nature between the self and its object; the knowledge to which it contributed was valid only for the self from which it drew its unifying principle. When, however, the imagination is conceived as recognizing the inherent interdependence of subject and object (as complementary aspects of a single reality), its dignity is immeasurably raised. How far such a function can be legitimately attributed to such a faculty, is another question. It should, however, be remembered, that the German word (Einbildungskraft[2]) does not etymologically imply the power of dealing with images as sensuous representations, but merely the power of immediate apprehension in general, and therefore its application to an act of pure intelligence would not present the same difficulty as in the case of the word 'imagination'. It was no doubt because he felt this difficulty that Coleridge coined the term 'esemplastic power', a term which he apparently owed to his erroneous translation of the word 'Einbildungskraft', as signifying 'the unifying power'.[3] But in spite of his false etymology Coleridge rightly apprehended the agreement of Schelling's conception, in its cardinal features, with his own; to unify and so to create is, in the view of both writers, the characteristic function of the imagination. And of this unification the principle is found in the self, conceived not abstractly but as the whole nature of man, or all that is essential to that nature. Thought and feeling, in their original identity, demand expression through an organ which itself partakes of both.

To Schelling's conception it has been objected, that in constituting the imagination the peculiar organ of philosophy, he countenances the claim of every visionary to a respectful hearing, be his system never so wild and fantastic. But this is to misinterpret his meaning, and to fall into the common error of confounding fancy with imagination. If the faculty of imagination be not equally active in all men, its activity is none the less independent of the idiosyncrasies of the individual, its witness is none the less a witness of universal validity. By calling it the organ of philosophy, Schelling means that philosophy must start from a fundamental experience, and that it is the imagination which renders this fundamental experience possible. And to Schelling this ultimate fact of experience appeared to be given, inwardly, in what he called the intellectual intuition, and outwardly, in the products of art. These, he asserted, were intuitions of truth which demanded universal acceptance.

But at the same time Schelling acknowledged that of these facts one at least (the object of intellectual intuition) could not be made universally conscious. He therefore started from a datum which it was not in the power of all men to realize. No appeal to a universal spiritual faculty was here possible. All that lay open to him was to point to the creations of art, as the guarantee and evidence (evidence made visible to all) of that ultimate ground of all knowledge and being which the philosopher alone could directly contemplate.

Now, that poetry and philosophy, if their message be true, must be founded on the same spiritual experience, Coleridge would have readily acknowledged; indeed, it was the truth for which he had been contending throughout his life. To this truth, moreover, his own mental history bore witness; for he was conscious that the same impulse lay at the root of his poetic and speculative creation, the impulse to give again that which he had felt and known. By his own confession in later years, it was the same 'spirit of power' which had stirred him throughout –

> A matron now, of sober mien,
> Yet radiant still and with no earthly sheen,
> Whom as a faery child my childhood woo'd
> Even in my dawn of youth – Philosophy;
> Tho' then, unconscious of herself, pardie,
> She bore no other name than Poesy.[4]

And his description of his poetic manner, given in that 'dawn of youth' which he here recalls, shows that he was conscious of his inclination to confuse these kindred modes of communicating truth.[5] It was the conviction that in either case the whole self must be active in the apprehension of reality,which in the first instance opened his eyes to the error of the empiricists in their one-sided interpretation of a partial aspect of things. And it was to a poet (to *the* poet of the age) that he looked for a final confutation of this false philosophy. In Wordsworth's *Excursion* he had anticipated 'the first genuine philosophic poem',[6] which in its conclusion was to have emphasized the message of which the age stood most in need. This message was none other than 'the necessity of a general revolution in the modes of developing and disciplining the human life by the substitution of life and intelligence . . . for the philosophy of mechanism, which, in everything that is most worthy of the human intellect, strikes *Death*, and cheats itself by mistaking clear images for distinct conceptions, and which idly demands conceptions where intuitions alone are adequate to the truth. In short, facts elevated into theory, theory into laws, and laws into living and intelligent powers, true idealism necessarily perfecting itself in realism, and realism refining itself into idealism.'

This task, however, Wordsworth had shown no inclination to undertake; and the sense that it was still waiting to be accomplished was present with Coleridge, when he was composing his literary life. And here the 'genial coincidence' of his opinions with those of Schelling stood him in good stead. For at this time at least he seems to have believed that in the transcendental philosophy was exemplified this process of 'true idealism perfecting itself in realism, and realism refining itself into idealism', and this through intuitions as 'alone adequate to the majesty of truth'. Hence it was that he incorporated into his book so much of Schelling's doctrines as suited his immediate purpose, without perhaps reflecting on their ultimate implications. A brief analysis of the relevant portions of the *Biographia Literaria* will show this more clearly.

After introducing, in chapter 4,[7] the distinction of imagination and fancy, Coleridge proceeds to investigate it psychologically. He begins with an historical discussion of the theory of association, and compares Aristotle's theory with that of Hartley; the inadequacy of the 'mechanical theory' is then exposed, and the true nature of association explained. Having thus cleared the

ground, Coleridge next purposed to show 'by what influences of
the choice and judgement the associative power becomes either
memory or fancy, and to appropriate the remaining offices of the
mind to the reason and the imagination'. But this promise of a
psychological treatment of the distinction is not fulfilled: indeed
we hear little more of the fancy until, in the final summing up, it is
defined side by side, or rather in contrast, with the imagination.
After some intervening chapters of general or biographical
interest, Coleridge advances to the statement of his system, from
which he proposes 'to deduce the memory with all other
functions of intelligence', but which, as a matter of fact, he views
in connexion with one faculty only – the imagination. In a series
of theses[8] he discovers the final principle of knowledge as 'the
identity of subject and object' in 'the SUM, or I AM', which 'is a
subject which becomes a subject by the act of constructing itself
objectively to itself; but which never is an object except for itself,
and only so far as by the same act it becomes a subject'.
Originally, however, it is not an object, but 'an absolute subject
for which all, itself included, may become an object'. It must,
therefore, be an act. Thus it follows that consciousness in its
various phases is but a self-development of absolute spirit or
intelligence. This process of self-development Coleridge asks us to
conceive 'under the idea of an indestructible power with two
counteracting forces, which by a metaphor borrowed from
astronomy, we may call the centrifugal and centripetal forces'.
Such a power he 'assumes for his present purpose, in order to
deduce from it a faculty the generation, agency, and application
of which form the contents of the ensuing chapter'.

This faculty is the imagination or esemplastic power. But the
promised deduction is cut short by the timely or untimely letter of
warning from Coleridge's fictitious friend. The chapter on the
imagination, 'which cannot, when it is printed, amount to so
little as an hundred pages', was laid aside, and we are left with the
mere conclusion, which is framed in the following words: –

The imagination, then, I consider either as primary or secondary. The
primary imagination I hold to be the living power and prime agent of
all human perception, and as a repetition in the finite mind of the

eternal act of creation in the infinite I Am. The secondary I consider as an echo of the former, coexisting with the conscious will, yet still as identical with the primary in the kind of its agency, and differing only in degree and in the manner of its operation. It dissolves, diffuses, and dissipates in order to recreate: or, where this process is rendered impossible, yet still, at all events, it struggles to idealize and to unify. It is essentially *vital* even as all objects (as objects) are esentially fixed and dead.[9]

The distinction here drawn is evidently between the imagination as universally active in consciousness (creative in that it externalizes the world of objects by opposing it to the self) and the same faculty in a heightened power as creative in a poetic sense. In the first case our exercise of the power is unconscious: in the second the will directs, though it does not determine, the activity of the imagination. The imagination of the ordinary man is capable only of detaching the world of experience from the self and contemplating it in its detachment; but the philosopher penetrates to the underlying harmony and gives it concrete expression. The ordinary consciousness, with no principle of unification, sees the universe as a mass of particulars: only the poet can depict this whole as reflected in the individual parts. It is in this sense (as Coleridge had written many years before) that to the poet 'each thing has a life of its own, and yet they have all our life'.[10] And a similar contrast is present to Schelling when he writes that 'through the objective world as a whole, but never through a single object in it, an Infinite is represented: whereas every single work of art represents Infinity'.[11]

With the definition of fancy which now follows we are already familiar. 'Fancy has no other counters to play with but fixities and definites. The fancy is indeed no other than a mode of memory emancipated from the order of time and space; and blended with and modified by that empirical phenomenon of the will which we express by the word choice. But equally with the ordinary memory it must receive its materials all ready-made from the laws of association.'[12] This distinction, which in its essentials Coleridge made so long before, need not be long dwelt upon here. As connected by the fancy, objects are viewed in their limitations and particularity; they are 'fixed and dead' in the sense that their connexion is mechanical and not organic. The law, indeed, which governs it is derived from the mind itself, but the links are supplied by the individual properties of the objects. Fancy is, in fact, the faculty of mere images or impressions, as imagination is the faculty of intuitions. It is in this sense that Coleridge sees in their opposition an emblem of the wider contrast between the mechanical philosophy and the dynamic, the false and the true.

But with all this we have nothing of the promised 'deduction' of the imagination, still less that of the memory and other 'functions of intelligence'. The definition of fancy is founded, apparently, on the psychological discussion of the earlier chapters, not on the theory of knowledge propounded later on. As to the imagination, it seems at first sight, from the close coincidence of Coleridge's statement with that of Schelling, that he had accepted Schelling's system wholesale and with it his account of that faculty. But the sudden termination of the argument, and the unsatisfactory vagueness of the final summary, in which he does not really commit himself to Schelling's position, suggest that that position was not in fact his own. And this suggestion is confirmed by other evidence.

That Coleridge's attitude from the first to Schelling's philosophy was by no means one of unqualified approval, we have already seen. But in the *Transcendental Idealism* which he studied at a time when he was deeply engaged in aesthetic problems, he found a peculiar attraction. Here for the first time the significance of 'the vision and the faculty divine' seemed to be adequately realized. At first it appeared to Coleridge that he had met with a systematized statement of his own convictions, the metaphysic of poetry of which he was in search. But he was soon to find that the supposed concurrence did not exist — that the Transcendentalism of Schelling in fact elevated the imagination at the expense of other and more important factors in our spiritual consciousness.

SOURCE: extract from Introduction to Shawcross's edition of *Biographia Literaria*, pp. lx–lxix.

NOTES

1. Schelling, *Transcendental Idealism*; in *Werke* (1858), vol. I, iii, p. 626.
2. From eins = one: whereas the 'ein' in 'Einbildungskraft' has an adverbial force, as in the phrase, 'ich bilde es mir ein'. Bilden = to shape or create in its widest sense.
3. Cf. *Anima Poetae*, ed. E. H. Coleridge (London, 1895) p. 236.
4. 'The Garden of Boccaccio' (1828) 46–51.
5. Letter to Thelwall: 'I seldom feel without thinking, or think without feeling. . . . My philosophical opinions are blended with or deduced from my feelings', etc. *Letters of S. T. Coleridge*, ed. E. H. Coleridge (London, 1895) p. 196. [*Collected Letters of S. T. C.*, ed. E. L. Griggs (1956–71) vol. I, p. 279–Ed.]
6. Ibid., p. 649.
7. [See above, Part One, section I. IV. – Ed.]
8. [See ibid., section I. VI.– Ed.]
9. *Biographia Literaria*, ed. Shawcross, vol. I, p. 202.
10. *Letters of S. T. Coleridge*, p. 405. [*Collected Letters of S. T. C.*, ed. Griggs, vol. II, p. 866; Shawcross quotes incorrectly: cf. original letter, Part One, section 1.1. above – Ed.]
11. *Werke*, i, p. 627.
12. *Biographia Literaria*, ed. Shawcross, vol. I, p. 202.

Basil Willey

IMAGINATION AND FANCY (1949)

One chief outcome of Coleridge's enquiry into 'what our faculties are, and what they are capable of becoming', was his distinction between Imagination and Fancy. I propose now to examine what Coleridge meant by this, and why he thought it so important.

A recent critic has referred to the distinction as 'celebrated but useless'. 'Celebrated' we know it to be; its 'usefulness', however, cannot be determined without raising some important questions. Are we interested in enquiring into the nature of poetry, and the ways in which it comes to be written? Do we wish to think seriously of poetry as in some sense an approach to truth? Has it any significant relationship with life in general? What place can we give it in our scheme of values? And if we decide that poetry can make a vital contribution to the good life, how can we determine which are the best kinds of poetry? It seems to me that Coleridge's distinction can be 'useful', not by furnishing us with final or explicit answers to such questions, but by deepening and enriching our understanding of their meaning. It is natural and right that questions like these should occasionally be asked, and it would be surprising if the greatest of our poet – critics had no light to throw upon them.

We can best begin by reminding ourselves of the passage in the *Biographia Literaria*, chapter 4, where Coleridge describes the birth of his own idea. It came to him, we find, as a direct result of his discovery of Wordsworth's poetry; here was a new poet, speaking with a superiority of accent which linked him with the great poets of a former age. To what was that superiority due? What was it that lifted Wordsworth above the eighteenth century level, and placed him with Shakespeare or Milton? Already, while an undergraduate at Cambridge, Coleridge had been greatly impressed by the *Descriptive Sketches*: 'seldom, if ever', he writes, 'was the emergence of an original poetic genius above the literary horizon more evidently announced'. But two years later came a more memorable experience: 'I was in my twenty-fourth year, when I had the happiness of knowing Mr Wordsworth personally, and while memory lasts, I shall hardly forget the sudden effect produced on my mind, by his recitation of a manuscript poem [afterwards incorporated in *Guilt and Sorrow*].'

What struck Coleridge in this poem was not so much the 'freedom from false taste'; it was

the union of deep feeling with profound thought: the fine balance of truth in observing, with the imaginative faculty in modifying the objects observed; and above all the original gift of spreading the tone, the *atmosphere*, and with it the depth and height of the ideal world around forms, incidents, and situations, of which, for the common view, custom had bedimmed all the lustre, had dried up the sparkle and the dew drops.

This peculiar excellence, he goes on to tell us, 'I no sooner felt than I sought to understand' — a phrase which (we may note in passing) epitomizes Coleridge's distinctive quality as a critic: he first feels keenly, and then tries to understand what he has felt.

Repeated meditations led me first to suspect (and a more intimate analysis of the human faculties . . . matured my conjecture into full conviction) that fancy and imagination were two distinct and widely different faculties, instead of being, according to the general belief, either two names with one meaning, or, at furthest, the lower and higher degree of one and the same power.

It is well known that when Coleridge felt himself confronted by an important duty he instinctively shrank from it, or postponed its performance to a more auspicious occasion. Hence his endless digressions and asides, both in writing and in conversation, and hence his habit of scattering his most pregnant remarks in marginalia or footnotes, where he could say the vital thing *tanquam aliud agendo*. Unfortunately this desynonymizing of Fancy and Imagination seemed to him a supremely important task, and he accordingly shies off at a tangent whenever he approaches it. We have therefore to be content with hints and glimpses, and must piece together his meaning from several scattered passages. All he vouchsafes here is that Milton had a 'highly *imaginative*' and Cowley a 'very *fanciful*' mind; that the distinction is analogous to that between *delirium* and *mania*; and that it can be illustrated by contrasting Otway's line

Lutes, lobsters, seas of milk and ships of amber

with Shakespeare's

What! have his daughters brought him to this pass?

These interesting suggestions are here left undeveloped, but they foreshadow the fuller account in chapter 13 and in the Shakespeare Lectures. In delirium the mind pours forth its contents incoherently, that is, with no unifying principle to order its sequences save the law of association; in mania, the mind, obsessed by a fixed idea, sees and interprets all things in relation to that idea, and so has (though in a morbid form) a co-ordinating power. If we translate disease into health, delirium becomes Fancy, and mania Imagination: Fancy assembling and juxtaposing images without fusing them; Imagination moulding them into a new whole in the heat of a predominant passion.

We may now turn to chapter 13, where Coleridge, face to face at last with his central problem, and alarmed by his own chapter heading: 'On the imagination, or esemplastic power', slips lizard-like into a thicket of learned excerpts, and vanishes from sight, leaving in our hands his tail only – a letter from himself to himself about his forthcoming masterpiece. But the tail is not without a sharp point – the last two paragraphs, and these we must now inspect. First, what of the distinction here introduced between the two kinds of Imagination, the Primary and the Secondary? I fear that some readers are misled by the oracular sublimity of Coleridge's definition of the former: 'The primary Imagination', he declares (in oft-quoted words), 'I hold to be the living Power and prime Agent of all human Perception, and as a repetition in the finite mind of the eternal act of creation in the infinite I AM.'

This is not to be dismissed as metaphysical babble; a weight of thought, indeed a whole philosophy, lies beneath each phrase. Coleridge is here summarizing the great struggle and victory of his life — his triumph over the old tradition of Locke and Hartley, which had assumed that the mind in perception was wholly passive, 'a lazy looker-on on an external world'. We should here recall the letter to Poole, written in March 1801, in which Coleridge announces the overthrow of 'the doctrine of associ-ation as taught by Hartley, and with it all the irreligious metaphysics of modern infidels'. The mind, he now teaches, works actively in the mere act of perception; it knows its objects not by passive reception, but by its own energy and under its own necessary forms; indeed, it knows not mere objects as such, but itself in the objects: 'If the mind be not *passive*, if it be indeed made in God's Image, and that, too, in the sublimest sense, the *Image of the Creator*, there is ground for suspicion that any system built on the passiveness of the mind must be false, as a system.'[1]

In speaking thus of the Primary Imagination, then, Coleridge is affirming that the mind is essentially and inveterately creative: 'we receive but what we give', and in the commonest everyday acts of perception we are making our own world. We make it, indeed, not *ex nihilo*, but out of the influxes proceeding from Nature, or as Coleridge preferred to say, 'the infinite I AM'. Whatever we perceive is what we have made in response to these stimuli; perception is an activity of the mind, not a merely mechanical registering of impressions. However (and this is now the point to be emphasized), it is the Secondary Imagination, not the Primary, which he proceeds to contrast with Fancy; it is the Secondary Imagination which is at work in the making of poetry. For how does it operate? 'It dissolves, diffuses, dissipates, in order to recreate . . . it struggles to idealize and to unify. It is essentially *vital*, even as all objects (*as* objects) are essentially fixed and dead.' Here speaks the seer, the poet and the romantic; not content with the automatic 'poetry' which we all create, and which we call the world of everyday appearances, he would transcend this for a vision more intense, more true, than is afforded by the light of common day. The daily routine world may be the product of a faculty essentially creative — indeed, in opposition to Locke and Hartley, Coleridge asserts that it is — yet in itself it is cold and inanimate, filled only with 'the many shapes of joyless daylight'. As Sidney had expressed it in his *Apologie*, Nature's world is brazen, 'the poets only deliver a golden'. To retain the Midas-touch, to be constantly in possession of the transforming power, this for Coleridge meant life, and joy, and triumph; to lose it meant failure and spiritual death, the reduction of existence to a state of somnambulism; in which we languish amidst

> The repetitions wearisome of sense
> Where soul is dead, and feeling hath no place.
> (Wordsworth, *Excursion*, IV 620—1)

Coleridge knew all too well the misery of this condition; it was the mood of dejection which he describes in the Ode of that title, where, like Wordsworth (but without the Wordsworthian compensation), he laments the passing of the visionary gleam:

> And would we aught behold, of higher worth,
> Than that inanimate cold world allowed
> To the poor loveless ever-anxious crowd,
> Ah! from the soul itself must issue forth
> A light, a glory, a fair luminous cloud
> Enveloping the Earth. . . .

If we ask, then, what it is which the Secondary Imagination must 'dissolve, diffuse, and dissipate', the answer is given here: it is the 'inanimate cold world' of the Primary Imagination; all that is allowed to the daily, prosaic consciousness of average humanity, and to poets themselves when power deserts them. I shall say a word more on this topic later, but I would suggest here, in passing, that this desire (as Wordsworth expresses it)

>   for something loftier, more adorned,
> Than is the common aspect, daily garb
> Of human Life   (*Prelude*, v 575−7)

is no mere romantic escapism, though it may sometimes take that
form; it is the originating impulse of poets at all times (including
our own time), and not merely of poets, but of seers and saints and
scientists as well − of all whose task it is to fight the habit of

> Viewing all objects unremittingly
> In disconnection dead and spiritless.
>   (*Excursion*, iv 961−2)

   The Imagination, then (we may now drop the word 'secondary'), is the mind in its highest state of creative insight and
alertness; its acts are acts of growth, and display themselves in
breaking down the hard commonplaceness which so easily besets
us, and in remoulding this stubborn raw material into new and
living wholes. And now, what of Fancy? These are Coleridge's
well-known words:

Fancy, on the contrary, has no other counters to play with, but fixities
and definites. The Fancy is indeed no other than a mode of Memory
emancipated from the order of time and space. . . . But equally with the
ordinary memory the Fancy must receive all its materials ready made
from the law of association.

In so far as it involves acts of selection and of arrangement ('that
empirical phenomenon of the will, which we express by the word
Choice'), Fancy is on a higher level than mere perception or mere
memory. But it is below Imagination in that, instead of making
all things new, it merely constructs patterns out of *ready-made*
materials, 'fixities and definites'. It juxtaposes images, but does
not *fuse* them into unity; its products are like mechanical mixtures
(as of salt with iron filings), in which the ingredients, though close
together, remain the same as when apart; whereas those of
Imagination are like chemical compounds (say, of sodium and
chlorine), in which the ingredients lose their separate identities in

a new substance, composed of them indeed, but differing from them both. We may fitly use, as an illustration, the two passages quoted by Coleridge himself from 'Venus and Adonis', on which Dr I. A. Richards has ably commented in his *Coleridge on the Imagination*. The first, illustrating Fancy, is:

> Full gently now she takes him by the hand,
> A lily prison'd in a gaol of snow,
> Or ivory in an alabaster band;
> So white a friend engirts so white a foe.

On this Dr Richards observes that the activity of putting together these images is, as Coleridge has said, that of choice, 'an empirical phenomenon of the will'; it is 'an exercise of selection from amongst objects already supplied by association, a selection made for purposes which are not then and therein being shaped, but have been already fixed'. 'Lily' and 'snow', 'ivory' and 'alabaster', are drawn out from the storehouse of memory and juxtaposed, but they remain themselves, not passing into each other, nor becoming one with the hands of Venus and Adonis with which they are compared. We may note here another remark of Coleridge on Fancy: its images, he says, 'have no connexion, natural or moral, but are yoked together by the poet by means of some accidental coincidence' (*Table Talk*, June 23, 1834). Many of the conceits of the Metaphysical poets, and of some modern poets, could be classified in this way as fanciful: for instance Donne's comparison of his mistress's hair with his own spinal cord, or Herbert's comparison of his sins with rocks in the stream of the Redeemer's blood. Two other examples, one serious and one frivolous, may serve to clarify the point:

> (*a*) So, when the Sun in bed,
> Curtain'd with cloudy red,
> Pillows his chin upon an Orient wave.
> (Milton, 'Ode, On the Morning of Christ's Nativity')

> (*b*) And, like a lobster boiled, the morn
> From black to red began to turn.
> (Butler's *Hudibras*)

The juxtapositions of 'chin' and 'pillow' with 'Sun' and 'Orient wave', and of the boiling lobster with dawn, are products of the faculty which, in another phrase of Coleridge's, brings together 'images dissimilar in the main by some one point or more of likeness'. In neither example is there any plastic stress shaping the images into one; the poets are not *realizing* a situation nor compelling us to do so.

Coleridge's second Shakespearean example, illustrating Imagination, is this:

> Look! how a bright star shooteth from the sky,
> So glides he in the night from Venus' eye.

His comment is: 'How many images and feelings are here brought together without effort and without discord – the beauty of Adonis – the rapidity of his flight – the yearning yet helplessness of the enamoured gazer – and a shadowy ideal character thrown over the whole.' This is 'imaginative', according to Coleridge, because Shakespeare is here seen in the act of realizing, making real to himself and to us, the departure of Adonis from Venus; the fall of the shooting star and the flight of Adonis become one in a flash of creative vision, and are henceforth inseparable. Or take a well-known line from *The Merchant of Venice*:

> How sweet the moonlight sleeps upon this bank!

In saying that the moonlight 'sleeps', Shakespeare has said an imaginative thing; the more one dwells upon the metaphor, the more intimate become the links between sleep and moonlight – silence, the prone position of sleeper and moonlit bank, tranquillity, unconsciousness, a trance-like or enchanted state: Shakespeare has seen that all these (and more) are qualities which sleep and moonlight have in common, and in a single word he has made them permanently one. Here is a final pair of illustrations, taken this time from Keats:

(Fancy)   When Cynthia smiles upon a summer's night,
And peers among the cloudlets jet and white,
As though she were reclining in a bed
Of bean blossoms, in heaven freshly shed.

                          ('To Charles Cowden Clarke')

(Imagination)   . . . the moon, lifting her silver rim
Above a cloud, and with a gradual swim
Coming into the blue with all her light.

                                   ('I stood tiptoe . . .')

I suggest that the first passage is fanciful, because in spite of the *curiosa felicitas* of the comparison (it is based upon accurate observation), moonlit cloudlets do not really fuse with bean blossoms, chequered though they both are. The black-and-white is their only link; the warmth and scent of the beanfield and all its suggestions of summer daytime and luxury are unwanted here, whereas in Imagination all the essential qualities of the images are made to interpenetrate. In the second passage I think this actually happens; the keyword is 'swim', which is emphasized by its position at the end of the line. Here everything connected with the movement of a swimmer is apt and relevant to the moon: slow, smooth, steady, purposive motion, and motion in a blue, liquid medium (the night sky is well realized as a sea, with clouds as islands). It is significant that when Keats is treating the moon thus imaginatively he does not need to call her Cynthia.

The Imagination was concerned not merely in the creation of living metaphor (as in the examples quoted above); as the coadunating, shaping power its function was to see all things as one, and the one in all things. It was typically displayed in 'the balance or reconcilement of opposite or discordant qualities'. What discordant qualities? Here are some given by Coleridge: 'a sense of novelty and freshness with old and familiar objects'; 'a more than usual state of emotion with more than usual order'; 'to make the external internal, the internal external, to make nature thought, and thought nature'; 'sameness with difference'; 'truth in observing with the imaginative faculty in modifying the object observed'; 'reducing multitude to unity' or 'succession to an instant'. These are all modes of the fundamental imaginative activity: dissolving in order to re-create, struggling to idealize and to unify 'dead' objects. Objects, taken as such, are fixed and dead, but it is the uncreative mind which fixes and kills them. They need not be so taken; when imaginatively seen they can be vitalized with an energy which comes indeed from within the mind, but which is also, mysteriously, their *own* life so revealed. The cold world of objects will not seem alive unless the poet takes the initiative.

'Extremes meet' was a favourite maxim with Coleridge; indeed, he saw in the interpenetration of opposites the very meaning and inmost process of existence. Life itself, abstractly considered, consists in the tension between polar opposites, the One becoming the Many, and the Many being resolved into the One. 'Subject' and 'Object' coalesce in Knowing; and in Art, Nature becomes Thought and Thought Nature.

Every power in nature and in spirit must evolve an opposite, as the sole means and condition of its manifestation: and all opposition is a tendency to re-union. . . . The identity of thesis and antithesis is the substance of all being. . . . It is the object of mechanical, atomistic philosophy to confound synthesis with synartesis, or rather with mere juxtaposition of corpuscles separated by invisible interspaces.[2]

Coleridge must needs postulate a Faculty: Imagination (or Reason, as we shall see later), whose special function it is to see parts as a whole, and the whole in the parts. It is not surprising, then, to find that, as a critic, Coleridge conceives himself to be engaged in uniting opposites in a new synthesis, or, as he puts it, 'acting the arbitrator between the old school and the new school'.[3] He wished to preserve what was valuable in the 'classical' tradition, while infusing into it the new life and passion of his own age. In that concluding passage of the *Biographia Literaria* (ch. 14) from which I have already quoted phrases, 'classical' and 'romantic' are reconciled and transcended: Coleridge welcomes the passion and the life, but he will have it expressing itself in a greater, not a less, degree of organization – 'a more than usual state of emotion' *with* 'more than usual order', 'the individual' *with* 'the representative', 'judgement ever awake and steady self-possession' *with* 'enthusiasm and feeling profound or vehement'.

The fusion of subject and object in the act of imagination may be attained in a number of ways, though all may be reduced to the 'balance or reconcilement of opposite or discordant qualities'. For instance, while Shakespeare 'darts himself forth, and passes into all the forms of human character and passion', Milton 'attracts all forms and things into himself, into the unity of his own ideal. All things and modes of action shape themselves anew in the being of Milton; while Shakespeare becomes all things, yet for ever remaining himself' (*Biographia Literaria*, ch. 15). In both poets, though in opposite ways, the external becomes internal, and the internal external. Again, both Coleridge and Wordsworth make use of the antithesis of 'sameness with difference', or 'similitude with dissimilitude', in their theories of metrical language – language which is at once 'the same' as, yet other than, the language of 'speech'. Coleridge applies the principle in his psychological account of the origin of metre; here, the 'balance of antagonists' lies between *passion*, which demands a heightened mode of utterance, and *will*, which seeks to master and 'hold in check the workings of passion'. Out of this interpenetration of passion and will springs that organization, that 'ordonnance' of language which we call metre. But he applies it still more widely to the whole relation between subject-matter and treatment, where the synthesis is to be sought in 'the balance of truth in observing with the imaginative faculty in modifying the object observed'. This 'balance', first noted by Coleridge as the distinctive mark of Wordsworth's poety (see above, p. 120), is the topic of several celebrated passages in the Preface to *Lyrical Ballads* and in the *Biographia Literaria*, where the aim of both poets is said to be to combine the truth of Nature with the modifying colours of the Imagination. Moonlight or sunset over a 'known and familiar landscape' proved an apt symbol for the imaginative act as they conceived it; hence, perhaps, the prevalence of the moon in their poetry of 1798. Everyone knows Coleridge's statement of Wordsworth's purpose, a statement which deepens the principle of sameness-and-difference into the notion of awakened insight into the life of common things:

> to give the charm of novelty to things of every day, and to excite a feeling analogous to the supernatural, by awakening the mind's attention from the lethargy of custom, and directing it to the loveliness and the wonders of the world before us; an inexhaustible treasure, but for which, in consequence of the film of familiarity and selfish solicitude, we have eyes, yet see not, ears that hear not, and hearts that neither feel nor understand.[4]

The 'colouring' without the 'truth of Nature' could yield nothing but fanciful kaleidoscope-patterns; 'Nature' alone, on the other hand, would be inanimate and cold. The authentic miracle occurred only when mind and matter, Imagination and observation, fused together to produce that which was neither the one nor the other, but both at once: a living compound, not a mechanical mixture. It is noteworthy that 'the sense of novelty and freshness with old and familiar objects' could be achieved especially by carrying on 'the feelings of childhood into the powers of manhood', by combining 'the child's sense of wonder and novelty with the appearances, which every day for perhaps forty years had rendered familiar'. The power to do this, Coleridge believes, is 'the character and privilege of genius, and one of the marks which distinguish genius from talents'.[5] How distinctive this view is of Coleridge's period may be gauged by imagining what, say, Ben Jonson, Dryden, Boileau or Dr Johnson would have thought of it.

The specific function of the 'esemplastic' or 'coadunating' faculty—the one-making or 'shaping' power—is the fusion of the many into one: its energy is eminently seen, as Coleridge puts it, in the reducing of multitude to unity or succession to an instant. And this in turn is a form of the fusion of subject and object, since the usual mode of its operation is the subordination of the multitude of 'things' to a predominant mood in the poet. Examples of these aspects of Imagination could be collected from any of the major poets: e.g. (multitude to unity)

> As when far off at sea a fleet descried
> Hangs in the clouds, by equinoctial winds
> Close sailing from Bengala . . .
> > (*Paradise Lost*, 1 636 ff.)

or

> the visible scene
> Would enter unawares into his mind
> With all its solemn imagery, its rocks,
> Its woods, and that uncertain heaven received
> Into the bosom of the steady lake.
> > (Wordsworth, 'There Was a Boy', 21–5)

or (succession to an instant)

> The fierce confederate storm
> Of sorrow barricadoed ever more
> Within the walls of cities.
> > (*Excursion*, Prospectus, 78–80)

or (both at once)

> And all that mighty heart is lying still.
> > ('Composed upon Westminster Bridge')

All these extracts probably illustrate also the subordination of multiplicity to the poet's mood; this is perhaps more clearly seen in

> The moving waters at their priestlike task
> Of pure ablution round earth's human shores.
> > (Keats, 'Bright Star')

or in

> April is the cruellest month, breeding
> Lilacs out of the dead land. . . .
> > (Eliot, *The Waste Land*)

But every reader must test Coleridge for himself; whoever will do so attentively, will generally find his understanding of the creative process deepened and clarified.

To grasp the significance of Fancy in this wider context, we must remember that in Coleridge's view the mental habits of the previous century had resulted in the exclusion of Imagination from poetry. Since Milton, poets had on the whole ceased to maintain the creative interchange between mind and object, and had been content to use ready-made material created in earlier, more imaginative times, or at best to say supremely well what had been greatly imagined by others, but less perfectly uttered. As we have seen, the essence of the Imagination was that it involved the poet's whole soul in a creative act; Fancy merely used the results of previous activity. This, for Coleridge, was the only kind of poetic activity possible in the eighteenth century climate; it had taken the form of selecting images from older poets—from the ancients, from Milton, and later from Celtic, Norse or mediaeval sources. 'The Gothic' was at first fancifully used rather than imaginatively, but it helped, in virtue of its unfamiliarity, to evoke new imaginative life. It encouraged the poet (in a phrase of Mrs Radcliffe) 'to send forward a transforming eye into the distant obscurity'. If we remind ourselves of the age in which Coleridge lived, we shall not wonder that notions of life, growth and *transformation* were in the ascendant. In the first half of the eighteenth century life was conducted, on the whole, within a framework which was accepted as fixed and final. Fixities and definites were the order of the day: in society, the appointed hierarchy; in religion, the establishment; in Nature, the admirable order with its Chain of Being and its gravitational nexus which was mirrored in humanity by 'self-love and social'; in art, the rules and the proprieties. The aim of politics, religion and philosophy was not to transform, but to demonstrate and confirm existing perfection; the aim of poetry was to decorate. But with the onset of the revolutionary age all this was altered; the fixities yielded to flux, mechanics to life and organism, order to process, and the imaginative mouldings of the poets reflected on the ideal plane the great social changes which were proceeding on the material level. Life, and growth, and consciousness – those very mysteries which had never fitted comfortably into the mechanical scheme, now came into their own. Poets could feel, as seldom before, and hardly since, that they were allies of the ascendant forces, the leaders and legislators of mankind, instead of being elegant triflers or refugees from reality:

> O pleasant exercise of hope and joy!
> For mighty were the auxiliars which then stood
> Upon our side, us who were strong in love!

Within the life-span of Wordsworth and Coleridge most of this transforming energy of love and hope was deflected by events from political into imaginative and ideal channels; the soul comforted itself for political disillusionment by exulting in its own 'mighty and almost divine powers' (Wordsworth, 1815 Preface). Nothing, it seemed, could be more important than exertions of such powers, nothing more satisfying than their results – so satisfying, that they could only be expressed in terms of 'Truth'. For the human mind, for better or worse, does call by the name of Truth whatever deeply satisfies, as well as that which, on the practical level, is found to *work*. But – and this is where Fancy comes in again – not all such transformations were found to satisfy; there were those which merely amused or titillated, as well as those which seemed meaningful. The first were fanciful, the second imaginative. The business of the Imagination was not to generate chimaeras and fictions – the *imaginary* – but to 'disimprison the soul of fact'.'What the imagination seizes as beauty must be Truth', says Keats. Why must it? One can only reply in such terms as Wordsworth's that when the mind of man is 'wedded to the universe', and works 'subservient strictly to external things', the creation 'which they with blended might accomplish' does, in fact and in experience, produce a sense of something seen, something truly realized. Of course, there will be a metaphysical way of putting this, and naturally we find it in Coleridge: the world is really alive, and not dead; the life we project into it meets a life which is already there, and there is a mysterious link between man and Nature, whereby man, in

moulding Nature, can be *unfolding* Nature in the direction of its
own striving. 'Dare I add', says he, 'that genius must act on the
feeling that body is but a striving to become mind – that it is
mind in its essence!'[6] But whatever the metaphysical validity of
what is seen by the visionary light, it remains important for us
that the soul should be able to project upon the world 'the light,
the glory, the fair luminous cloud'. It is only in dejection that the
world seems cold and inanimate; if it can be transfigured (and the
poets know that it can), then why say that the cold world is the
real, the true world? Meanwhile, when joy and vision fail, there is
always the metaphysical consolation that perhaps Nature is not
naturata after all – not really fixed and dead, that it is *naturans*,
alive and growing, and ready to yield its secret to the eye that
brings with it the means of seeing.

I cannot therefore agree with those who call the
Fancy – Imagination distinction 'celebrated but useless'. It
seems to me to point, not only to an observable difference
between kinds of poetry, but to a profound distinction in our ways
of responding to experience. In our own time the task of poets has
become harder than ever; they must resist and subdue a world far
colder and more hostile than Coleridge's. But some of them are
doing it, even if each poem must be 'a fresh start and a fresh kind
of failure'; and we can still use Coleridge's theory to distinguish
between those who are genuinely performing this task and those
who are merely using bygone modes to produce what is
superficially or academically pleasing. Let us say, in conclusion,
that no poetic output demonstrates the distinction more strik-
ingly than Coleridge's own. The difference between his 'great
three' poems and most of his other verse is so extraordinary that it
can only be called a difference in kind, and only accounted for on
the supposition that in them he was using faculties and powers
which lay dormant at other times. Professor Lowes has demonstrated that in the 'great three' poems the images stored in
Coleridge's mind had undergone alchemical change by being
plunged in the deep well of his subconsciousness, whereas
elsewhere they are merely produced by a deliberate choice of the
will, and rhetorically juxtaposed. Today we talk familiarly about
the subconscious, and think we are speaking more scientifically

than our predecessors who discoursed about 'the soul'. But the difference remains valid, however we describe it or account for it, between poetry which is merely made or contrived in the top layer of the consciousness and that which springs from the energy of the poet's whole being, and in us (the readers) 'calls the whole soul into activity, with the subordination of the faculties to each other according to their several worth and dignity'.

SOURCE: extract from essay in *Nineteenth Century Studies* (1949; reprinted 1955, 1961) pp. 19–35.

NOTES

1. *Letters of S. T. Coleridge*, ed. E. H. Coleridge (London, 1895) vol. I, p. 352.
2. Coleridge, *The Friend* (London, 1818); Bohn ed. (1865) pp. 57–8 n.
3. *Letters*, vol. I, p. 387.
4. *Biographia Literaria*, ed. Shawcross, vol. II, p. 6.
5. Ibid., vol. I, p. 59.
6. 'On Poesy or Art', in ibid., vol. II, p. 258.

Barbara Hardy

DISTINCTION WITHOUT DIFFERENCE: COLERIDGE'S FANCY AND IMAGINATION (1951)

Coleridge's famous definition by distinction had its roots in aesthetic experience: it was his first contact with Wordsworth's poetry which, if we are to believe the account in chapter 4 of the *Biographia Literaria*, set him off on this analysis of creative activity. He claimed to be investigating both terminology and mental faculties, and though he speaks of the 'collective, unconscious good sense working progressively to desynonymize those words originally of the same meaning . . .' he was doing rather more than recording this process. Coleridge liked nothing better than giving the Genius of the Language a push, and he often does it under the cover of investigation.

Here he had a threefold motive for pushing. He wanted to explain what had moved him so deeply in Wordsworth, he wanted also to make an anti-associationist manifesto, and, as always, he wanted to pay full tribute to a power which could satisfy his thirst for unity. For Coleridge the imagination was an *active* power, independent of the fixed associations of memory and experience, and it was also a *unifying* power. His hatred of passive association and his hatred of the disconnected ('The universe seems a heap of little things', he shudders once), made him take a very special interest in this particular piece of desynonymization, since, if he exaggerated the distinction between the two terms, he would be provided with a purer Imaginative activity, which could be freed of any suggestion of mechanical work by a judicious use of the waste-bin of Fancy. The fixed patterns of association must play some part in aesthetic creation, but he refused to admit that Imagination had any responsibility for this part. Not all the processes of writing a poem can be explained as unifying processes, so he leaves the little disconnected things to the scapegoat Fancy, and finds in Imagination the sign or the symbol of universal unity.

In his list of the operations of Imagination in chapter 13 of the *Biographia* he has his eye on unity. 'It dissolves, diffuses, dissipates, in order to re-create: or where this process is rendered impossible, yet still at all events it struggles to idealize and to unify. It is essentially *vital*. . . .' It dissolves or dissipates because the artist can neither copy nor assimilate in wholes: the whole is an obstacle to selection and change, and destruction is the first step in re-creation. This holds good for an art like literature where the material is not raw (like marble) but already cooked by experience. The power over experience and the urge to unify are both implicit in this destructive process. And the same power is implicit in the process of modifying, which he mentions in chapter 4 and elsewhere. The Imagination modifies its materials because it organizes them into unity, and they have to be adapted to each other and to the total poetic effect. In other words, the Imagination has to make good neighbours of dramatic characters or poetic images so that no 'unit' disturbs the unity. Idealizing and vitalizing (we meet the latter again under the name of 'humanizing') are less obviously unifying processes, but sooner or later the implication creeps in. Milton unifies by stamping his materials with the magnificent trade-mark of his own image; Shakespeare withdraws his own image and penetrates to the essence of the object — his unity is that of the universe, which his generalizing power permits him to reveal. Coleridge is often more concerned with this prophetic revelatory function than with the simple power to create aesthetic harmony, but that does not matter here. What matters is his interest in any kind of unity.

For, when we turn to Fancy's syllabus, we find that there is no suggestion of unity: 'FANCY, on the contrary, has no other counters to play with, but fixities and definites. The Fancy is indeed no other than a mode of memory emancipated from the order of time and space . . . equally with the ordinary memory the Fancy must receive all its materials ready made from the law of association.' Any operation not characteristic of the power to transform or to unify is attributed to Fancy.

In chapter 12 Coleridge made one very important delegation
to Fancy. In Southey's *Omniana* (1812) he had called Fancy 'the
aggregative and associative power', and Wordsworth's objection
in the preface to the 1815 *Poems* that 'to aggregate and to
associate, to evoke and to combine, belong as well to the
Imagination as to the Fancy' called out an indignant denial: 'I
reply, that if, by the power of evoking and combining, Mr.
Wordsworth means the same as, and no more than, I meant by
the aggregative and associative, I continue to deny, that it
belongs at all to the Imagination.' Aggregating or collecting is
beneath the dignity of Imagination because it is not necessarily
an act of unifying. It is necessary, of course: the materials have to
be assembled before Imagination can get to work and make the
transformation and the synthesis. Fancy has to do it, because the
collector may collect at hazard, for fun, or for reasons so thin as to
be patently mere excuses for the act of collecting. The Fancy who
in 'Venus and Adonis' collects lilies, snow, ivory, alabaster and
doves, is the kind of collector who is more interested in the
collecting than in the things (tram-tickets, car-numbers,
cigarette-cards, autographs) collected. The suggestion of the
white hands of Venus and Adonis is enough for the enthusiastic
collector. 'Let's collect white things' says Fancy, and the one
common quality of whiteness is the link. But a linking together is
not necessarily a unity.

The links in Fancy's collections are like the links between the
objects in a free association game, and Fancy's work is both a
game (the counters are there 'to play with') and an act of free
association. The play of Fancy is often the play of life's
incongruous assemblies: the disconnected and fantastic associations of sandwiches and sunsets and blisters and half-forgotten
conversations. Imagination can rise above these jostling associations, or break them up, selecting the sunset and ignoring the
undignified remainder. Coleridge must attack Hartley's associationism with all the fervour of the Kantian convert, and so he
denies that Imagination can ever touch these fixtures of memory
or of unconscious pattern. Just as Fancy must have all the jobs not
directly connected with the making of unity, so that
Imagination's unifying power can be emphasized, so Fancy must

have all the blind, capricious, playful juxtapositions of casual association as its material, so that the emphasis can be placed on Imagination's ability to control and change the experience of poet and reader.

These are some of the differences between Fancy and Imagination and some of the reasons for Coleridge's emphasis of the differences. But are there no better reasons for the distinction? What of the aesthetic evidence?

Coleridge began by reading Wordsworth. He began with effect and worked back to cause. And, as we should expect, his aesthetic evidence is plausible: he chooses illustrations of Fancy and Imagination which seem different in kind. Butler's reddening lobster which describes the sunset is so different from the bright shooting star which gives all the passionate loss of Venus and the elusive beauty of Adonis, that we are tempted to argue with Coleridge that two poetic effects so different must be produced by two separate mental faculties. But this argument from effect has dangers: we are in the position of the man who is neither a scientist nor a cook, and who deduces from the qualitative difference between hot water and steam that there must be a qualitative difference between the cause of steam and the cause of hot water. Lowes believed that the poetic cause changed only quantitatively, as the cause of hot water differs only quantitatively from the cause of steam, but it is not so easy to refute Coleridge as it is to show the ignorant man the gas-ring beneath the kettle. In spite of the backing given to Coleridge (in very different ways) by I. A. Richards, D. G. James, and Basil Willey, I believe that Lowes was right and Coleridge wrong. We have to look for the equivalent of the gas-ring beneath the kettle.

Garrod called the distinction useless, and useless it may be for us, though it is not very easy to say why, but it was of enormous use to Coleridge. It was because he needed and wanted the separation of the two faculties that he was so fussy about keeping their work separate, and insisted somewhat arbitrarily that though they might work together they never did the same job. Wordsworth left open the door between Fancy and Imagination by allowing that they might both associate and combine, and Ruskin (who knew Wordsworth's theory, even if he did not know

Coleridge's) opened the door even wider, and allowed free passage. But Coleridge slammed it. And the result was that he is left with a very curious relationship which begins to disintegrate as soon as we inspect it.

The co-operation of Fancy and Imagination is the co-operation of delegator and delegate. (It is hard not to be anthropomorphic about mental activities.) And the delegator is in the not very happy position of being forced to delegate by his inability to do a certain menial job. Imagination is the great administrator who can never never do the work of his clerk. This means, of course, that his clerk has enormous power. Imagination can work wonders with the material supplied, but can never facilitate the wonder-working by choosing and assembling the material for himself. Or, to change the metaphor, Imagination is like a host who can modify the habits and temperaments of his guests — sever a memory here, amputate an opinion there — but who can never facilitate the work of creating the perfect party by choosing the guests.

This means, of course, that, although the menial has power, he is as restricted as his superior. For he is eternally unpromotable. Fancy can never do the work of Imagination. This may seem a smaller flaw in the theory than the strange limitation of Imagination, but it is just as fatal.

If Imagination and Fancy are always and essentially different in kind, what happens when Imagination fails? If it fails to unify, may the result not bear a strong resemblance to the casual connections of Fancy? If its vital function fails, and its characters or metaphors do not come to life, will they not be mistaken for the stillborn children of Fancy, who cannot give life? If it fails to modify one image by using a second (if Wordsworth had failed to block the associations of the stone image by using the more animated but still inhuman image of the sea-beast so as to give us both the mystery and the humanity of the leech-gatherer), will it not seem as though the unchecked associations of Fancy are at work? This failure to discriminate — or to recognize that we may be unable to discriminate — between the success of Fancy and the failure of Imagination is one of the weak spots of this belief in a qualitative difference. For once we recognize the similarity or the identity of the successes of Fancy and the failures of Imagination, we begin to wonder whether the door between *can* be slammed.

Once we have begun to doubt, we are tempted to look outside Coleridge's convincing illustrations for our own evidence of the two faculties. For, if it is true that each has its separately apportioned task, then it should be possible to recognize the workmen by the work – particularly when we remember that Coleridge, and any critic who knows little psychology and less physiology, can infer the separate existence of the workmen only by showing the traces of two hands in the work.

Coleridge believed that the Imagination left its mark wherever it worked. Not only could we trace it in the harmonious unity of the poem or play but also in the presence of microcosmic imaginative unities within the major aesthetic whole. Within the poem the image would have a compressed and complex reference; within the play the individual scene or the individual character would be packed with a variety of harmonious functions and characteristics. Coleridge's respect for complexity, like his aching longing for unity or his scorn for the associationists' poetic passiveness, shows itself in the favouritism of his terminology. Imagination is always complex, Fancy is not. Fancy, like Hazlitt's Wit, which is probably a direct descendant from it, connects dissimilar objects by one tenuous connecting similarity. So the fanciful simile or metaphor (the lobster) tells us only one thing about the object or experience it expresses (the sun), unlike the imaginative image which will concentrate our attention upon the thing described because it has a manifold relevance.

This respect for complexity in detail, for a continual imaginative pressure within character and image, is less acceptable than the familiar and well-tested aesthetic demand for variety in unity in the whole. If each character in a play or a novel is given the maximum complexity, the unity of the whole may well be sacrificed to the warring unities of the separate parts. If each image in a poem has the maximum complexity of reference, the pace of the poem will inevitably be slowed up. What happens if the poet wants speed? We are, of course, often unwittingly moved by a complex meaning whose separate suggestions we may not disentangle until after the aesthetic event, but there seems no very obvious reason for the assumption which began with Coleridge (or, more probably, with Walter Whiter), that *local* complexity is necessarily a virtue.

Coleridge was the first serious complexity-hunter, and the hunt was an important part of the Imagination theory. But it can have two unhappy results. The first is the occasional neglect of the poem as an organic whole. The attention to the complex detail which produced the brilliant analysis of the shooting-star image, produced also the comment on the flattery metaphor in the sonnet beginning

> Full many a glorious morning have I seen
> Flatter the mountain-tops with sovereign eye.

Coleridge is so interested in the imaginative evidence of the metaphor with its complex suggestions of royal condescension and sunlit summits that he forgets the more important business of relating the image to the rest of the poem, and misses the imaginative integrity which results from our introduction to an image which is later applied, in all its complex suggestions of glory and flattery, to the lover and the beloved.

More important for my present purpose is the general weakness of Coleridge's case for the imaginative detail. Is there any reason why the complexity of the part (unless we can relate it to the complexity of the whole) is Imaginative? If complexity is one of the marks of Imagination are we to assume that the playful image (the work of Fancy), or the image which does not hide or control its incongruous suggestions can never be complex? When Dylan Thomas (in the eleventh poem in *18 Poems*) speaks of the 'kissproof world' is he not deliberately playing on the incongruous associations with advertisements for lipstick? But is he not also loading the image with more than this one suggestion of a world where kissing is commercialized? The world of this poem about death's tracking down of love and life is kissproof in another sense: its decay resists love, is proof against a kiss. The trade-name is unmade and remade. Is this Fancy or Imagination? Complexity is not only a dangerous criterion, it is not even a satisfactory label for Imagination.

What about the other labels? Another proof of imagination, we are told in chapter 15 of the *Biographia*, is the image which is modified by 'a predominant passion'. Does this mean that the image so modified will never be playful or incongruous? What about Lady Macbeth's forced spark of bravado

> I'll gild the faces of the grooms withal;
> For it must seem their gilt?

Here is play, albeit grim, and here, as always in the pun, is the deliberate opening of the door as an invitation to the incongruous association. But the pun is the communication of the strained mind and the effort to belittle the reality of murder. Is it Fancy or Imagination? Or there are the swift-moving images of the last stanza of 'Modern Love':

> Thus piteously Love closed what he begat
> The union of this ever-diverse pair!
> These two were rapid falcons in a snare,
> Condemned to do the flitting of the bat.

The images are joined only by their relevance to the ever-diverse pair: not only is there a contradiction but it is contradiction essential to the poem, for only the clash of images could give the emotional clash. Like Lady Macbeth's pun the image is modified by predominant passion – indeed it communicates the passion – but it has the normal characteristic of Fancy.

Is the label more clearly recognizable if we turn from the image to the total structure? Coleridge said in Chapter 22 of the *Biographia* that the happiest example of the difference between Imagination and Fancy was a structural difference, and he contrasts 'the minute accuracy in the painting of local imagery' in *The Excursion* with Milton's description of the fig-tree, concluding that the second is imaginative because 'the co-presence of the whole picture flashed at once upon the eye, as the sun paints in a camera obscura' and that the first is Fancy, since it produces an effect of disconnection:

It seems to be like taking the pieces of a dissected map out of its box. We first look at one part, and then at another, then join and dove-tail them; and when the successive acts of attention have been completed, there is a retrogressive effort of mind to behold it as a whole.

It is an excellent example of the way in which Coleridge inferred cause from effect. It is also an excellent example of a difference in effect. But is it always so easy to put one's finger on imaginative and fanciful structure? How do we classify the coolly relaxed plot relations and smooth transitions of Lyly's plays? Or the scenic planning of Webster, where we can often displace scenes and events (the resistance to such displacement is another of Coleridge's signs of imagination), but where there is atmospheric and linguistic unity? What about the deliberate discord of the Porter in *Macbeth* or the removable keystone of the Hell scene in *Man and Superman?*

There is no point in piling up examples which resist the classification – they are easier to find than examples which can be fitted into it.

It is true, of course, that Coleridge insisted that Imagination used Fancy – he accused Wordsworth of confusing the work of both with the work of one. But if we are going to take the audacious step of inferring cause from effect we dare not be vague about the qualitative difference. We should be able to put the labels, if not on an entire play or poem, at least on single aspects of form or language. And can we do this often enough to make out any kind of case for the distinction? Will we not find ourselves, nine times out of ten, in a critical limbo where there is only the evidence of an enormous versatile creative power which refuses to stand still long enough for us to fix either label?

SOURCE: *Essays in Criticism*, I (1951) 336–44.

J. R. de J. Jackson

' "FANCY" RESTORED TO DIGNITY' (1969)

Coleridge's distinction betwen Imagination and Fancy in the thirteenth chapter of *Biographia Literaria* is his most detailed attempt to define the problem of probing the unconscious for the initiatives necessary to the Method of poetry. It is constantly quoted in a casual way in critical discussions, and it is the most exhaustively studied passage in all Coleridge's criticism. The distinction is phrased metaphorically, and it has long appeared to invite explication. The fact that analyses continue to be made, in spite of the attention lavished on it, is evidence of a sort that the results have not yet been entirely satisfactory: Some have suggested that the fault lies with the distinction itself; one is inclined to suggest that we do not yet understand the underlying philosophy well enough to be sure. Now that we have made an attempt to display the kind of thinking with which Coleridge was preoccupied, it may be possible to carry our interpretation of his terms a step farther. One of the most interesting effects will be, I believe, to restore Fancy to the dignity and power with which Coleridge originally endowed it — to present it once again as an integral part of great poetry, and to reject the too common misconception of it as a faculty appropriate to inferior verse only. . . .

[Quotes Fancy – Imagination distinction from *Biographia Literaria*; see above, Part One, section I. VII. – Ed.]

The prevailing explanation of these terms is the account given by Shawcross[1] in the introduction of his edition of *Biographia Literaria*. Shawcross uses Schelling's *Transcendentalen Idealismus* as the key to Coleridge's discussion, exaggerating, in my estimation, the extent to which Coleridge was passively reliant on the German philosopher when the *Biographia* was composed. He concludes from his comparison that the Primary Imagination is 'the imagination as universally active in consciousness (creative in that it externalizes the world of objects by opposing it to the self)', and that Secondary Imagination is 'the same faculty in a heightened power as creative in a poetic sense'. According to this view, Primary Imagination is the consciousness shared by all men, while Secondary Imagination is limited to poets who can project the unity they discern in their consciousness upon the particulars of their environment. Fancy, for Shawcross, is 'the faculty of mere images or impressions, as imagination is the faculty of intuitions'. He states that Coleridge sees in the opposition of Imagination and Fancy 'an emblem of the wider contrast between the mechanical philosophy and the dynamic, the false and the true'.

Shawcross's interpretation marked a significant advance in the study of Coleridge's criticism; there can be no doubt that it was the most profound and exhaustive analysis that had been made. But Shawcross knew his subject much too well to feel entirely satisfied with his explanation. He observes that the distinction between Imagination and Fancy understood in these terms hardly measures up to the ' "deduction" of the imagination' that Coleridge had promised. He proposes, therefore, noting that Coleridge was not altogether committed to Schelling's theory, that the abrupt interruption of the argument in chapter 13, and the 'unsatisfactory vagueness of the final summary', may be attributed to the position's being Schelling's and not Coleridge's.

Subsequent students have tended to accept the broad outlines of Shawcross's account and have devoted their attention to elaborating it or to developing its implications. I. A. Richards, for example, has made a courageous and remarkably successful effort to construct a viable critical instrument out of it.[2] Others, feeling that the distinction, understood as Shawcross presents it, is inadequate, have argued that it was not the distinction of kind which Coleridge had thought it, but rather one of degree.[3] T. S. Eliot has ventured the opinion that 'the difference between imagination and fancy amounts in practice to no more than the difference between good and bad poetry'.[4] There has been little fundamental opposition to Shawcross.

The first, and so far as I am aware, the only basic disagreement is voiced in Walter Jackson Bate's essay 'Coleridge on the Function of Art'. Passing by the apparent similarities to Schelling he concentrates on the terms of the distinction themselves, and maintains that Shawcross's rendering of them is not consistent with Coleridge's known attitudes. He expresses dissatisfaction with the idea that Coleridge could have meant the poetic imagination to be nothing more than an 'echo' of our consciousness of our surroundings (Shawcross's definition of Primary Imagination), and says that Secondary Imagination is 'rather the highest exertion of the imagination that the "finite mind" has to offer; and in its scope . . . necessarily includes universals which lie beyond the restricted field of the "secondary" imagination'.[5] Bate, then, is arguing that Primary Imagination is something more than the consciousness common to us all. This, as I shall try to show, is a very workable objection. He goes on to suggest that Primary Imagination may be connected to 'direct awareness of reason', and that the term may refer to 'that aspect of the creative capacity which draws down the rational insight of the universal into an individualized form of response, thus repeating "the eternal act of creation" '.[6]

Bate's dissatisfaction with Shawcross's interpretation of Primary Imagination focuses upon a most unfortunate and confusing ambiguity in Coleridge's definition. The account begins: 'The primary IMAGINATION I hold to be the living Power and prime Agent of all human Perception. . . .' By 'Perception' reasonably enough, Coleridge has been taken to mean sense perception. Bate, as we have seen, suggests that he means instead 'direct awareness of·reason'.[7] This is, even for Coleridge, an unusual usage, but it does occur in 1825 in *Aids to Reflection* with reference to perception of the unconscious. He remarks there that 'the lowest depth that the light of our Consciousness can visit even with a doubtful Glimmering, is still at an unknown distance from the Ground. . . . Conception is consequent on Perception. What we cannot *imagine*, we cannot, in the proper sense of the word, conceive.'[8] It seems possible at least that Coleridge is using the term 'perception' in this sense in his definition of Primary Imagination. It is worth adding that Coleridge does not in fact identify Primary Imagination with perception; it is rather 'the

living Power and prime Agent of all human Perception' – that is
to say, it is in some way a condition on which the act of perception
depends.

Having gone so far with the orthodox interpretation of the
distinction, and having noticed an important criticism of it, it is
time to step back for a moment in order to get a longer view.
Chapter 13, entitled 'On the imagination, or esemplastic power',
was apparently conceived of as a lengthy philosophical treatise.
In the interposed letter it is said to be so long that it *cannot, when it
is printed, amount to so little as an hundred pages*.[9] It is not surprising
that the 'main result' of such a chapter, presented without its
preamble, should prove obscure. Shawcross, as we have noticed,
called in the aid of Schelling; another useful approach is to enlist
the help of Coleridge himself, by drawing on his metaphysics as
we have reconstructed them.

A very helpful gloss, which encourages this approach, appears
written in Coleridge's hand on the endpapers of a volume of
Tennemann's *Geschichte der Philosophie*. It suggests an interpretation of Imagination markedly different from the ones we
have been examining. The note runs as follows:

The simplest yet practically sufficient order of the mental Powers is,
beginning from the

lowest	highest
Sense	Reason
Fancy	Imagination
Understanding	Understanding
―――――――	―――――――
Understanding	Understanding
Imagination	Fancy
Reason	Sense

Fancy and Imagination are Oscillations, *this* connecting R and U; *that*
connecting Sense and Understanding.[10]

Here we have a chart of the correct disposition of Imagination
between Subject and Object, Man and Nature, or, as they are
termed in this instance, Reason and Sense. Imagination, it will

be noted, is far removed from Sense. But in this list, Imagination
is not distinguished into Primary Imagination and Secondary
Imagination, and one is faced with the question of where they
could be fitted if the distinction were made. If one accepts
Shawcross's explanation, or Bate's, it is an awkward
problem – to be circumvented, perhaps, by the suggestion that
Coleridge was not thinking in the same terms when he drew up
the chart. Before rejecting the chart, however, we are well
advised to ponder the meaning of the three new terms which it
introduces – Reason, Understanding, and Sense – and to see
whether they are relevant to the definitions of chapter 13.

Coleridge discusses Reason and Understanding and their
relation to Sense in *The Statesman's Manual*[11] and in the fifth essay
of the third volume of the 1818 *Friend*. His treatment of Reason is
difficult to follow, because he generalizes the term so as to include
two similar and yet different faculties. 'I should have no
objection,' he says, 'to define Reason with Jacobi, and with his
friend Hemsterhuis, as an organ bearing the same relation to
spiritual objects, the Universal, the Eternal, and the Necessary,
as the eye bears to material and contingent phænomena'. That is
to say, Reason is the organ (or faculty) through whose agency we
are permitted to perceive 'the Universal'. Coleridge immediately
qualifies this statement: 'But then it must be added, that it is an
organ identical with its appropriate objects. Thus, God, the Soul,
eternal Truth, &c. are the objects of Reason; but they are
themselves *reason*. We name God the Supreme Reason; and
Milton says, "Whence the Soul *Reason* receives, and Reason is her
Being".'[12] Reason, then, means both the Absolute and the
faculty which permits us to look at the Absolute. It is in the latter
sense that Coleridge is using the term when he concludes that
'Whatever is conscious *Self*-knowledge is Reason. . . .' He adds,
'in this sense it may be safely defined the organ of the
Supersensuous'.[13] The same distinction is made in *The Statesman's
Manual*, where Coleridge speaks of:

The REASON, (not the abstract reason, not the reason as the mere *organ* of
science, or as the faculty of scientific principles and schemes a priori; but
reason) as the integral *spirit* of the regenerated man, reason sub-

stantiated and vital, . . . the breath of the power of God, and a pure influence from the glory of the Almighty. . . .'[14]

We have, then, Reason itself, and the same word to mean the organ of Reason – another regrettable ambiguity.

In chapter 13, as in the manuscript chart, Coleridge is, I believe, referring to both senses of the word 'Reason' and giving them different names. In *Biographia Literaria*, Primary Imagination is Reason itself, while Secondary Imagination is the organ of Reason; in the chart, Reason is Reason itself, while Imagination is the organ of Reason. This interpretation of Coleridge's definition of Imagination varies sharply from the interpretations offered by Shawcross and Bate; it will, therefore, be necessary to display at some length the grounds for accepting it. What I am suggesting, to revert to the diagrammatic aid of the chart, may be represented as follows:

lowest	highest
Sense	Reason (Primary Imagination)
Fancy	organ of Reason (Secondary Imagination)
Understanding	Understanding

Understanding	Understanding
organ of Reason (Secondary Imagination)	Fancy
Reason (Primary Imagination)	Sense

Such an interpretation does not affect our general understanding of Coleridge's thought in any radical way, but it does alter the meaning of the distinction between Imagination and Fancy very considerably. It hinges essentially on a different account of the relation of Primary and Secondary Imagination to the unconscious and to physical phenomena.

We have already mentioned the sense in which Reason is taken by Coleridge to mean 'God, the Soul, eternal Truth, &c'.[15] So understood it is identical with the unconscious repository of divine knowledge, or Revelation, which we have shown to be the medium for the Human mode of the Communicative Intelligence. Coleridge calls Primary Imagination, 'a repetition in the finite mind of the eternal act of creation in the infinite I AM'. The description recalls a similar one in a letter written to Humphry Davy in 1809, in which Coleridge mentions 'the moral connection between the finite and infinite Reason, and the aweful majesty of the former as both the Revelation and the exponent Voice of the Latter, immortal Time-piece [of] an eternal Sun'.[16] Here we have a triple division: infinite Reason (God); and finite Reason, both as Reason itself (in man) and as the organ of Reason. In his definition of Primary Imagination, Coleridge makes no allusion to the transmission of the 'repetition in the finite mind', nor does he say that Primary Imagination is conscious. It is, in fact, 'the IMMEDIATE, which dwells in every man', and 'the original intuition, or absolute affirmation of it (which is likewise in every man, but does not in every man rise into consciousness)'.[17] Primary Imagination may be taken as the literary term for the consciousness, and for an unconscious which has the characteristic traces of the Communicative Intelligence which Coleridge has ascribed to it.[18]

In *Biographia Literaria* Coleridge forgoes discussion of the unconscious as 'something, which must lie beyond the possibility of our knowledge' and as of no concern to us as 'transcendental philosophers'.[19] In his 'Treatise on Logic', however, he speculates about it, with the property of 'synthetic unity'.[20] He then considers the relationship between this primary act and consciousness. He begins by asserting that 'Without the primary act or unity of apperception we could have nothing to be conscious of.' He adds that 'Without the repetition of representation of this act in the understanding completes the consciousness we should be conscious of nothing.' Here the will evidently plays a part. Coleridge concludes by saying that

It will appear . . . on a moment[']s self-examination that a mere repetition of this act, a mere representation of the product of the act, could in no respect differ from the former in kind[,] at least more than the second echo from the former or a secondary Rainbow, from the principal arch; something more must take place in order to constitute it a repetition by the Understanding and this something, is the act of reflection.[21]

The 'mere repetition of this act, a mere representation of the product of the act' is very much like the definition of Secondary Imagination: 'The secondary . . . I consider as an echo of the former, co-existing with the conscious will, yet still as identical with the primary in the *kind* of its agency. . . .'[22] Secondary Imagination is somewhere between Understanding in its full sense and the unconscious; it is not completely under the control of the mind, but it does 'co-exist' with 'the conscious will'. It is the power referred to simply as 'imagination' in chapter 14 of the *Biographia*, as being 'first put in action by the will and understanding, and retained under their irremissive, though gentle and unnoticed, controul (*laxis effertur habenis*)'[23]

Secondary Imagination is the faculty of mind involved in the difficult and mysterious activity of attaining the Ideas necessary to the Method of the Fine Arts; its activity is Passion. Elsewhere Coleridge calls it 'imagination' merely, and his differentiation between it and Primary Imagination in chapter 13 seems calculated to make its kinship with the Communicative Intelligence, its source in the unconscious, explicit. The most important point about the definition is that it excludes the possibility that the material world can contribute to the Secondary Imagination – except, perhaps, in so far as it may affect the unconscious.[24] Coleridge's assertion that 'It dissolves, diffuses, dissipates, in order to re-create; or where this process is rendered impossible, yet still, at all events, it struggles to idealize and to unify' refers to the process of deriving the 'Mental initiative' which in the Fine Arts 'must necessarily proceed from within', the process by which 'the obscure impulse' becomes 'a bright, and clear, and living Idea!'[25] Secondary Imagination is the faculty used to exploit the God-given resources hidden in the unconscious interior of the human mind.

In terms of Coleridge's chart, beginning with 'the highest', we have now moved from Reason (Primary Imagination) through

Imagination (Secondary Imagination). The next term to be considered is Understanding. Understanding is variously described by Coleridge, but he always seems to use it in the sense of the conscious regulation of knowledge — it is a means of control rather than a source of knowledge. As we have noticed, there are in Coleridge's view two kinds of knowledge — one derived from the unconscious, and the other from material phenomena. Understanding is the faculty which controls and regulates both kinds. That is probably why it appears twice on the chart, and the line drawn between its two appearances emphasizes the dichotomy of the sources of knowledge. Used consciously and intentionally, Understanding is the element of control necessary if the Secondary Imagination is to be put to good use. It corresponds to the faculty involved in the progression of Method based on the relation of Law.

We have followed and explained the progress of the chart from Reason to Understanding. The line which Coleridge now draws to separate his terms into two halves implies a bar to our moving any farther in the same direction. Instead we must start again, this time at 'the lowest', and work our way up from Sense, through Fancy, to Understanding.

By Sense, Coleridge means the faculty which allows us to perceive our environment, and which makes us aware of material things. He is fully conscious, as we have observed in our preliminary discussion of his treatment of Method in the Fine Arts, of the important role played by the evidence of the senses in poetry. He has admitted that the Fine Arts 'all operate by the images of sight and sound, and other sensible impressions; and [that] without a delicate tact for these, no man ever was, or could be, either a Musician or a Poet; nor could he attain to excellence in any one of these Arts'.[26] Coleridge's only restriction on the powers of Sense is that, unlike the powers of Reason, they cannot rightly be thought of as hints of the mind of God, and hence they are an unsatisfactory source of the initiatives of Method in the Fine Arts. They are the source material for Method based on the relation of Theory; they are the subject-matter of the Applied Sciences.

Sense cannot be converted into Fancy, the next term on the

chart, by a completely controlled act of the mind, any more than
Reason can be converted in a wholly conscious manner into
Secondary Imagination. Fancy is a poetic faculty, only less
promising than Imagination because it does not transmit
Revelation.[27] 'Fancy', Coleridge maintains, '. . . has no other
counters to play with, but fixities and definites.' That is to say, it is
derived from the objects which we observe around us. It is not,
however, derived from them directly. Coleridge goes on to say
that 'equally with the ordinary memory it must receive all its
materials ready made from the law of association'. The law of
association is discussed at considerable length in the *Biographia*,
and Coleridge's treatment of it is a much more adequate preface
to his description of Fancy than his abortive preamble to the
definition of Imagination is for his description of that faculty. The
burden of Coleridge's account is to question the theory, put
forward by Hartley, that contemporaneity is the sole de-
terminant of what is essentially an unconscious process. Were
there no limiting power, were the association entirely mechanical, Coleridge argues, the result would resemble delirium.[28]

In a telling section of chapter 7, Coleridge demonstrates
convincingly that the law of association is more complicated and
devious in its operation than Hartley's account of it would allow.
He offers his own 'true practical general law of association':

whatever makes certain parts of a total impression more vivid or distinct
than the rest, will determine the mind to recall these in preference to
others equally linked together by the common condition of contemporaneity, or (what I deem a more appropriate and philosophical
term) of *continuity*. But the will itself by confining and intensifying the
attention may arbitrarily give vividness or distinctness to any object
whatsoever. . . .[29]

Fancy is the result of this kind of association. It is, Coleridge tells
us, 'a mode of Memory emancipated from the order of time and
space'.[30] An important emancipation if we recall the words of
Coleridge's original announcement of his overthrow of de-
terminist philosophy in his letter to Poole of March 16th, 1801: 'I
have . . . completely extricated the notions of Time, and

Space; . . . [I] have overthrown the doctrine of Association, as taught by Hartley, and with it all the irreligious metaphysics of modern Infidels — especially, the doctrine of Necessity.'[31] Association is also, according to Coleridge, 'blended with, and modified by that empirical phænomenon of the will which we express by the word CHOICE'. Fancy is based on a semi-conscious process of association, which in turn is predicated on the 'fixities and definites' of nature that are perceived by Sense; Fancy is 'modified', but not quite determined, by the will.[32]

The poet attains the images he needs from nature by means of Fancy; as a result he can convey the Ideas he has from God. This is the 'observation' of true poetry, and it is dependent on the indirect, half-understood, half-conscious, mental activity that is Association. If Method in the Fine Arts is the reconciliation of the Method based on the relation of Law and the Method based on the relation of Theory, with the former calling the tune, Fancy is the poetic faculty which transmits the relation of Theory. Such an interpretation not only fits the general pattern which we have found in Coleridge's thought, it also makes sense of Coleridge's characterization of a writer such as Spenser — whose work he admired — as fanciful.[33]

The final item on the chart is once more Understanding — this time the completely conscious control of the products of Fancy. It is that other manifestation of Understanding which Coleridge had described in 1806 in a letter to Clarkson as

that Faculty of the Soul which apprehends and retains the mere notices of Experience, as for instance that such an object has a triangular figure, that it is of such or such a magnitude, and of such and such a color, and consistency, with the anticipation of meeting the same under the same circumstances, in other words, all the mere $\phi \alpha \iota \nu \acute{o} \mu \varepsilon \nu \alpha$ of our nature. . .[34]

He describes it in similar terms in *The Statesman's Manual*, calling it 'the science of phænomena, and their subsumption under distinct kinds and sorts. . . . Its functions supply the rules and constitute the possibility of EXPERIENCE; but remain mere logical *forms*, except as far as *materials* are given by the senses or sensations.'[35]

The two Understandings are, of course, really only one faculty – 'wakefulness of mind'. Coleridge divides it in order to show that it may be applied to two quite different sorts of perception – the perception of the interior intellect, and the perception of external nature. Both kinds play a part in the poetic process, and they can be combined in the same poem. Given such an interpretation it is difficult to see how one could disagree with Coleridge's conviction that Imagination and Fancy are 'two distinct and widely different faculties, instead of being . . . either two names with one meaning, or at furthest, the lower and higher degree of one and the same power'.[36] The Method of poetry is the due reconciliation of the two, in which the Imagination must predominate. The concluding sentence of chapter 14 of the *Biographia* seems to be a much more carefully weighed statement than one had realized: 'Finally, GOOD SENSE [Understanding] is the BODY of poetic genius, FANCY its DRAPERY, . . . and IMAGINATION the SOUL that is everywhere, and in each; and forms all into one graceful and intelligent whole'.[37]

SOURCE: extract from chapter 5 of *Method and Imagination in Coleridge's Criticism* (1969) pp. 109–21.

NOTES

1. [Reprinted here as the first extract in Part Two – Ed.]
2. *Coleridge on Imagination* (London, 1934; 3rd ed. 1962).
3. E.g. John Livingston Lowes, *The Road to Xanadu* (London, 1930) p. 103. [See above, Introduction – Ed.]
4. *The Use of Poetry and the Use of Criticism* (London, 1933) p. 77.
5. 'Coleridge on the Function of Art', in *Perspectives of Criticism*, ed. Harry Levin (Cambridge, Mass., 1950) p. 145.
6. Ibid., p. 146. Bate's account of Secondary Imagination, however, seems to me to be misleading. He states that the 'appointed task of the "secondary" imagination is to "idealize and unify" its objects. . . . Indeed, its field is explicitly stated to consist of "objects" which (*as objects*) are essentially fixed and dead' (pp. 145–6). But

Coleridge does not say that Secondary Imagination struggles to 'idealize and unify' objects, but only that it struggles to 'idealize and unify'. In fact, he makes an oblique contrast between it and objects in the next sentence: 'It is essentially *vital*, even as all objects (*as* objects) are essentially fixed and dead.' The view that Secondary Imagination is directed towards the world of material phenomena seems to me an erroneous one. J. V. Baker's account of the contribution of the unconscious is, I think, relevant to Fancy alone, and not, as he supposes, to Imagination. (See *The Sacred River*, pp. 152–63.)

7. Ibid.

8. Coleridge, *Aids to Reflection* (London, 1825) p. 73. Cf. his glossary in *The Statesman's Manual* (London, 1816) p. xlvii: 'A conscious Presentation, if it refers exclusively to the *Subject*, as a modification of his own state of Being, is = SENSATION. The same if it refers to an OBJECT, is = PERCEPTION. A PERCEPTION, immediate and individual is = INTUITION.'

9. *Biographia Literaria*, ed. Shawcross, I, pp. 293–4; Everyman ed., ed. G. Watson (1906, reset 1956) p. 166.

10. British Museum copy (C. 43. c. 24) VIII ii 960, note. This note can be dated with some confidence as belonging to the period between the beginning of July 1818, and the end of March 1819.

11. [See above, Part One, section 1. XI.– Ed.]

12. *The Friend* (London, 1818) vol. I, p. 266.

13. Ibid., pp. 266–7. Cf. a passage in one of Coleridge's manuscripts: 'The Reason and it's Objects do not appertain to the World of the Senses, outward or inward – i.e. they partake neither of Sense nor of Fancy. Reason is *Supersensuous*: and here th' Antagonist is the *Lust of the Eye*.' (British Museum MS., Egerton 2801, fo. 218v.)

14. *The Statesman's Manual*, Appendix, p. xii.

15. *The Friend*, vol. I, p. 266.

16. *Collected Letters*, ed. E. L. Griggs (Oxford, 1956–71) vol. III, p. 172.

17. *Biographia Literaria*, ed. Shawcross, vol. I, p. 246; Everyman ed., p. 140. Cf. *Statesman's Manual*, Appendix, pp. xii–xiii.

18. Cf. the statement in 'On Poesy or Art' that 'there is in genius itself an unconscious activity; nay, that is the genius in the man of genius' (Shawcross edition, vol. II, p. 258).

19. *Biographia Literaria*, ed. Shawcross, vol. I, p. 273; Everyman ed., p. 154.

20. British Museum MS., Egerton 2826, fo. 56.

21. Ibid., fo. 59–60.

22. *Biographia Literaria*, ed. Shawcross, vol. I, p. 202; Everyman ed., p. 167. [See above, Part One, section I. VIII. – Ed.]

23. Ibid., vol. II, p. 12; Everyman ed., p. 174. [See above, Part One, section I. IX. – Ed.]

24. Coleridge toys with a paradox in *Aids to Reflection* (p. 216): 'Reason indeed is far nearer to SENSE than to Understanding: for Reason . . . is a direct Aspect of Truth, an inward Beholding, having a similar relation to the Intelligible or Spiritual, as SENSE has to the Material or Phenomenal.'

25. *Treatise on Method*, ed. Alice D. Snyder (London, 1934) pp. 62–3.

26. Ibid., p. 62.

27. See, for example, *Shakespearean Criticism*, ed. T. M. Raysor (London, 1960) vol. II, p. 102: 'there is a language not descriptive of passion, not uttered under the influence of it, which is at the same time poetic, and shows a high and active fancy'.

28. *Biographia Literaria*, ed. Shawcross, vol. I, pp. 110–12; Everyman ed., pp. 63–5.

29. Ibid., vol. I, pp. 126–7; Everyman ed., p. 73.

30. It might be interesting to compare this with Wordsworth's 'emotion recollected in tranquillity'.

31. *Collected Letters*, ed. Griggs, vol. II, p. 706.

32. There is, I believe, a basic confusion in J. V. Baker's objection to this aspect of Coleridge's theory. According to him, 'The weakness of Coleridge's theory is using "fancy" as a name for the associative power and assuming that the associative power is "mechanical"' (*The Sacred River*, p. 217). Coleridge does neither. Association for him provides the materials for fancy; the associative power (as Baker is clearly aware when he is discussing it specifically – e.g. pp. 35–9) is not in Coleridge's view mechanical, in fact this is the point of his quarrel with the Hartleyan account.

33. For example, see *Coleridge's Miscellaneous Criticism*, ed. T. M. Raysor (London, 1936) p. 38.

34. *Collected Letters*, ed. Griggs, vol. II, p. 1198.

35. *Statesman's Manual*, Appendix, p. v.

36. *Biographia Literaria*, ed. Shawcross, vol. I, pp. 86–7; Everyman ed., p. 50.

37. Ibid., vol. II, p. 12; Everyman ed., p. 174). I omit the phrase 'MOTION its LIFE', because I do not understand it in any technical sense. Coleridge does not seem to have left any trace of a developed theory for it, and it does not receive much attention in the *Biographia*. [See above, Part One, section I. IX. – Ed.]

René Wellek

'VARIETIES OF IMAGINATION IN WORDSWORTH' (1955)

In many pronouncements imagination is substantially the eighteenth-century faculty of arbitrary recall and willful combination of images. In others it is the neo-Platonic intellectual vision. There is apparently no chronological progress from one conception to the other. The idea of imagination as vision occurs both early and late. There seems to be a distinction between statements in prose and statements in verse. The neo-Platonic metaphysical conception permeates the last books of *The Prelude* and *The Excursion*, the psychological the Preface of 1815. The discussion in *The Prelude*, and *The Excursion*, in verse, can hardly be treated as literary theory without falsifying its tone and implication. The distinctions there between imagination in general and the poetic imagination are so fluid and obscure that it seems impossible to extract a coherent doctrine for poetics. Wordsworth disconcertingly vacillates among three epistemological conceptions. At times he makes imagination purely subjective, an imposition of the human mind on the real world. At other times he makes it an illumination beyond the control of the conscious mind and even beyond the individual soul. But most frequently he takes an in-between position which favors the idea of a collaboration,

> An ennobling interchange
> Of action from within and from without.
>
> [*Prelude* (1850) XIII 375-6]

The many passages which suggest an extreme subjectivism, an activity of the imagination exerting itself against the world, must be always interpreted in the light of the other conceptions which

assume a continuity between mind and nature. When Wordsworth speaks of throwing a 'certain coloring of imagination' over
'incidents and situations from common life', he justifies his choice
of subject matter. Even when he says that the duty of poetry is 'to
treat things not as they *are*, but as they *appear*, not as they exist in
themselves, but as they *seem* to exist to the *senses*, and to the
passions', he defends the poet's emotion and transfiguration of
reality and not psychological solipsism or illusionism,[1] which
may seem to follow if we press the terms 'appear' and 'seem'.

The famous vision on Mount Snowdon suggests a parallelism
between the workings of nature and imagination: nature,
represented by the moon, 'moulds, endues, abstracts, combines'.
It has a 'genuine counterpart' in the imaginative faculty of
'higher minds' (geniuses, especially poets) who, like nature, can
'create a like existence'. These higher minds can hold 'communion with the invisible world'. They have genuine liberty,
genuine free will. This imagination is identified with

> absolute strength
> And clearest insight, amplitude of mind.
> And reason in her most exalted mood.[2]

It is then associated very closely with intellectual love. Imagination is here conceived as intellectual intuition, as a higher
faculty of knowing, as reason, *nous*, *Vernunft*, which demands the
association of love, the love of mankind and of God. On occasion
Wordsworth adopts the language of idealism and calls imagination 'the faculty by which the poet conceives and
produces – that is, images – individual forms in which are
embodied universal ideas or abstractions'.[3] But such an approximation
to the idea of poetry as a symbolism of abstractions is rare. More
common is the view that imagination 'turns upon infinity',
'incites and supports the eternal', and thus suggests religion or, at
least, religious feelings.[4]

Only the 1815 Preface brings the concept of imagination into
closer relation with actual literary texts. There Wordsworth
defends the ordering of his poems by explaining imagination and
fancy in psychological terms. He objects to the usual definitions

as making imagination and fancy only modes of memory and then tells that it rather means 'processes of creation or of composition'. His illustrations are, however, curiously inept: they merely cite very ordinary metaphorical transfers. Thus the samphire gatherer in *King Lear* 'hangs' on the cliff, which, according to Wordsworth, shows imagination, because 'hanging' is not to be understood as actual support from above but refers, presumably, to the precariousness of the man's hold on the rocks. Other examples are drawn from Wordsworth's own poetry. The stock-dove's voice is described as 'buried among trees'; the phrase is not literally accurate but suggests the love of seclusion of the bird and the effect of the 'voice being deadened by the intervening shade'. Similarly, calling the cuckoo a 'wandering voice' is an instance of imagination, as 'voice' is here a substitution depriving the creature almost of a corporeal existence, while 'wandering' suggests seeming ubiquity. Wordsworth then proceeds to an analysis of more complex instances and discusses his own leechgatherer, who is compared to both a 'huge stone' and a 'sea-beast'. The stone is given some measure of life to make it similar to the beast, and the sea-beast is deprived of some life to assimilate it to the stone. Thus imagination is defined, in a quotation from Charles Lamb, as 'drawing all things to one', as 'consolidating numbers into unity' but also as 'dissolving and separating unity into number'.[5] It seems thus both a unifying and an analyzing power. Elsewhere Wordsworth discusses his sonnet 'With Ships the Sea' as another example of the mind fastening on an individual object (a ship) among a multitude of others, as if the poem were an elementary lesson in the psychology of attention.[6] Wordsworth here seems not to go beyond the idea that imagination dissolves, endows, modifies, and abstracts, and when he speaks of imagination as shaping and creating, he seems to think of nothing more than 'consolidating numbers into unity'.

Next comes the distinction between fancy and imagination, for which Wordsworth quotes Coleridge's passing reference in *Omniana*.[7] Wordsworth argues that Coleridge's definition of fancy as the 'aggregative or associative power' (in contrast to imagination as the 'shaping or modifying power') is too general. He maintains that imagination, as well as fancy, aggregates and associates, evokes and combines, and that fancy, as well as imagination, is a creative faculty. But actually Wordsworth's own theory is well in agreement with Coleridge's, at least, as that theory was developed or put on paper a little later.[8] Both Wordsworth and Coleridge make the distinction between fancy, a faculty which handles 'fixities and definites', and imagination, a faculty which deals with the 'plastic, the pliant and the indefinite'.[9] The only important difference between Wordsworth and Coleridge is that Wordsworth does not clearly see Coleridge's distinction between Imagination as a 'holistic' and fancy as an associative power and does not draw the sharp distinction between transcendentalism and associationism which Coleridge wanted to establish. His own examples lead to a rather naive revival of the difference between the beautiful and sublime. We are in the presence of fancy when definite sizes are indicated, in the presence of imagination when we hear that the Archangel's 'stature reached the sky' or when the firmament is called 'illimitable'.[10] Chesterfield's conceit of referring to the 'dews of the evening' as the 'tears of the sky' is dismissed as fancy, while Milton's sky weeping 'sad drops' at the completion of Adam's fall is approved as imagination because 'the mind acknowledges the justice and reasonableness of the sympathy in nature'.[11] In practice this amounts to a rating of imagery in terms of seriousness. Fancy is disparaged because it is based on some kind of deceit. Fancy is recognized by the rapidity with which she scatters her thoughts and images, and by the 'curious subtility and the successful elaboration with which she can detect the lurking affinities' of thoughts and images.[12] Fancy is thus a sleight of hand and an intellectual exercise. Combinatory power, intellectual subtlety are unpoetic compared to the slow workings of imagination dealing with indefinite illimitable objects. The distinction serves to devalue the whole line of wit – both seventeenth and eighteenth century poetry – though Wordsworth concludes by quoting an 'admirable composition', Cotton's 'Ode upon Winter', as an example of fancy.

The distinction between fancy and imagination is parallel to a distinction between the animating metaphors or personifications of the eighteenth century of which Wordsworth disapproves and the metaphors which he himself uses. This is not very clear theoretically but is apparently based on some final test of truth. Chesterfield is wrong, because the 'dews of the evening ' are not the 'tears of the sky'. Milton is right because it is spiritually true that the sky should weep at Adam's fall. 'I have never given way to my own feelings in personifying natural objects', says a late letter, 'without bringing all that I have said to a rigorous after-test of good sense.'[13] But surely Wordsworth's good sense is not that of other men: it includes the belief in a profound identity of man and nature, in the good heart of the ass, in the flower enjoying the air it breathes, and in the 'unutterable love in the silent faces of the clouds'.[14] Imagination is thus linked and fused with Wordsworth's view, or rather feeling, of the world as a unity and community of living beings.

Wordsworth rarely uses what is the critically most fruitful element in the theory of imagination: the insight into the wholeness and totality of a work of art. After alluding to August Wilhelm Schlegel, he praises Shakespeare's 'judgment in the selection of his materials, and in the manner in which he has made them, heterogeneous as they often are, constitute a unity of their own, and contribute all to one great end'.[15] His objections to eighteenth century poetry are frequently directed against something which could be called its atomism: the 'glaring hues of diction' which show no appreciation of a 'pure and refined scheme of harmony'; or the imagery of Macpherson, 'defined, insulated, dislocated, in absolute independent singleness'.[16] A standard of unity or rather of continuous flow is also at the basis of his criticism of *ottave rime* in an epic poem such as Tasso's, or behind his praise of the sonnet for its 'pervading sense of intense unity'. 'Instead of looking at this composition as a piece of architecture, making a whole out of three parts, I have been much in the habit of preferring the image of an orbicular body, a sphere, or a dewdrop'.[17] The analogy from building is rejected in favor of an analogy, not from an organism but from the roundness of a geometrical sphere.

Wordsworth thus holds a position in the history of criticism which must be called ambiguous or transitional. He inherits from neoclassicism a theory of the imitation of nature to which he

gives, however, a specific social twist; he inherits from the
eighteenth century a view of poetry as passion and emotion
which he again modifies by his description of the poetic process as
'recollection in tranquillity'. He takes up rhetorical ideas about
the effect of poetry but extends and amplifies them into a theory
of the social effect of literature, binding society in a spirit of love.
But he also adopts, in order to meet the exigencies of his mystical
experiences, a theory of poetry in which imagination holds the
central place as a power of unification and ultimate insight into
the unity of the world. Though Wordsworth left only a small
body of criticism, it is rich in survivals, suggestions, anticipations,
and personal insights.

SOURCE: extract from *A History of Modern Criticism:
1750–1950* (London, 1955) vol. II, pp. 144–50.

NOTES

1. *Wordsworth's Literary Criticism*, ed. N. C. Smith (London, 1905)
pp. 13, 169.

2. *Prelude* (1805 version) XIII, 79, 88–9, 94–5, 105, 121–2,
166–70.

3. Crabb Robinson's Diary, 11 Sep 1816; a similar explanation in
Diary, 31 May 1812; *H. C. Robinson on Books and Their Writers*, ed. E. J.
Morley (London, 1938) vol. I, p. 191. Ibid., p. 89: 'The poet first
conceives the essential nature of his object and strips it of all casualties
and accidental individual dress, and in this he is a philosopher; but to
exhibit his abstraction nakedly would be the work of a mere philosopher; therefore he reclothes his *idea* in an individual dress which
expresses the essential quality, and has also the spirit and life of a sensual
object, and this transmutes the philosophic into a poetic exhibition.' It
is perhaps significant that these most intellectualist formulations come
from Robinson, who knew German idealism and its vocabulary.

4. Letter to Landor, 21 Jan 1824; *Wordsworth's Literary Criticism*,
p.165.

5. *Wordsworth's Literary Criticism*, pp. 157, 162. The quotation from
Lamb comes from 'On the Genius and Character of Hogarth' (1811);
Works, ed. T. Hutchinson (Oxford, 1924) vol. I, pp. 95–6. The

example of 'hanging' comes from Goldsmith's essay 'Poetry Distinguished from Other Writing'. See J. L. Lowes, 'Wordsworth and Goldsmith', *The Nation*, xc11 (1911) pp. 289–90.

6. *Wordsworth's Literary Criticism*, pp. 52–4; Letter to Lady Beaumont, 21 May 1807.

7. *Omniana* (London, 1812) pp. 2, 13. It might be added that the earliest distinction in Wordsworth between fancy and imagination comes from the note to 'The Thorn' in the 1800 edition of *Lyrical Ballads*. It differs in emphasis. 'Imagination [is] the faculty which produces impressive effects out of simple elements; . . . fancy . . . the power by which pleasure and surprise are excited by sudden varieties of situation and an accumulated imagery' – *Poetical Works*, ed. E. de Selincourt (London, 1940–9) vol. ii, p. 512.

8. I am not convinced by Clarence D. Thorpe's argument that on this point there is a deep disagreement between Wordsworth and Coleridge. See 'The Imagination: Coleridge versus Wordsworth', *Philological Quarterly*, xviii (1939) 1–18.

9. Fancy's 'fixities' in *Biographia Literaria*, ed. Shawcross, vol. i, p. 202; 'the plastic', in *Wordsworth's Literary Criticism*, p. 164.

10. *Wordsworth's Literary Criticism*, p. 164.

11. Ibid., pp. 165–6.

12. Ibid., p. 164.

13. To W. R. Hamilton, 23 Dec 1829; *The Letters of William and Dorothy Wordsworth: The Later Years*, ed. E. de Selincourt (Oxford, 1939), vol. i, pp. 436–7.

14. Allusions to 'Peter Bell', 'Lines written in Early Spring', and *The Excursion*, i 204–5.

15. *Wordsworth's Literary Criticism*, p. 178.

16. Ibid., pp. 171, 191.

17. Ibid., pp. 224, 247; letter to Southey (1815); letter to A. Dyce (1833).

J. A. W. Heffernan

'WORDSWORTH AND THE TRANS-FORMING IMAGINATION' (1969)

For Wordsworth, imagination is a power that acts upon the objects of the visible world. Once set in motion by creative sensibility, it behaves like a natural force, dominating the universe by transforming its sights and sounds. As mist converts a rolling landscape into a ghostly sea, the imagination turns the call of a cuckoo into a voice of mystery. It transfigures the world, investing natural phenomena with an almost supernatural phosphorescence. But its impact is just as powerful on the words the poet uses. In the years that followed the Preface of 1800, Wordsworth came to realize that if the imagination is to work its alchemy on natural objects, it must also make its mark on 'the real language of men'.

Wordsworth's concept of the imagination as a power is based on his belief that nature provides a model for the creative transformations wrought by man. In the days when his conversations with Coleridge 'turned frequently on the two cardinal points of poetry', the two men found in nature a sanction or archetype for the poetic fusion of novelty and truth. Coleridge reported their discovery years later. 'The sudden charm', he wrote, 'which accidents of light and shade, which moon-light or sun-set diffused over a known and familiar landscape, appeared to represent the practicability of combining both' (*BL*, vol. II, sig. B$_3$).[1] This movement to nature as guide and authority, so typical of Wordsworth in all of his thinking, is fundamental to his concept of the imagination.

We have seen that Wordsworth postulates a perfect harmony between nature and the mind of man. But we should note with care the basis of this harmony, the reason why the two are so compatible. As early as 1802, Wordsworth wrote that the poet 'considers man and nature as essentially adapted to each other, and the mind of man as naturally the mirror of the fairest and most interesting properties of nature' (*PW*, vol. II, p. 396). The key word here is 'mirror'. It clearly indicates that the consonance of mind and universe is founded on a vital correspondence, a profound *analogy* between their respective powers. In Wordsworth's view, man is the image and likeness of nature.

Wordsworth's sense of this vital correspondence permeates his poetry. Writing of his Cambridge days in Book III of *The Prelude*, completed in 1804, he tells us that 'deep analogies by thought supplied' enabled him to see moral and spiritual qualities in the natural objects about him (III 121–39).[2] Elsewhere he is more explicit. In a passage of the same period as the lines just cited, he suggests that a consciousness of analogy originates in the mind of the 'favored' child, gradually emerging and expanding with the passage of time. As the child matures, he finds 'his image' in the universe; the 'inexhaustible' majesty of nature, abundantly manifest in the beauty, excellence, and sublimity of her countenance, appears before him as a fitting counterpart to the 'insatiate' power, aspiration, and dignity of his own mind.[3] The child discovers much more than a simple harmony of attributes. Nature renders back to him his deepest self, so that what he sees is a vital analogy between the energies within him and the energies without. So it is with the American frontiersman described in *The Excursion*. Gazing down the mighty ribbon of the Mississippi, he beholds in it the image of 'his own unshackled life, / And his innate capacities of soul' (III 933–5).

Because of this dynamic correspondence of forces, Wordsworth held that the creation of poetry imitates the action of creative power in the visible world. Coleridge, of course, had similar ideas; in 1801 he called the human mind 'the *Image of the Creator*' (*LC*, vol. II, p. 709), and three years later he described 'Imagination or the *modifying* Power' as 'a dim Analogue of Creation' (*LC*, vol. II, p. 1034). But Wordsworth need not have borrowed these insights from his formidable friend. By October, 1800, he had completed Book II of *The Prelude*,[4] and in this book he clearly indicates that perception is for him an *active* process. The infant shown to us is a 'creator' of the world about him, operating on it as 'an agent of the one great mind' (II 272–3). Furthermore, this operation demonstrates 'the first / Poetic spirit of our human life' (II 275–6), and therefore constitutes a paradigm of the creative act. Like the infant, the poet must imitate the living power manifest in nature herself; the exercise of imagination then becomes – as Wordsworth later called it – a 'God-like [function] of the Soul'.[5]

We can see this more clearly by examining Wordsworth's comments on the relation between poetry and nature. Plainly, he believed the two inseparable. In the Preface of 1800, when he says in effect that his poetry makes its appeal to 'certain inherent and indestructible qualities of the human mind', he links those qualities to 'certain powers in the great and permanent objects that act upon it, which are equally inherent and indestructible' (*PW*, vol. II, p. 389). But the link is more specific in *The Prelude*. There he explains that natural forms themselves infuse poetry with passion. With their noble influence, these forms can sway the poet's heart and mind; and if he captures the spirit of their influence in a work of his own, it becomes 'a power like one of Nature's' (XII 289–312). The words are more than empty abstractions, for throughout his life, Wordsworth believed that the energy of nature is precisely what the poet should incorporate in his work. Counseling a correspondent as late as 1830, he writes: 'You feel strongly; trust to those feelings, and your poem will take its shape and proportions as a tree does from the vital principle that actuates it'.[6]

Wordsworth's analogy does not simply involve the *form* of the tree and that of the poem. Instead, it embraces the kinds of *energy* that produce these forms. Each of them, tree and poem, is in Wordsworth's mind a living organism. Each is the outward articulation of an inner creative power, the manifestation of what he called 'divine vitality' in a sonnet of his later years (*PW*, vol. III, p. 52). By the power of his imagination, therefore, he seeks to imitate in his poems the power of nature – revealed most vividly whenever it suddenly changes the face of an object. Such a change can have electric impact. 'By abrupt and unhabitual influence', he writes, nature sometimes

Doth make one object so impress itself
Upon all others, and pervade them so
That even the grossest minds must see and hear
And cannot chuse but feel.   (*Prelude*, XIII 80–4)

This was the kind of transformation that excited Wordsworth's imitative instincts. Many years after his composition of 'The Thorn', he told Isabella Fenwick: '[The poem] arose out of my observing, on the ridge of Quantock Hill, on a stormy day, a thorn which I had often passed in calm and bright weather without noticing it. I said to myself, "Cannot I by some invention do as much to make this Thorn permanently an impressive object as the storm has made it to my eyes at this moment?" ' (*PW*, vol. II, p. 511). Clearly, Wordsworth saw himself as a kind of translator. To use the words of Coleridge, he had been struck by the 'sudden charm' of an arresting metamorphosis, by the action of change in a 'known and familiar' sight; his poem would be an imitation of that action, rendering into poetic terms an 'impressive' transformation wrought by nature.

We can see this process in a brief examination of the poem itself. An apparently negligible object emerges with sharp detail in the opening stanzas, graphically defined as if by a camera in perfect focus: it is an old, gray, knotted, and apparently stunted little tree – overgrown with tufts of moss that seem determined to drag it down. By this photographic concentration alone, of course, Wordsworth makes the object seize our attention. But what especially arrests us is the atmosphere of pathetic desolation which surrounds the tree, stubbornly erect and yet 'a wretched thing forlorn'. Even before we learn of its connection with the forsaken mother, the appeal of the object is instantly affective, because the poet transforms it into something implicitly human. In so doing, he attempts to make it as striking for the reader as the storm has made it for him. And he was clearly thinking of this attempt when he gave his earliest definition of the imagination. In 1800, in a note to 'The Thorn', he called it 'the faculty which produces impressive ideas out of simple elements' (*PW*, vol. II, p. 512).

Wordsworth knew, of course, that subtle transformations did

not penetrate 'the grossest minds'. They could impress the sensitive alone, who would cooperate with nature to receive her gift, and 'catch it by an instinct / Say rather by an intellectual sense / Or attribute, inevitably fine.'[7] Newton Stallknecht is right when he says that Wordsworth often thought of man as a spectator to the artistry of nature; but the spectator must be singularly equipped to appreciate that artistry. Above all, a poet must be able to recognize a transformation when he sees one, catching from it what Wordsworth calls an 'impression'. Only then can he translate into poetry the power of nature. Describing the background of *Descriptive Sketches*, Wordsworth said in 1843: 'Nothing that I ever saw in nature left a more delightful impression on my mind than that which I have attempted, alas, how feebly! to convey to others in these lines' (*PW*, vol. I, p. 324). Wordsworth has sought to create for his reader the kind of impression that nature has made upon him. But because of his creative sensibility, the impression he has received is itself, in part, one of his own making. He illustrates this point in his late remarks on another poem – 'Yarrow Unvisited'. Commenting on his description of a single swan, floating 'double, swan and shadow', on a still lake, Wordsworth reportedly spoke as follows to Aubrey de Vere:

Never could I have written 'swans' in the plural. The scene when I saw it, with its still and dim lake, under the dusky hills, was one of utter loneliness: there was *one* swan, and one only, stemming the water, and the pathetic loneliness of the region gave importance to the one companion of that swan, its own white image in the water. It was for that reason that I recorded the Swan and the Shadow. Had there been many swans and many shadows, they would have implied nothing as regards the character of the scene; and I should have said nothing about them. (*PrW*, vol. III, pp. 487–8)

This passage surely explains why Wordsworth sometimes speaks of 'imaginative impressions' as the sources of his poetry.[8] Whatever the precise meaning of the phrase, it is evident that such impressions are in part the products of his own creative energy. As he receives the scene, he intensifies the atmosphere of loneliness with which nature has already invested it. He then conveys this impression in his poetry by imitating the action of nature's power, by transforming the objects of the universe even as nature herself has transformed them. Wordsworth describes the process in an early book of *The Prelude*. At Cambridge, he says, he sought

> To apprehend all passions and all moods
> Which time, and place, and season do impress
> Upon the visible universe, and work
> Like changes there by force of my own mind.
>
> (III 85–88)

The language is clear, if a little abstract. But with the cunning of a true poet, Wordsworth saves his richest treatment of transformation for the concluding book of *The Prelude*. He tells us there the story of an unforgettable experience – the sight of hills one summer evening in a heavy mist. It is true, of course, that others had commented on phenomena like this, noting the harmonizing and beautifying effect of vapor upon a landscape.[9] But it remained for Wordsworth – profoundly convinced as he was of the correspondence between nature and the human mind – to see in the transformation wrought by mist a perfect model of imaginative transformation, an archetypal embodiment of imaginative power. This is why his account of a known and familiar spectacle has extraordinary impact.

First of all, Wordsworth describes what he saw from the peak of Snowdon, when the hills about him were quilted by a moonlit fog and the roar of distant waters ascended through a chasm in the vapor. Nature had transformed nearly everything. The mist appeared to him a 'huge sea', and the hundred hills were living things, heaving up 'their dusky backs . . ./All over this still Ocean' (XIII 43–6). After a time the mist dissolved, and the poet meditated on the meaning of the scene. It seemed to him, he says, the 'perfect image of a mighty Mind' (XIII 69), for it showed

> That domination which [Nature] oftentimes
> Exerts upon the outward face of things,

. . . moulds them, and endues, abstracts, combines. . . .

(XIII 77−9)

Nature was sculptor, painter, and poet at once, magisterially transforming the landscape 'as if with an imaginative power'.[10] This 'as if 'line is crucial. It appears only in a fragmentary draft of the Snowdon passage, but it gives us a clue to one of the most vexing questions raised by that passage: just what is the 'mighty Mind' of the early version, or the lower-case 'mind' of the later one? The answer, I think, can be best approached by means of an algebraic proportion. What Wordsworth witnessed at Snowdon was the transforming effect of mist and moonlight upon distant hills. This effect struck him as very similar to the transforming effect that he, as a poet, often had upon the images he used in his poetry. In poetry, he believed, such an effect was produced by the imagination. But what produced it in nature? We have three givens and one unknown – all the requisites for a standard algebraic proportion:

$$\frac{\text{human imagination}}{\substack{\text{transformation of} \\ \text{images in poetry}}} = \frac{X}{\substack{\text{transformation of natural} \\ \text{objects in actual experience}}}$$

In ordinary English, the human imagination is to the transformation of images in poetry as X is to the transformation of natural objects in actual experience. With a formula something like this, not articulated but certainly felt, Wordsworth groped his way toward a definition of X, the unknown factor. What he concluded, I think, was this: the transformation of natural objects before his very eyes was 'presumptive evidence' – a favorite phrase of Wordsworth's – that something like the human imagination was at work upon them. It was a mighty mind, an archetype of the human imagination; it exercised itself on natural objects 'as if' with imaginative power. What Wordsworth saw at Snowdon was an image, emblem, or shadow of that mind, a demonstration of its power for the human senses. But only in the visible demonstration – only in the emblem – could he perceive the mighty mind. In the Platonic language of the later *Prelude*, therefore, he ascended from 'sense . . . to ideal form' (xiv 76). He went from the known to the unknown, believing that in its ideal form as in its sensible manifestation, the transforming power of nature must somehow correspond to the transforming power of his own imagination.

Can we give the 'mind' a specific name? It is extremely tempting to call it God, for at various times elsewhere, Wordsworth himself suggests that the human imagination is a 'godlike' faculty. It is tempting, too, to explain his concept of nature's 'imaginative power' in Coleridgean terms: to say that for Wordsworth also, the archetype of the human imagination is 'the eternal act of creation in the infinite I AM' (*BL*, vol. i, p. 202). But in fairness to Wordsworth, we must resist these temptations. In the early version of *The Prelude*, Wordsworth tells us that the mighty Mind is exalted by 'the sense of God' (xiii 72), which surely implies that it is not identical with God. Further, even though Wordsworth seems to separate the human imagination from the 'Power' of nature, which is its 'Counterpart / And Brother' (xiii 89–90), he does not clearly separate it from the 'mighty Mind'. There are troublesome ambiguities in both versions of the Snowdon passage. In interpreting either version, can we impute absolute infinity to a mind that 'feeds upon infinity'(xiii 70 and xiv 71)? In the later version, can we impute absolute transcendence to 'a mind *sustained* / By recognitions of transcendent power' (xiv 74–5; italics mine)? And can we impute immortality to a mind which is 'in soul of more than mortal privilege' (xiv 77)? None of these questions, I think, can be answered with certainty or precision. They show us that Wordsworth was stuck on the horns of the human dilemma, yearning to define the infinite but able to do so only in finite, anthropomorphic terms. He could not escape the limitations of language itself. Consequently, even if he thought of the 'mind' as the divine, transcendent *archetype* of the human imagination, he seems to describe it as if it were the human imagination itself.

Yet one thing is clear. Wordsworth definitely finds in nature evidence for the existence of a 'Power' which behaves like the human imagination. His own experience — as both a poet and an observer of nature — tells him that this power is the duplicate of 'the glorious faculty / Which higher minds bear with them as their own'. These exalted creatures rival the feats of nature. 'They . . . send abroad', he says, 'Like transformation, for themselves create / A like existence' (xiii 89–95). Wordsworth wrote these lines about 1805, but he might well have been thinking of them when he composed the first of his essays on epitaphs in 1810. Advising against detailed biography in an epitaph, he states: 'The character of a deceased friend or beloved kinsman is not seen, no – nor ought to be seen, otherwise than as a tree through a tender haze or a luminous mist, that spiritualises and beautifies it' (*PrW*, vol. ii, p. 36). Instinctively, Wordsworth explains the art of sympathetic portraiture by reference to a natural phenomenon. From the summit of Snowdon he had witnessed living proof of the analogy between natural power and poetic creation; the experience left a permanent stamp upon his mind. For the rest of his life, he firmly believed that when a poet transforms the visible universe by the power of his imagination, he imitates the creative action of nature herself.

Source: extract from *Wordsworth's Theory of Poetry: The Transforming Imagination* (Ithaca, N.Y., and London, 1969) pp. 95–105.

NOTES

1. [The following abbreviations are used in the text and notes:

BL   Coleridge, *Biographia Literaria*, ed. Shawcross.
LC   *Collected Letters of Samuel Taylor Coleridge*, ed. E. L. Griggs, 6 vols (Oxford, 1956–71).
PrW   *The Prose Works of William Wordsworth*, ed. A. B. Grosart, 3 vols (London, 1876).
PW   *The Poetical Works of William Wordsworth*, ed. E. de Selincourt and H. Darbishire, 5 vols (Oxford, 1940–9) – Ed.]

2. [Unless otherwise stated, all references to *The Prelude* are to the text of 1805 – Ed.]

3. I refer to lines 126, 171–81 and 200–1 in the MS. Y version of *The Prelude*, VIII 159–61. See *The Prelude*, ed. E. de Selincourt and H. Darbishire (Oxford, 1959) pp. 574–6.

4. See *The Prelude*, ed. de Selincourt and Darbishire, pp. xlvi – xlvii.

5. 'To the Utilitarians,' composed in 1833 (*PW*, vol. IV, p. 388). In the 'Christabel' notebook of 1798–9, he speaks of man's 'godlike faculties' and 'godlike senses' (*PW*, vol. V, pp. 343–4). Cf. also the Preface of 1815, in which he indicates that certain acts of the imagination call into play the 'almost divine powers' of the soul (*PW*, vol. II, p. 439).

6. *The Letters of William and Dorothy Wordsworth: The Later Years*, ed. E. de Selincourt (Oxford, 1939) vol. I, p. 537.

7. MSS. A² and B² variant of *Prelude*, XIII 96–7, in *Prelude*, ed. de Selincourt and Darbishire, p. 485, textual notes.

8. See his note on the late sonnet, 'Cave of Staffa', in *PW*, vol. IV, p. 407.

9. See Z. S. Fink, *The Early Wordsworthian Milieu* (Oxford, 1958) pp. 45–7, 58–9, 124–5.

10. This line appears in the MS. W elaboration of *The Prelude*, XIII 93–4; see *The Prelude*, ed. de Selincourt and Darbishire, p. 623. In MS. W, Wordsworth traces the 'analogy betwixt / The mind of man and nature', giving several examples besides that of Snowdon to show how nature's 'imaginative power' operates (pp. 623–5). Coleridge may be referring to some of these examples when he reports that Wordsworth helped him to clarify his own views on the imagination 'by many happy instances drawn from the operation of natural objects on the mind' (*BL*, vol. I, p. 64).

C. D. Thorpe

'KEATS ON THE IMAGINATION' (1926)

I

In both his letters and his poems Keats has, first to last, many things to say about the imagination. Always he understood it to be the supreme active principle in poetic composition. But how decisively with the rapid maturity of his intellect and critical judgment during the brief, fitful working period of his life did his ideas change and develop. Through the unquiet days and restless nights of burning thought, the puerile, vaporish notions of the 1815–1816 period became alchemized into sinewy convictions which, expressed in vigorous and picturesque language, stand as some of the most striking comments upon the nature of the imagination to be found in critical literature. In previous chapters I have pointed out how Keats's early notions of the ecstatic trance and 'direct divination' methods of imaginative activity merged into the later more ripened conception of insight based on knowledge and experience. But in both of these views the imagination is all important as the vital element in poetic activity; Keats has merely arrived in his later thinking at a more comprehensive understanding of the intuitive faculties.

An analysis of his utterances on the subject from the middle of 1817 on, reveals that he has reached two significant conclusions as to the nature and function of the imagination. First, the imagination as an instrument of intuitive insight is the most authentic guide to ultimate truth; second, the imagination in its highest form is a generative force, in itself creative of essential reality.

II

Plato has said, 'Not by wisdom do poets write, but by a sort of genius and inspiration.' If by *wisdom* Plato means knowledge through reasoning, and I think he does, Keats would have been in complete agreement. For, though he believed firmly in the wisdom that springs from close contact with a harsh world and flowers into gracious human sympathy, Keats had no faith in mere cold knowledge and reason. 'One of the first characteristics of the genuine and healthy poetic nature', declares Professor Shairp, 'is this — it is rooted rather in the heart than in the head.' So Keats thought. For to him poetry has its genesis in imagination, and feeling is both its rudder and its sails. Deep feeling makes possible thinking with our whole selves, soul and body. It emancipates the poet's mind from the incidental and temporary, leaving it free to probe the deeper mysteries of existence.

Imagination, with its springs in the heart rather than the head, though the head too has its place, becomes with Keats the highest and most authentic guide to truth. Not only is the imagination to be trusted more implicitly than reason in matters where both are operative, but there are even things clear to the imagination of which the reason knows nothing. As Joubert says, in words that well express Keats's thought on this subject, 'Heaven, seeing that there were many truths which by our nature we could not know, and which it was to our interest, nevertheless, not to be ignorant of, took pity on us and granted us the faculty of imagining them.'

'Keats', says James Russell Lowell, 'certainly had more of the penetrative and sympathetic imagination which belongs to the poet, of that imagination which identifies itself with the momentary object of its contemplation, than any man of these later days.' If this be true, Keats had realized in achievement one of his favorite poetic theories. For, supplementary to his demand for a detached state of spirit for poetic experience, was his conception of the poetic nature as a free entity with capacity to penetrate wherever it may choose, able to project itself into and merge itself in complete identification with the objects of its contemplation, yet in that mingling never losing its proper native qualities of unity and power.

In *Endymion*, torn by conflicting earthly and immortal loves, perplexed by a confusing, tangled web of circumstances, drawn by feeling and instinct in one direction, by reason in another, and, withal, carried out of himself by the power of his emotions, the poet cries out –

> What is this soul then? Whence
> Came it? It does not seem my own, and I
> Have no self-passion or identity.   (IV 475–7)

This is Keats himself speaking, uttering a thought that often came into his mind with the teasing interest of the novel and unexplained. 'Nothing startles me beyond the moment', he declares to Bailey, evidently when thinking in this vein. 'The Setting Sun will always set me to rights, or if a Sparrow come before my Window, I take part in its existence and pick about the gravel.' Again he writes, 'One of the most mysterious of semi-speculations is, one would suppose, that of one Mind's imagining into another.' And these reflections at once suggest to our minds his definition of a poet –

> Where's the Poet? Show him! show him,
> Muses nine! that I may know him.
> 'Tis the man who with a man
> Is an equal, be he King,
> Or poorest of the beggar-clan,
> Or any other wondrous thing
> A man may be 'twixt ape and Plato;
> 'Tis the man who with a bird,
> Wren, or Eagle finds its way to
> All its instincts; he hath heard
> The Lion's roaring, and can tell
> What his horny throat expresseth,
> And to him the Tiger's yell
> Comes articulate and presseth
> On his ear like mother-tongue.

Through the power of the imagination, then, the poet is one who in spirit intimately lives with the feathered and wild creatures of the forest, who shares the identity of, hence, in thought and imagination, becomes equal to, king or beggar, or any that wear the semblance of man, and who, because he has partaken of the existence of bird or beast of prey, can understand the meaning of its every move or cry.

In a second passage in *Endymion*, there is suggested the other imaginative extreme — from the very earthy, we ascend at a leap to the ethereal. 'Wherein lies happiness?' the poet has asked. It is, he replies, in that which raises our ready minds to a 'fellowship with essence', leaving us completely 'alchemized and free of space'.

> Feel we these things? — that moment have we stept
> Into a sort of oneness, and our state
> Is like a floating spirit's. But there are
> Richer entanglements, enthralments far
> More self-destroying, leading, by degrees,
> To the chief intensity.   (I 795 – 800)

Here plainly is implied a complete identity with the infinite, when the mind of the poet shall merge itself imaginatively into the spirit of the universe, to lose itself in a divine 'fellowship with essence'.

In a self-revelatory letter to Richard Woodhouse, written October 27, 1818, Keats presents further evidence. Here we find that this power of identification is reciprocal; not only does the poet's self go out to others, but the identity of others forces itself upon him, until he is helpless before its might. [Quotes from the letter to Woodhouse: see above, Part One, section 4. IV. – Ed.]

Keats's conception is that the poet's being is a sort of detached entity — an unfettered spirit-like thing — independent of earthy circumstances and vision, free to take leave of the body to roam about where it will, penetrating into the mysterious chambers of the soul's deepest recesses, or, soaring into the shadowy and illimitable spaces of the universe, to mingle with 'essence' in 'fellowship divine'; its delight is ever fresh, adventurous speculation, whether down into the darker regions of existence or up into the majestic realm of 'Saturn and old Ops'. This process with Keats is not merely a submergence of one's self into another; it is not a substitution where the poet puts himself in the place of the object of his contemplation: it is rather a sort of etherized penetration, in which the poetic soul, acting as an ethereal chemical operating on man and the physical world, liberates the fine essence of spiritual being in its purest and freest state, to be condensed, through the agency of beautiful verse, into new elements of living truth. 'Men of Genius', declares Keats, writing to Bailey, 'are great as certain ethereal Chemicals operating on the Mass of neutral intellect – but they have not any individuality, any determined Character.'

The remarks on the reciprocal phase of identity are an interesting commentary on the insistence with which life crowded itself upon Keats. Whether he would or no, the personalities about him pressed upon him, absorbed him, annihilated him.

How far may a poet's utterances be taken as expressing himself? Keats would seem to say, 'Not in the least'; for, except in the rare instances of the 'Wordsworthian egotistical sublime', the true poet has no permanent identity to express, and therefore cannot, if he would, lay bare the rooms of his house, nor can he with sonnet or any other key unlock his own heart. Elsewhere Keats declares, 'The only means of strengthening one's intellect is to make up one's mind about nothing – to let the mind be a thoroughfare for all thoughts, not a select party.' What type of mind better fitted for this thoroughfare than that of a poet who has no self-identity, but whose penetrative mind can roam whither it will, can see and apprehend all clearly, and bring home its fruits of truth untainted by bias or prejudice? Is it not a pleasing thought that the mind of the greatest poet may be a sort of filter through which the great truths of the eternal universe are clarified, organized, and given to the world? Keats's logic would lead one to consider the poet as so closely identifying himself with his object, his own identity being submerged, that his utterance really becomes a true and unhampered expression of the object itself. Keats 'does not put himself on an equality' with Nature, says Reynolds. 'You do not see him, when you see her.'[1] This seems to be Keats's ideal – to represent things as they are without putting himself into the picture.

To such a poet, able to imagine himself into any living thing, mere life itself and the things of life that lead to speculation are alone adequate to pleasurable activity. So he knows no good and evil; he is as delighted to contemplate and portray the villainy of an Iago as to share in and represent the white virtue of an Imogen. For each one embodies life and a bit of the passion and truth of life, and for a poet that is enough.

[In a letter written to Benjamin Bailey (November, 1817), Keats addresses himself directly to the subject of the nature, function, and importance of imaginative activity,] and his observations are of all the worth that a real thinker's unpremeditated, spontaneous utterance on any subject close to his heart always is – utterance where we arrive at the crux of a matter directly without the sophistications of studied delivery.

But I am running my head into a subject which I am certain I could not do justice to under five Years' study, and 3 vols. octavo – and moreover, long to be talking about the Imagination . . . O! I wish I was as certain of the end of all your troubles as that of your momentary start about the authenticity of the Imagination. [Quotation continues as cited above in Part One, section 4. II. – Ed.]

Here Keats is confessing, perhaps to the point of exaggeration, his complete faith in the authenticity of the imagination. It is a faith that wavers somewhat in the mental shake-up of 1818, when the young poet's conception of what constitutes imagination is altered as he perceives ever more and more that barren dreams are vain and breed only mawkishness in verse; but even when under the influence of the insistent conviction that a poet must understand the 'Mystery', and must know life to the core, Keats perceives that the final way to great poetry is through the imagination. Milton was his exemplar in philosophic attainment; yet when he writes in the very spiritual presence of the 'old scholar of the spheres', he still adheres to his faith in the intuitive as the last resort for poets:

> But vain is now the burning and the strife
> Pangs are in vain, until I grow high-rife
>   With old Philosophy,
> And mad with glimpses of futurity.
>   ('On a Lock of Milton's Hair')

To grow 'high-rife / with old philosophy' is only a preparation for, and an accompaniment of, the highest type of seer-like vision – the vision of a prophet to whom all veils are rent in 'glimpses of futurity'.

This does not mean that Keats would in the end minimize the importance of knowledge. He came to see that for the poet every avenue to the fullest and most complete knowledge of reality should be left open. He realized, as Mr. Herford, in his *Is There a Poetic View of the World?*, puts it, that 'What distinguishes poetic from religious or philosophic apprehension is not that it turns away from reality, but that it lies open to and in eager watch for reality at doors and windows which with them are barred or blind. The poet's soul resides, so to speak, in his senses, in his emotions, in his imagination, as well as in his conscious intelligence; and we may provisionally describe poetic apprehension as an intense state of consciousness in which all these are concerned.' Most of this Keats understood when he wrote this letter. His instinct taught him that the doors and windows to reality barred to the scientists and philosopher – men of 'consecutive minds' – are the very ones the poet most uses, those of 'Sensation', or intuitive perception; only at this time he had not yet realized the importance of 'his conscious intelligence'. That was to come when he should grow to see the necessity for the 'gradual ripening of all the intellectual powers'.

One word that follows is used carelessly and is confusing: 'And yet such a fate can only befall those who delight in sensation, rather than hunger as you do after Truth.' But taken in connection with the preceding sentences, it appears that it is truth from reason alone that is meant, without respect to imaginative truth, and this, of course, is quite consistent with Keats's whole thought.

Santayana has shown in his admirable way the right relation between reasoning and philosophy and poetry:

In philosophy itself investigation and reasoning are only preparatory and servile parts, means to an end. They terminate in insight, or what in the noblest sense of the word may be called *theory*, θεωρια, – a steady contemplation of all things in their order and worth. Such contemplation is imaginative. No one can reach it who has not enlarged his mind and tamed his heart. A philosopher who attains it is, for the moment, a poet; and a poet who turns his practised and passionate imagination on the order of all things, or on anything in the light of the whole, is for the moment a philosopher.[2]

This is a doctrine to which Keats would have heartily subscribed. For in this larger sense he was always an intuitionist. The imaginative is the highest, and most generative, of all poetic functions. Reason and knowledge are requisites, it is true; but only as educators of the imagination. They are but guides to point the way. In the end the pupil far outruns the master.

In his eager pursuit of truth Keats believed that intuitive insight rather than reason is to be trusted as the authentic guide to the hidden mysteries of the poetic world. To sound the sea of imaginative reality to the depths was the passionate longing of his soul. To see, to know, as did Shakespeare, Milton, Homer, – such was his young Parnassian dream. And he believed the magic open sesame to all the fair realms beyond to be the feelings, refined and spiritualized into poetic imagination. We recognize this ideal in these lines to Homer:

> Standing aloof in giant ignorance,
> Of thee I hear and of the Cyclades,
> As one who sits ashore and longs perchance
> To visit dolphin-coral in deep seas.
> So thou wast blind! – but then the veil was rent;
> For Jove uncurtain'd Heaven to let thee live,
> And Neptune made for thee a spermy tent,
> And Pan made sing for thee his forest-hive;
> Aye, on the shores of darkness there is light,
> And precipices show untrodden green;
> There is a budding morrow in midnight, –
> There is a triple sight in blindness keen;
> Such seeing hadst thou, as it once befel
> To Dian, Queen of Earth, and Heaven, and Hell.

The poet is one before whose insistent spirit the veils of heaven are rent; through the power of imagination – for what else can be this 'triple sight in blindness keen?' – the poet has power to ascend into the empyrean or to find a home in the bottomless depths of the ocean; his seeing is like that of the Gods, to whom all things, in 'Earth and Heaven and Hell', are clear. Reason could not do this. All his lifetime Keats earnestly, passionately, sought truth, but not truth through reason alone. Reason could never carry a poet to the heart of man,

>   Be he King
>   Or poorest of the beggar clan,

nor help him find his way to all the instincts of bird, wren, or eagle; and reason could never uncurtain 'heaven', nor guide in exploring the 'passages all dark' that lead to the inner 'Penetralium' of the 'Burden of the Mystery', where the miseries and agonies of the world are bared. Keats could not trust reason to reveal ultimate reality to him.

It was this instinctive conviction which Keats held from the very first that prompted his almost savage attack in 'Sleep and Poetry' upon the classical poets and their verse of reason and good taste. It evolved naturally from his reflections on the place of intuition and feeling in poetry; he could not help contrasting the high imaginative power of the older poetry with its decline in the verse of poets like Boileau and Pope. He insists upon a return to imagination:

>   Is there so small a range
>   In the present strength of manhood, that the high
>   Imagination can not freely fly
>   As she was wont of old . . .
>   . . . Has she not shown us all?
>   From the clear space of ether, to the small
>   Breath of new buds unfolding? From the meaning
>   Of Jove's large eye-brow, to the tender greening
>   Of April meadows? Here her altar shone,
>   E'en in this isle; and who could paragon
>   The fervid choir that lifted up a noise

> Of harmony, to which it aye will poise
> Its mighty self of convoluting sound
> Huge as a planet, and like that roll round,
> Eternally around a dizzy void.

And then follows the indignant denunciation:

> Could all this be forgotten? Yes, a schism
> Nurtured by foppery and barbarism,
> Made great Apollo blush for this his land.

There came a time when the highest honors were paid to men who had not the slightest understanding of real poetry; but in sublime self-deception,

> . . . with a puling infant's force
> They sway'd about upon a rocking horse,
> And thought it Pegasus. Ah, dismal soul'd!
> The winds of heaven blew, the ocean roll'd
> Its gathering waves — ye felt it not. The blue
> Bared its eternal bosom and the dew
> Of summer nights collected still to make
> The morning precious: beauty was awake!
> Why were ye not awake? But ye were dead
> To things ye knew not of, — were closely wed
> To musty laws lined out with wretched rule
> And compass vile: so that ye taught a school
> Of dolts to smooth, inlay, and clip, and fit,
> Till, like the certain wands of Jacob's wit,
> Their verses tallied. Easy was the task:
> A thousand handicraftsmen wore the mask
> Of Poesy. Ill-fated, impious race!
> That blasphemed the bright Lyrist to his face,
> And did not know it, — no, they went about
> Holding a poor, decrepid standard out
> Mark'd with most flimsy mottos, and in large
> The name of one Boileau!
>
>   ('Sleep and Poetry', 181–201)

Here Keats expresses his allegiance to freedom-giving, truth-revealing intuitive imagination as the informing spirit of poetry, and his deep-rooted antagonism to the idea of verse coldly thought out, cut by feet and chiseled by rule, all unwarmed by the penetrative fires of feeling. In this the young poet is much in accord with the poetic thought of his day. In these lines there are distinct echoes of Wordsworth's sonnet beginning 'The World is too much with us', with its emphasis upon a fresh imaginative enjoyment of beauty; and there is expressed the same impatience of studied formalism in art that Wordsworth voices in his 'A Poet! He hath put his heart to school' —

> A Poet! He hath put his heart to school,
> Nor dares to move unpropped upon the staff
> Which Art hath lodged within his hand — must laugh
> By precept only, and shed tears by rule.
> Thy Art be Nature; the live current quaff,
> And let the groveller sip his stagnant pool,
> In fear that else when Critics grave and cool
> Have killed him, scorn should write his epitaph.

But Keats is not merely echoing Wordsworth. Young as he is, he is declaring what was to him from first to last a basic tenet of his poetic creed. To follow the teachings of Boileau, he instinctively felt, would be to take the surest possible route to artistic blight and stultification. To put such reins upon the poetic faculties as the classical school proposed was, to him, to falsify nature and to destroy the imagination.

Yet, Keats and Boileau agreed on one essential: each knew that nothing is more dangerous than for a poet to write with the imagination only; Boileau believed this firmly, and Keats, at least after 1818, came to know that the highest poetry could not be written in this way. But Keats took the more balanced view. Where Boileau would make the imagination subordinate, Keats would have the imagination and the intellect work together, like twin sisters, as it were, except that the imaginative sister should have the stronger, clearer eyes and the deeper, more accurate seeing power, and so should always be the authority in case of dispute. In fact Keats refused to trust the intellectual sister's vision at all until he had appealed to the imaginative twin to corroborate her judgment – 'I can never be sure of a truth except by a clear conception of its beauty.' On the other hand he will even discredit or ignore the intellect if the imagination's penetrative vision has pierced some misty haze and caught gleams that her slower sister's eye cannot detect: 'What the imagination seizes as Beauty must be truth. . . .' Boileau's mistake, as Brunetière points out in a statement with which Keats would agree, is that he failed to 'recognize that, in spite of all its excesses, the imagination, that is to say the faculty of transcending nature, of even seeing in it what is not there, provided only that he make us see it, that imagination remains the supreme faculty of the poet, his original aptitude, one whose place can be supplied by no other, without which one may indeed be artist, writer, orator, but never poet – for this it is we are bound to upbraid him. The reason is that he himself was not a poet. . . .'[3]

So it was not that Keats discarded knowledge; we have seen how earnestly he sought to know and understand: it was not that he despised concious craftmanship in verse building; we shall see how much thought he himself gave to fitting form for poetic substance: it was simply that he felt that without the operation of the imagination there could be no artistic perception nor revelation. In the education of the imagination, all knowledge and intellect have a place. But Keats would maintain firmly with Leigh Hunt that 'thought by itself makes no poetry at all'.[4] For the conclusions of the understanding can at best be only so many matters of fact. 'Sensation', on the other hand, in that it gives a sense of deepest truth through direct emotionalized intuition, is a fundamental to all real poetry; though without knowledge as a ballast, it leads to lack of balance, and to irresponsible, giddy soaring. In other words, 'sensation' without knowledge is mere fancy, with knowledge it becomes creative imagination, the basis of all true art.

And now we come to those other lines that are so often quoted to show how Keats elevated the 'paradise of the sensations over the mind':

> . . . Do not all charms fly
> At the mere touch of cold philosophy?
> There was an awful rainbow once in heaven:
> We know her woof, her texture; she is given
> In the dull catalogue of common things.
> Philosophy will clip an angel's wings,
> Conquer all mysteries by rule and line,
> Empty the haunted air, and gnomed mine –
> Unweave a rainbow, as it erewhile made
> The tender-person'd Lamia melt into a shade.
>
> (*Lamia*, ii 229–38)

It is possible to interpret this passage by the application of a fact earlier developed in this treatise – the fact that Keats had a sort of dual nature, one half of which cried for the untrammeled sway of instinctive creative fancy, the other of which turned toward wisdom and knowledge.

But there is a more satisfactory explanation. We must interpret the passage in the light of all that Keats says elsewhere. Then it is cold 'reason unmitigated by the warmth of intuitive imagination' that Keats condemns, as he does always. Just as we have seen that feeling or 'sensation' by itself is not enough until balanced by reason and knowledge, so 'cold philosophy' out of sympathy with the human heart and natural beauty he as a poet rightly despises. As Goethe declares, the Significant 'must have a soul breathed into it before it can be art.'

Keats realized that poetry has a peculiar province of knowledge all her own, her proper realm being the imaginative as opposed to the scientific. He probably felt as he may have heard Hazlitt declare in his lectures of the spring of 1818, that the progress of scientific knowledge and refinement has a tendency to circumscribe the limits of the imagination, and 'to clip the wings of poetry'. Jacob's dream was a product of imagination, but, says Hazlitt, 'There can never be another Jacob's dream. Since that time, the heavens have gone farther off, and grown astronomical.' Hard, dry, scientific fact, then, must be indeed antagonistic to poetry. But that does not apply to 'philosophy' in its broader sense of spiritual wisdom and knowledge of humanity. On the contrary, a proper union of this sort of philosophy with feeling and sensation becomes imagination, the great revealer of poetic truth. 'What then shall we say?' inquires Coleridge. 'Even this; that Shakespeare, no mere child of nature; no automaton of genius; no passive vehicle of inspiration, possessed by the spirit, not possessing it; first studied patiently, meditated deeply, understood minutely, till knowledge, become habitual and intuitive, wedded itself to his habitual feelings, and at length gave birth to that stupendous power by which he stands alone, with no equal or second in his own class.' It was such a power as this that Keats longed to possess; and had he lived who knows but that finally he would have realized his dream.

III

Keats's poetic world was an imaginative one. Byron 'describes what he sees', he declared, 'I describe what I imagine. Mine is the hardest task.' This was written in September, 1819, just when Keats was at the peak of his poetic powers, and may be trusted as a final utterance. Keats was not in any sense confessing that the objects of his verse were lacking one whit of the reality to be found in Byron's; indeed he would have contended that his own poetry reflected the greater truth and reality, in that his was universal, while Byron's was only particular. Keats believed that the imagination of the true poet was capable not only of perceiving, but of creating essential reality. Sometimes it appears that he thinks of this imaginative power as extending to the point of actual new creations, as when he boldly announced, 'What the imagination seizes as Beauty must be truth – whether it existed before or not.' At other times, it would seem that he has reference to a re-creative force able to seize visible materials and truth that lies hidden and combine them into new forms, as when he writes in elevated vein of his 'readiness to measure time by what is done and to die in six hours could plans be brought to conclusions – the looking upon the Sun, the Moon, the Stars, the Earth and its contents, as materials to form greater things – that is to say ethereal things – but here I am talking like a Madman – greater things than our Creator himself made.'

Keats would logically hold that true art, the product of this generative power of the mind, embodies both the visible sensuous and the generative unseen spiritual, combined in a single imaginative creation. In this Keats is Hegelian. Note Hegel's own comment:

Genuine reality is only to be found beyond the immediacy of feeling and of external objects. Nothing is genuinely real but that which is actual in its own right, that which is the substance of nature and of mind, fixing itself indeed in present and definite existence, but in this existence still retaining its essential and self-centered being, and thus and no otherwise attaining genuine reality. . . . Art liberates the real import of appearances from the semblance and deception of this bad and fleeting world, and imparts to phenomenal semblances a higher reality, born of mind. The appearances of art, therefore, far from being mere semblances, have the higher reality and the more genuine existence in comparison with the realities of common life.

With Keats the essential reality of these imaginative conceptions was not at all dependent on their expression in art forms; it was only necessary for them to exist in the mind of the poet, who, beginning with the appearances of men and things, constructs for himself a world of his own, which includes but transcends the things of sense. 'What creates the pleasure of not knowing?' Keats reflects, as he reads Book I of *Paradise Lost*. 'A sense of independence, of power, from the fancy's creating a world of its own by the sense of probabilities', he replies.

There is no room to doubt Keats's conviction as to the capacity of the imagination to create spiritual reality. It is made evident in the letter concerning the 'mighty abstract idea of beauty', where the poet declares that he feels more and more as his imagination strengthens that he does 'not live in this world alone but in a thousand worlds'; the idea is clearly conveyed in the passages just quoted – in his explanation that where Byron describes the visible, he describes what he imagines; in his epigrammatic 'What the imagination seizes as Beauty must be Truth for I have the same idea of all our passions as of Love, they are all in their sublime creative of essential beauty'; in his declaration that the poet has power to create 'ethereal things greater than those of the

Creator himself' – and it is even more explicitly stated in the following:

I want to hear very much whether Poetry and literature in general has gained, or lost interest with you – and what sort of writing is of the highest gust with you now. With what sensation do you read Fielding? – and do not Hogarth's pictures seem an old thing to you? Yet you are very little more removed from general association than I am – recollect that no Man can live but in one society at a time – his enjoyment in the different states of human society must depend upon the Powers of his Mind – that is you can imagine a Roman triumph or an Olympic game as well as I can. We with our bodily eyes see but the fashion and Manners of one country for one age – and then we die. Now to me manners and customs long since passed whether among the Babylonians or the Bactrians, are as real, or even more real than those among which I now live. My thoughts have turned lately this way. The more we know the more inadequacy we find in the world to satisfy us – this is an old observation; but I have made up my Mind never to take anything for granted – but even to examine the truth of the commonest proverbs.

In such passages as these we not only discover a complete confession of Keats's idealism, but we find revealed the important function of the imagination in combining and creating into forms of beauty the truths that lie beyond the visible. The world of sense is imperfect and incomplete: 'The more we know the more inadequacy we find in the world to satisfy us.' Therefore, every appearance must be scrutinized for its possible implications as to the larger reality. Perceptions of this reality can come only through the operation of the imaginative faculty; only through the imagination can the poet see the world true and see it whole, and only through the imagination can he create and re-create new forms of beauty. This holds in the realm of imaginative literature and history as well as in relation to the real and ideal worlds; and the capacity to create is largely independent of time or place or circumstances. George and Georgiana Keats are in remote America; yet – 'recollect that no man can live but in one society at a time – that is, you can imagine a Roman triumph or an Olympic game as well as I can'. Man's real ability to know life to the full rests upon the resources of his imagination. Art treasures and general cultural environment are not necessary to the fullest appreciation of the beauty of the world. Give a man the gift of imagination, and in the Sahara desert as well as London the whole universe is at his command. Roman and Egyptian civilizations long since melted away, are re-created at the call of this divine faculty, and form a portion of the aggregate of all reality to make an ideal whole.

From what has just been said it is evident that the creative power of the imagination is in no wise restricted by inability to see with the physical eyes that which it creates or the materials with which it works. This fact is thrown into stronger relief by a suggestive remark Keats made concerning Milton, occurring in a note on the early lines of *Paradise Lost*. 'A poet', declares Keats, 'can seldom have justice done to his imagination − for men are as distinct in their conceptions of material shadowings as they are in matters of spiritual understanding: it can scarcely be conceived how Milton's blindness might here aid the magnitude of his conceptions as a bat in a large gothic vault'. Keats's statement is incomplete, yet as Mr. Forman has pointed out,[5] the general sense is clear. Milton is working with vast conceptions, the materials for which are visible only to the imaginative eye. How are such transcendent conceptions to be accounted for? Keats's suggestion is 'that Milton's blindness might so sharpen his imagination as to give him the same advantage in the realm of the unseen as a bat has in the darkness of a gothic vault', that is, the ability to imagine ultimates − infinite spaces peopled by personages of infinite scope and power.

'Imagination then', says Professor Mackail, in his *Lectures on Poetry*, 'is the power or faculty which creates, in so far as creation is within human power. It is the likeness or echo of the divine creative power; like it, according to its measure, it gives shape and substance to what had neither, what was without form and void.[6] It dissolves in order to re-create, or if the word create be too strong, to unify and idealize.' This perhaps would sum up fairly well Keats's thoughts as to the creative imagination. He would have added, as he matured in intellect, that the authenticity of these creations must be governed by the extent to which the poet knows the world of men.

But the creations of the imagination are none the less real because they are thus limited. No, 'What the imagination seizes as Beauty must be Truth – whether it existed before or not. . . .' That is, what the imagination constructs for itself as reality is truth. Note the real significance of certain phrases in the letter quoted: 'Now to me manners and customs long since passed, whether among the Babylonians or the Bactrians, are as real, or even more real than those among which I now live.' 'Even more real', Keats says, for he ever trusted to the light of imagination more fully than to the voice of reason. And things imagined are never reasoned; they are felt. To Keats, things of the mind, creations of the imagination, were as real as to Wordsworth when he wrote:

> Paradise, and groves
> Elysian, Fortunate Fields, like those of old
> Sought in the Atlantic Main – why should they be
> A history only of departed things,
> Or a mere fiction of what never was?
> For the discerning intellect of Man,
> When wedded to this goodly universe
> In love and holy passion, shall find these
> A simple produce of the common day.
>
> (*The Recluse*, 799–808)

In his *Sartor Resartus*, Carlyle has most vigorously and succinctly expressed a similar idea:

To clap on your felt, and, simply by wishing you were Any*where*, straightway to be *There!* Next to clap on your other felt, and, simply by wishing you were Any*when*, straightway to be *Then!* This were indeed the grander: shooting at will from the *Fire-Creation* of the World to its Fire-Consummation; here historically present in the first century, conversing face to face with Paul and Seneca; there prophetically in the Thirty-first, conversing also face to face with other Pauls and Senecas, who as yet stand hidden in the depths of that late Fire.

Or thinkest thou it were impossible, unimaginable? Is the Past annihilated then, or only past; is the Future non-extant, or only future? Those mystic faculties of thine, Memory and Hope, already answer: already through those mystic avenues, thou the Earth-blinded summonest both Past and Future, and communist with them, though as yet darkly, and with mute beckonings. The curtains of Yesterday drop down, the curtains of tomorrow roll up; but Yesterday and Tomorrow both *are*. Pierce through the time-element, glance into the Eternal, Believe what thou findest written in the sanctuaries of Man's soul, even as all Thinkers, in all ages, have devoutly read it there: that Time and space are not God, but creations of God; that with God as it is a universal Here, so it is an everlasting Now.

And again:

Was Luther's Picture of the Devil less a Reality, whether it were formed within the bodily eye, or without it? In every the wisest Soul lies a whole world of internal Madness, an authentic Demon-Empire; out of which, indeed, his world of Wisdom has been creatively built together, and now rests there, as on its dark foundations does a habitable flowery Earth-rind.

Keats's belief is quite as thorough-going as Carlyle's. So far from depending upon the sensuous world about him for mental food and spiritual substance, he asserts in effect that the poet's power rests largely on a subjective basis, upon his ability to create from the materials of his own brain, his intellect operating upon things of the visible world, in close relation with ideal truth and beauty, a new spiritual reality that embraces and comprehends both the known and the unknown verities, like, yet unlike, each — ethereal substance 'greater even than our Creator himself has made'. Of this the world of environment need furnish but a fractional part; yet, let us remember how vital a part it is. The world we see is entirely real, and, though it is but a small portion of a much larger unseen whole, a thorough knowledge of it is necessary to an understanding of the ideal entity to whose inner workings it gives the clue.

Such is the power of creative imagination, a seeing, reconciling, combining force that seizes the old, penetrates beneath its surface, disengages the truth lying slumbering there, and, building afresh, bodies forth anew a reconstructed universe in fair forms of artistic power and beauty.

SOURCE: chapter 7 of *The Mind of John Keats* (New York, 1926; reissued 1964) pp. 104–26.

NOTES

1. Alfred, *West of England Journal*; quoted in *The Complete Works of John Keats*, ed. H. B. Forman (London, 1901) vol. IV, p. 178.
2. George Santayana, *Three Philosophic Poets* (Cambridge, Mass., 1910) p. 10.
3. 'L'Esthétique de Boileau', *Revue des deux Mondes*, XCIII (1889); quoted in A. S. Cook, *The Art of Poetry* (Boston, 1892) p. L.
4. Hunt, *Imagination and Fancy*, 2nd ed. (London, 1845) p. 63.
5. *Works*, ed. Forman, vol. III, p. 258.
6. 'Must not the imagination weave garments, visible garments, wherein the else invisible creations and inspirations of our reason are, like spirits, revealed . . .' – Thomas Carlyle, *Sartor Resartus* (1833–4).

W. J. Bate

'KEATS'S "NEGATIVE CAPABILITY" AND THE IMAGINATION' (1963)

[Keats's 'Negative Capability' letter to George and Tom Keats of 21 December 1817] distills the reactions of three months to the dimension of thinking that had opened to him in September. A background that helps to clarify these rapid, condensed remarks is provided by the long letter written to Bailey only a month before,[1] just after Keats had arrived at Burford Bridge determined to 'wind up' the last five hundred lines of *Endymion*.

For weeks the ideal of 'disinterestedness' about which they had talked at Oxford had eluded his impulsive efforts to apply it to his own personal experience. Given the complexities, the unpredictable problems even in one month of life, no simple formula could serve. But perhaps that realization was itself a further argument for the need of 'disinterestedness' and a further indication of the futility, in a universe of uncertainties, of the brief, assertive postures we assume. The result, as he told Bailey, was a healthful increase in 'Humility and the capability of submission'. The significant word is 'capability', not 'submission'. 'Negative' was to be the next word he would apply to the 'capability' he had in mind – 'submission' could have very different connotations – though even 'negative' would still be far from adequate. Meanwhile he goes on:

I am certain of nothing but of the holiness of the Heart's affections and the truth of Imagination – What the imagination seizes as Beauty must be truth – whether it existed before or not – for I have the same Idea of all our Passions as of Love they are all, in their sublime, creative of essential Beauty. . . . The Imagination may be compared to Adam's dream [*Paradise Lost*, VIII 452–90] – he awoke and found it truth. I am the more zealous in this affair, because I have never yet been able to perceive how any thing can be known for truth by consequitive reasoning – and yet it must be – Can it be that even the greatest Philosopher ever arrived at his goal without putting aside numerous objections – However it may be, O for a Life of Sensations rather than of Thoughts!

Two general premises interweave here. Though they were common enough in the more thoughtful writing of the period, Keats has acquired them partly through self-discovery. Hence, far from being what Whitehead calls 'inert ideas', they are invested with possibilities. The first is the premise of all objective idealism: what the human mind itself contributes to what it assumes are direct perceptions of the material world – supplementing, channeling, even helping to create them – is not, as the subjective idealist argues, something imposed completely *ab extra*, something invented or read into nature that is not really there. Instead, this cooperating creativity of the mind has, to use a phrase of Coleridge's, 'the same ground with nature': its insights are to this extent a valid and necessary supplement in attaining the reconciliation or union of man and nature that constitutes knowledge. Keats, of course, knew nothing of contemporary German idealism, objective or subjective. He had dipped into a little of Coleridge: Bailey had been reading the *Lay Sermons*, and Keats in early November borrowed the *Sybilline Leaves* from Charles Dilke. But he seems to have caught very little from Coleridge at this point, and associated him a month later with an 'irritable reaching after fact and reason' the contrasts with the ideal he is naively but brilliantly evolving throughout the next half year.

It is primarily from Wordsworth that Keats has picked up enough hints to enable him to go ahead with this 'favorite Speculation', as he calls it. He was naturally unaware of the massive treatment of man's relation to nature in the *Prelude*, into which Wordsworth was putting so much that he was never satisfied that it was ready for publication. But what Keats had read of Wordsworth he had recently approached in a very different spirit from the way he had been reading poetry the year before. He was quicker to note what he was beginning to call the 'philosophical' implications of poetry. By now this speculation

about the mind's creativity has become peculiarly his own, and
to such an extent that he has begun to toy with the possible
antecedence or foreshadowing, through imaginative insight, 'of
reality to come'. The mention of this and of 'Adam's dream'
introduces

another favorite Speculation of mine, that we shall enjoy ourselves here
after by having what we called happiness on Earth repeated in a finer
tone and so repeated − And yet such a fate can only befall those who
delight in sensation rather than hunger as you do after Truth − Adam's
dream will do here and seems to be a conviction that Imagination and
its empyreal reflection is the same as human Life and its spiritual
repetition. But as I was saying − the simple imaginative Mind may
have its rewards in the repeti[ti]on of its own silent Working coming
continually on the spirit with a fine suddenness.

The second general premise involves the familiar romantic
protest on behalf of concreteness and the conviction that the
analytic and logical procedures of what Keats calls 'consequitive
reasoning' violate the organic process of nature. They abstract
from the full concreteness, reduce the living process to static
concepts, and substitute an artificial order.

Here again the immediate suggestions have come to Keats
from Wordsworth but are further substantiated by what he has
been reading of Hazlitt. More than any other literary critic of his
day, Hazlitt continued the brilliant psychological tradition of
eighteenth-century British empiricism, rephrasing and supplementing a descriptive study of the imagination that had been
developing for at least sixty years, and applying it even more
suggestively to genius in the arts, especially poetry. The great
contribution of English psychological criticism throughout the
later eighteenth century had been to describe and justify
confidence in the imaginative act − an act whereby sensations,
intuitions, and judgments are not necessarily retained in the
memory as separate particles of knowledge to be consulted one by
one, but can be coalesced and transformed into a readiness of
response that is objectively receptive to the concrete process of

nature and indeed actively participates in it. This entire approach to the imagination naturally involved a corollary protest against the sort of thing implied in Wordsworth's famous phrase, the 'meddling intellect'. The protest anticipates Whitehead's remarks on the 'fallacy of misplaced concreteness': abstraction by its very nature fails to conceive the full concreteness; it draws out particular elements for special purposes of thought; and the 'misplaced concreteness' comes when these necessary 'short-cuts' in thinking – as Hazlitt calls them – are regarded as equivalent to the concrete reality.

Keats had just begun to catch some of the implications of these ideas during his Oxford visit. Hazlitt's *Essay on the Principles of Human Action* had lit up a large zone of possibilities. Its persuasive argument on the possible 'disinterestedness' of the mind, and its brilliant treatment of the sympathetic potentialities of the imagination, had especially won him. But it is enough for the moment to point out how quickly it led him to read other works of Hazlitt. Within a few weeks after he wrote this letter to Bailey, he was telling both Haydon and his brothers that 'the three things to rejoice at in this Age' were Wordsworth's *Excursion*, Haydon's pictures, and 'Hazlitt's depth of Taste'. Hazlitt, by now, had completely replaced Hunt in the triumvirate of the year before.

Finally, Hazlitt's constant use of the word 'sensations' in the traditional empirical sense – as virtually equivalent to concrete experience – added a new term to Keats's own habitual vocabulary (hence the remark at the moment about the 'Life of Sensations': the bookish Bailey, inclining more toward philosophical analysis, 'would exist' – says Keats – 'partly on sensation partly on thought'). 'Consequitive reasoning' applies to the piecemeal, step-by-step procedures of the analytic and selective intelligence. But though Keats himself cannot perceive how truth can be known by this reductive means, and wonders whether the most astute reasoner 'ever arrived at his goal without putting aside numerous objections', he is far from pushing the matter, and grants that it 'must be' possible.

This letter to Bailey [21 November 1817], written at Burford Bridge as he begins his determined seven-day effort to complete

Endymion, has a sequel of its own. For Bailey seems to have been a little disturbed by portions of it – at least by the speculation about an afterlife in which the 'old Wine of Heaven' may consist of 'the redigestion of our most ethereal Musings on Earth', and 'what we called happiness on Earth repeated in a finer tone and so repeated'. Bailey saw Keats in London in January and may have talked with him about the letter. If not, he certainly wrote to him in some detail, and may have taken some time to do so.

At all events, the matter is picked up again in a letter Keats wrote to him on March 13. This letter gives every indication that Keats has been trying to think over some of the remarks he had made before. What he is most eager to state is that he is not a dogmatist in his skepticism – that he is not, as he thinks, a complete skeptic at all. He wishes he could 'enter into' all of Bailey's feelings on the matter, and write something Bailey would like (Keats was too 'transparent', said Bailey, ever to be able to hide anything); and if he had appeared to be substituting the poetic imagination for religion as a means of arriving at truth, he is now beginning to have moments of doubt about poetry itself.

Then he turns to what he had been trying to express about the validity of the imagination's own contribution to its perception. Some things, certainly 'real', may not require this 'greeting of the Spirit' from the human mind or heart. But others – at least 'things semireal' – do require that greeting, that contribution, for their fulfillment; and this union of the perceiving mind and the perceived object should not be confused with mere 'Nothings' that are solely the product of human desires. He begins:

You know my ideas about Religion – I do not think myself more in the right than other people and that nothing in this world is proveable. I wish I could enter into all your feelings on the subject merely for one short 10 Minutes and give you a Page or two to your liking. I am sometimes so very sceptical as to think Poetry itself a mere Jack a lanthern to amuse whoever may chance to be struck with its brilliance – As Tradesmen say every thing is worth what it will fetch, so probably every mental pursuit takes its reality and worth from the ardour of the pursuer – being in itself a nothing – Ethereal thing[s] may at least be thus real, divided under three heads – Things

real – things semireal – and no things – Things real – such as existences of Sun Moon & Stars and passages of Shakespeare – Things
semireal such as Love, the Clouds &c which require a greeting of the
Spirit to make them wholly exist – and Nothings which are made Great
and dignified by an ardent pursuit – Which by the by stamps the
burgundy mark on the bottles of our Minds, insomuch as they are able
to '*consec[r]ate what'er they look upon*'.

The theme of much of the greater poetry to come – certainly
of the 'Ode on a Grecian Urn' and the 'Ode to a
Nightingale' – may be described as the drama of the human
spirit's 'greeting' of objects in order 'to make them wholly
exist' – a drama in which the resolutions are precarious, as in life
itself, and the preciousness of the attainment ultimately crossed
by tragedy. But for the moment he is unable to go further, and
least of all to go further theoretically. In his remarks to Bailey,
particularly about the 'semireal' as distinct from 'Nothings', he is
trying to grope toward a distinction that Locke could not make
and that Hume thought it impossible to make. He can end only
with a plea for openness, and by recurring to a thought that has
been growing on him for some time: that the heart's hunger for
settlement, for finality, cannot be answered unless we shut
ourselves off from the amplitude of experience, with all its
contradictory diversity. All he can do is to proceed honestly and
empirically in this adventure of speculation, of openness, and (as
he later phrased it) of 'straining at particles of light in the midst of
a great darkness'.

Quite plainly he will 'never be a Reasoner'; every point of
thought quickly opens some further unexpected vista; and how
could he be confident therefore of 'the truth of any of my
speculations'? His comic sense is suddenly aroused by the
ineffectiveness of his discourse, which he burlesques for a
moment; and he ends with a characteristic pun.[2]

The 'Negative Capability' letter is best understood as another
phrasing of these thoughts, with at least three further extensions.
First, the problem of form or style in art enters more specifically.
Second, the ideal toward which he is groping is contrasted more

strongly with the egoistic assertion of one's own identity. Third, the door is further opened to the perception – which he was to develop within the next few months – of the sympathetic potentialities of the imagination.

He begins by telling his brothers that he has gone to see Edmund Kean, has written his review, and is enclosing it for them. Then on Saturday, December 20, he went to see an exhibition of the American painter, Benjamin West, particularly his picture, 'Death on the Pale Horse'. Keats was altogether receptive to any effort to attain the 'sublime', and West's painting had been praised for succeeding. Yet it struck Keats as flat – 'there is nothing to be intense upon; no women one feels mad to kiss; no face swelling into reality'. Then the first crucial statement appears:

The excellence of every Art is its intensity, capable of making all disagreeables evaporate, from their being in close relationship with Beauty & Truth – Examine King Lear & you will find this exemplified throughout; but in this picture we have unpleasantness without any momentous depth of speculation excited, in which to bury its repulsiveness.

In the active cooperation or full 'greeting' of the experiencing imagination and its object, the nature or 'identity' of the object is grasped so vividly that only those associations and qualities that are strictly relevant to the central conception remain. The irrelevant and discordant (the 'disagreeables') 'evaporate' from this fusion of object and mind. Hence 'Truth' and 'Beauty' spring simultaneously into being, and also begin to approximate each other. For, on the one hand, the external reality – otherwise overlooked, or at most only sleepily acknowledged, or dissected so that a particular aspect of it may be abstracted for special purposes of argument or thought – has now, as it were, awakened into 'Truth': it has been met by that human recognition, fulfilled and extended by that human agreement with reality, which we call 'truth'. And at the same time, with the irrelevant 'evaporated', this dawning into unity is felt as 'Beauty'. Nor is it a unity solely of the object itself, emerging untrammeled and in its full significance, but a unity also of the human spirit, both within itself and with what was at first outside it. For in this 'intensity' – the 'excellence', he now feels, 'of every Art' – we attain, if only for a while, a harmony of the inner life with truth. It is in this harmony that 'Beauty' and 'Truth' come together. The 'pleasant', in the ordinary sense of the word, has nothing to do with the point being discussed; and to introduce it is only to trivialize the conception of 'Beauty'. Hence Keats's reference to *Lear*. The reality disclosed may be distressing and even cruel to human nature. But the harmony with truth will remain, and even deepen, to the extent that the emerging reality is being constantly matched at every stage by the 'depth of speculation excited' – by the corresponding release and extension, in other words, of human insight. 'Examine King Lear & you will find this exemplified throughout. . . .'

Hazlitt's short essay 'On Gusto' had aroused his thinking about style when he read it at Oxford in the *Round Table*; and what he is saying now is partly the result of what he has assimilated from Hazlitt. By 'gusto', Hazlitt means an excitement of the imagination in which the perceptive identification with the object is almost complete, and the living character of the object is caught and shared in its full diversity and given vital expression in art. It is 'power or passion defining any object'. But the result need not be subjective. By grasping sympathetically the over-all significance of the object, the 'power or passion' is able to cooperate, so to speak, with that significance – to go the full distance with its potentialities, omitting the irrelevant (which Keats calls the 'disagreeables'), and conceiving the object with its various qualities coalescing into the vital unity that is the object itself. One result is that the attributes or qualities that we glean through our different senses of sight, hearing, touch, and the rest are not presented separately or piecemeal, but 'the impression made on one sense excites by affinity those of another'. Thus Claude Lorrain's landscapes, though 'perfect abstractions of the visible images of things', lack 'gusto': 'They do not interpret one sense by another. . . . That is, his eye wanted imagination; it did not strongly sympathise with his other faculties. He saw the atmosphere, but he did not feel it.' Chaucer's descriptions of natural scenery have gusto: they give 'the very feeling of the air, the coolness or moisture of the ground'. 'There is gusto in the colouring of Titian. Not only do his heads seem to think – his bodies seem to feel.'

This interplay and coalescence of impressions was to become a conscious aim in Keats's own poetry within the next six months, and, by the following autumn, to be fulfilled as richly as by any English poet of the last three centuries. Meanwhile, only a few days before he wrote the 'Negative Capability' letter to his brothers, he had followed Hazlitt's use of the word 'gusto' in his own review 'On Edmund Kean as a Shakespearian Actor' (though he later returns to the word 'intensity' – 'gusto' perhaps suggesting a briskness or bounce of spirit he does not have in mind). He had been trying in this review to describe how 'a melodious passage in poetry' may attain a fusion of 'both sensual and spiritual', where each extends and declares itself by means of the other:

The spiritual is felt when the very letters and points of charactered language show like the hieroglyphics of beauty; – the mysterious signs of an immortal free-masonry! . . . To one learned in Shakespearian hieroglyphics, – learned in the spiritual portion of those lines to which Kean adds a sensual grandeur: his tongue must seem to have robbed 'the Hybla bees, and left them honeyless'.

Hence 'there is an indescribable gusto in his voice, by which we feel that the utterer is thinking of the past and future, while speaking of the present'.[3]

    Keats is here extending the notion of 'gusto' in a way that applies prophetically to his own maturer style – to an imaginative 'intensity' of conception, that is, in which process, though slowed to an insistent present, is carried in active solution. So with the lines he had quoted a month before to Reynolds as an example of Shakespeare's 'intensity of working out conceits':

          When lofty trees I see barren of leaves
          Which erst from heat did canopy the herd,

>   And summer's green all girded up in sheaves,
>   Borne on the bier with white and bristly beard.

Previous functions, and the mere fact of loss itself, are a part of the truth of a thing as it now is. The nature of the 'lofty trees' in this season, now 'barren of leaves', includes the fact that they formerly 'from heat did canopy the herd'; nor is it only the dry, completed grain of the autumn that is 'girded up in sheaves', but the 'Summer's green' that it once was. This entire way of thinking about style is proving congenial to Keats in the highest degree; for though it has independent developments, it has also touched and is giving content to the ideal briefly suggested a year before in 'Sleep and Poetry' – even before he saw the Elgin Marbles for the first time: an ideal of poetry as 'might half slumb'ring on its own right arm'. The delight in energy caught in momentary repose goes back to the idea he had 'when a Schoolboy . . . of an heroic painting': 'I saw it somewhat sideways', he tells Haydon, 'large prominent round and colour'd with magnificence – somewhat like the feel I have of Anthony and Cleopatra. Or of Alcibiades, leaning on his Crimson Couch in his Galley, his broad shoulders imperceptibly heaving with the Sea.' So with the line in *Henry VI*, 'See how the surly Warwick mans the Wall'.[4] One of the comments he wrote in his copy of Milton during the next year gives another illustration:

Milton in every instance pursues his imagination to the utmost – he is 'sagacious of his Quarry', he sees Beauty on the wing, pounces upon it and gorges it to the producing his essential verse. . . . But in no instance is this sort of perseverance more exemplified than in what may be called his *stationing or statu[a]ry*. He is not content with simple description, he must station, – thus here, we not only see how the Birds '*with clang despised the ground*', but we see them 'under *a cloud in prospect*'. So we see Adam '*Fair indeed and tall – under a plantane*' – and so we see Satan '*disfigured – on the Assyrian Mount*'.[5]

The union of the ideal of dynamic poise, of power kept in reserve, with the ideal of range of implication suggests one principal development in his own style throughout the next year and a half.

The very triumph of this union — as triumphs often tend to do — could have proved an embarrassment to later ideals and interests had it become an exclusive stylistic aim. However magnificent the result in the great odes, in portions of *Hyperion*, or in what Keats called the 'colouring' and 'drapery' of the *Eve of St. Agnes*, it carried liabilities in both pace and variety that would have to be circumvented for successful narrative and, above all, dramatic poetry. But even at the moment, and throughout the next year, what he calls 'intensity' — the 'greeting of the Spirit' and its object — is by no means completely wedded to a massive centering of image through poise and 'stationing'. If his instinctive delight in fullness was strengthened in one direction by the Elgin Marbles — which he still made visits to see[6] — other, more varied appeals to his ready empathy were being opened and reinforced by his reading of Shakespeare.

The second and longer of the crucial parts of the 'Negative Capability' letter is preceded by some more remarks about what he has been doing since his brothers left, and the remarks provide a significant preface. He had dinner — 'I have been out too much lately' — with 'Horace Smith & met his two Brothers with [Thomas] Hill & [John] Kingston & one [Edward] Du Bois'.

Partly because he himself was so direct and — as Bailey said — 'transparent', he was ordinarily tolerant of the more innocent affectations by which people hope to establish superiority. Moreover, such affectations appealed to his enormous relish for the idiosyncratic. As the next year passed, the very futility of such brief postures — the pointless intricacy of these doomed stratagems — against the vast backdrop of a universe of constantly unfolding 'uncertainties, Mysteries, doubts', was also to take on a pathos for him. In fact, only a month after he tells his brothers about this dinner with Horace Smith and his literary friends, he was to write Bailey, speaking of 'Reynolds and Haydon retorting and recriminating — and parting for ever — the same thing has happened between Haydon and Hunt':

Men should bear with each other — there lives not the Man who may not be cut up, aye hashed to pieces on his weakest side. The best of Men have but a portion of good in them — a kind of spiritual yeast in their frames which creates the ferment of existence — by which a Man is propell'd to act and strive and buffet with Circumstance.[7]

Even so, during these important transitional months he is entering, moments inevitably occur when the familiar comic sense and the deepening charity are suspended. Affectations particularly bother him at such moments. It is a great pity, as he tells Haydon (March 21), that 'people should by associating themselves with the fine[st] things, spoil them — Hunt has damned Hampstead [and] Masks and Sonnets and [I]talian tales — Wordsworth ha[s] damned the lakes', and so on. Hazlitt is 'your only good damner', because he damns in a different spirit. And Keats was enormously — almost amusingly — disturbed when Reynolds told him that his self-defensive Preface to *Endymion* savored of 'affectation' in its own way. Keats kept protesting that, whatever else it showed, it certainly did not show 'affectation', though he at once began anxiously to rewrite it.

So at Horace Smith's dinner, which he describes to George and Tom, where he met five other men of literary interests. Their entire way of talking about literature fatigued him for the moment. The possible uses of literature seemed frozen into posture, into mannerism. Given his attempts to approach his new ideal of 'disinterestedness', and the thoughts of 'Humility' and of openness to amplitude that had become more specific, even more convinced, within the last few months, the gathering typified the exact opposite of what was wanted:

They only served to convince me, how superior humour is to wit in respect to enjoyment — These men say things which make one start, without making one feel, they are all alike; their manners are alike; they all know fashionables; they have a mannerism in their very eating & drinking, in their mere handling a Decanter — They talked of Kean & his low company — Would I were with that company instead of yours said I to myself! I know such like acquaintance will never do for me.

But his humor was to return when he found himself again in

Kingston's company at Haydon's a week and a half afterwards. The 'mannerism' in the 'mere handling a Decanter' had caught his fancy as a symbol of the entire evening. At Haydon's, as he gleefully told George and Tom, 'I astonished Kingston at supper . . . keeping my two glasses at work in a knowing way.'

Shortly after Smith's literary party, he went to the Christmas pantomime at Drury Lane with Charles Brown and Charles Dilke. Walking with them back to Hampstead, he found himself having

not a dispute but a disquisition with Dilke, on various subjects; several things dovetailed in my mind, & at once it struck me, what quality went to form a Man of Achievement especially in Literature & which Shakespeare possessed so enormously − I mean *Negative Capability*, that is when man is capable of being in uncertainties, Mysteries, doubts, without any irritable reaching after fact & reason − Coleridge, for instance, would let go by a fine isolated verisimilitude caught from the Penetralium of mystery, from being incapable of remaining content with half knowledge. This pursued through Volumes would perhaps take us no further than this, that with a great poet the sense of Beauty overcomes every other consideration, or rather obliterates all consideration.

Using what we know of the background, we could paraphrase these famous sentences as follows. In our life of uncertainties, where no one system or formula can explain everything − where even a word is at best, in Bacon's phrase, a 'wager of thought' − what is needed is an imaginative openness of mind and heightened receptivity to reality in its full and diverse concreteness. This, however, involves negating one's own ego. Keats's friend Dilke, as he said later, 'was a Man who cannot feel he has a personal identity unless he has made up his Mind about every thing. The only means of strengthening one's intellect is to make up ones mind about nothing − to let the mind be a thoroughfare for all thoughts. . . . Dilke will never come at a truth as long as he lives; because he is always trying at it.'[8] To be dissatisfied with such insights as one may attain through this openness, to reject them unless they can be wrenched into a part of a systematic structure of one's own making, is an egoistic assertion of one's own identity. The remark, 'without any irritable reaching after fact and reason', is often cited as though the pejorative words are 'fact and reason', and as though uncertainties were being preferred for their own sake. But the significant word, of course, is 'irritable'. We should also stress 'capable' — 'capable of being in uncertainties, Mysteries, doubts' without the 'irritable' need to extend our identities and rationalize our 'half knowledge'.[9] For a 'great poet' especially, a sympathetic absorption in the essential significance of his object (caught and relished in that active cooperation of the mind in which the emerging 'Truth' is felt as 'Beauty', and in which the harmony of the human imagination and its object is attained) 'overcomes every other consideration' (considerations that an 'irritable reaching after fact and reason' might otherwise itch to pursue). Indeed, it goes beyond and 'obliterates' the act of 'consideration' — of deliberating, analyzing, and piecing experience together through 'consequitive reasoning'.

SOURCE: extract from chapter 10 of *John Keats* (Cambridge, Mass., 1963) pp. 237–50.

NOTES

1. 22 Nov 1817. [See above, Part One, section 4. 11. – Ed.]

2. The speculation about 'ethereal things' — the division into real, semireal and nothings — 'may be carried — but what am I talking of — it is an old maxim of mine and of course must be well known that eve[r]y point of thought is the centre of an intellectual world — the two uppermost thoughts in a Man's mind are the two poles of his World he revolves on them and every thing is southward or northward to him through their means — We take but three steps from feathers to iron. Now my dear fellow I must once for all tell you I have not one Idea of the truth of any of my speculations — I shall never be a Reasoner because I care not to be in the right, when retired from bickering and in a proper philosophical temper — So you must not stare if in any future letter I endeavour to prove that Appollo as he had a cat gut string to his Lyre used a cats' paw as a Pecten — and further from said Pecten's reiterated and continual teasing came the term Hen peck'd.'

3. *The Poetical Works and Other Writings of John Keats*, ed. H. B. Forman, revised by M. B. Forman (1938–9) vol. v, pp. 229–30.

4. *The Letters of John Keats*, ed. H. E. Rollins (Oxford, 1958) vol. I, p. 265.

5. *Poetical Works*, ed. Forman, vol. v, pp. 303–4. The comment is written next to the passage in *Paradise Lost*, VI 420–3:

> but feather'd soon and fledge
> They summ'd their pens, and, soaring the air sublime,
> With clang despised the ground, under a cloud
> In prospect.

6. 'He went again and again to see the Elgin Marbles', said Severn, 'and would sit for an hour or more at a time beside them rapt in revery.' One afternoon, as he delighted to tell Severn, a man who apparently knew Keats strolled by and viewed the sculptures 'condescendingly through an eye-glass', and at last said, 'Yes, I believe, Mr. Keats, we may admire these works safely' – William Sharp, *The Life and Letters of Joseph Severn* (1892) p. 32.

7. *Letters*, vol. I, p. 210.

8. Ibid., vol. II, p. 213.

9. The mention of Coleridge's allowing 'a fine isolated verisimilitude' to 'go by' seems ludicrously inept, though forgivable considering how little Keats had read of him. However much Coleridge yearned for system, he could never attain it simply because he was able to let so little 'go by'; and the glory of his critical writing consists in its numerous 'isolated verisimilitudes'.

M. T. Solve

'SHELLEY ON THE IMAGINATION' (1927)

. . . Shelley's was the type of mind which inclines instinctively toward the ideal, and hence, while he recognized that the senses supplied the materials of beauty, he came to believe more and more that the power of mind, the imagination, was the important factor in art. In the *Defence* he distinguishes between reason and imagination.[1] Both work with the materials supplied by sense, but only imagination has the power of making new combinations, or discovering new truth. Imagination is the poetic faculty. By its power the artist creates what is new, yet also relative to the age – new, yet related to the world of sense. As Shelley was more and more driven in upon himself – the things of this world being nothing but disappointments – he found refuge in the transcendental philosophy, and solace in a perfect world of ideas governed by love and beauty. Sometimes this world was thought of as almost wholly within the mind, as in *Prometheus Unbound*; sometimes it existed apart from both mind and the world of things, as in the 'Hymn to Intellectual Beauty', and cast its shadow here; in 'The Zucca', it was imagined as being apart from this low sphere, neither in heaven nor earth. Sometimes the poet confuses the various 'worlds' or slips unconsciously from one to the other, or vainly hopes to find the eternal in the mortal, as in the *Epipsychidion*. Time and space do not exist; human nature is metamorphosed in what seems a moment, and the universe is in an atom.

Shelley's tendency to idealize nature is as clearly shown in his 'Skylark' as anywhere. Really, the actual bird which may have suggested the poem has little place in it. Shelley is interested in an 'unbodied voice' which never was a bird. Yet there is some connection with the world of sense, for he asks,

> What objects are the fountains
>   Of thy happy strain?
> What fields, or waves, or mountains?
>   What shapes of sky or plain?
> What love of thine own kind? what ignorance of pain?

External nature, the life of sense experience, pleasure and pain are sources of song, and often the saddest experiences and thoughts produce the sweetest music. Yet this unbodied voice that sings from the ideal world, or near it, must surpass in joy anything mortal. Could the poet learn half this gladness he could utter such harmonious madness that the world would be forced to listen, as it never listened to Shelley in his lifetime. For most readers would prefer the homely, not the ethereal. Even for our time Burroughs probably expressed the sentiment of the majority when he said he preferred Wordsworth's lark, which joined the kindred points of heaven and home, to Shelley's idealization. His story of the American tourist who went about English fields with Shelley's poem as a guide to the lark's song, and who reported that he found no lark, offers one of the most interesting commentaries ever made on Shelley as a nature poet.[2]

Another interesting commentary on Shelley and his relation to mundane facts has been made by one of the best-known students of Keats. Shelley's *Adonais*, says this critic, is unsurpassed as an utterance of abstract pity and indignation; 'its strain of transcendental consolation for mortal ears contains the most lucid exposition of his philosophy. But of Keats as he actually lived the elegy presents no feature, while the general impression it conveys of his character and fate is erroneous.'[3] Shelley wrote his poem from scant data, and had he possessed the particulars which Gisborne later sent him, his teeming imagination would have been so painfully stimulated that the elegiac sentiment, now so successfully expressed in the poem, would have been destroyed; as he says: 'The enthusiasm of the imagination would have overpowered the sentiment.'[4] The sentiment inspired by the contemplation of the untimely and sudden withdrawal of a noble spirit, Shelley would have agreed, is the valuable part of the poem, 'poetry having nothing to do with the invention of facts'.[5]

These statements must be disconcerting to the realists who hold that good art imitates by holding the mirror up to nature. But Shelley thought that the truth (which is ideal) can be seen only in the imaginative mirror which distorts the facts of nature. Burroughs was himself enough of a poet to recognize that the truth of poetry is of an ideal character. If one knows how to read the poets, he says, they are the best natural historians. But they translate the facts largely and freely. A celebrated lady once said to Turner, 'I confess I cannot see in nature what you do.' 'Ah, Madam,' said the complacent artist, 'don't you wish you could!'[6] . . .

Poetry and the other arts are imitative, but the imitation is the result of desiring to prolong or make permanent an effect which something in nature, or in the relations between men, had made upon the observer. This desire for prolongation of pleasure may coincide with the desire for communication, or merely for expression. The basis of art is, in either case, emotional and not intellectual. Facts as such, while they may be of importance in history or philosophy, would be of no importance in art unless they had a definite emotional value. The marshaling of facts is the work of reason; the selection and combination of materials of sense so as to produce a unified and harmonious result is the work of the poetic faculty, imagination. This power inherent in the mind is able to make out of the materials which it has, forms approaching to ideal perfection, and hence is genuinely creative.[7] Poetry and the other arts in their approximations to the perfect and enduring are thus concerned with the highest truth. When the veiled maid appeared to the Poet in *Alastor*, singing in tones 'like the voice of his own soul',

> Knowledge and truth and virtue were her theme,
> And lofty hopes of divine liberty.

But the imaginative truths of poetry always have to be referred to the emotions in order to determine their validity. Consciously or not it is the satisfaction of an emotional craving which the artist is trying to achieve in a work of art, and when he has found it he recognizes it instantly by the pleasure which attends the representation. Shelley believed that the spark of divinity, the white radiance of eternity which was in everyone, and which could not be entirely obscured by the dome of many-colored glass, made all people aspire toward a more perfect world. Everyone has some imagination, some ability to find truth and beauty, and hence happiness, but poets have this faculty most highly developed. Men in a society find the passions and pleasures of life greatly enriched, and equality, diversity, unity, contrast, and mutual dependence, which are the principles determining their wills to action, also are the principles which 'constitute pleasure in sensation, virtue in sentiment, beauty in art, truth in reasoning, and love in the intercourse of kind'. Love of truth and beauty, hatred of falsehood and error are the underlying principles of society and of art alike. Poetry is the expression of the imagination; the imagination enables us to put ourselves in the place of others, to find what is good in them and to love it. Poetry develops the imagination as exercise develops a limb, and hence is the best socializing agent. Poets, as those having most imagination, are the discoverers of all knowledge, the pioneers in all fields of learning. As they are most sensitive to harmony and best able to produce it, they are the originators of laws, the lawgivers to the world. The arts, then, are in the very closest relationship to life, to morality, to knowledge, and can never become obsolete or useless, as Peacock contended they had already become.[8] They bridge the gap between the temporal and the infinite.

Source: extracts from chapters 4 and 5 of *Shelley: His Theory of Poetry* (New York, 1927; reissued 1964) pp. 103–6, 124–6.

NOTES

1. [See above, Part One, section 4. IV. – Ed.]

2. John Burroughs, 'Birds of the English Poets', *Scribner's Monthly*, VI (1876) 568.

3. Sidney Colvin, *Keats*, 'English Men of Letters' Series (1887) p. 207.

4. To John Gisborne, 16 June, 1821.

5. To Mary, 11 Aug 1821.

6. Burroughs, 'Birds of the English Poets', p. 569.

7. Shelley here was following Sidney. [See Sidney, *Apologie for Poetrie* (1595) – Ed.] Sidney in turn had followed Aristotle in defining poetry as imitation whose purpose was to teach and delight. However, some think that when Sidney explains that those who 'most properly do imitate . . . borrow nothing of what is, hath been, or shall be; but range only, reined with learned discretion, into the divine consideration of what may be and should be', he goes much further into the region of the ideal than Aristotle meant to go. Shelley without doubt agreed wholly with Sidney in this interpretation of the meaning of imitation. Like Sidney, he believed that the poet remade nature and man, creating things and characters superior to nature.

8. Cf. *The Four Ages of Poetry* (1820).

Graham Hough

'SHELLEY'S *DEFENCE OF POETRY*' (1953)

It remains to say something of Shelley's beliefs about the nature and functions of poetry. There is something to be found in the letters (though his letters are not nearly so illuminating as those of Keats); much in the prefatory notes to the poems; but the principal place is the *Defence of Poetry*. There seems always to have been some uncertainty in Shelley's mind between didactic and purely artistic aims; but there is little doubt that the first predominate. The preface to the *Revolt of Islam* describes the poem as an experiment on the public mind to discover 'how far a thirst for a happier condition of moral or political society' has survived the tempests of the times. Shelley goes on to say, 'I have sought to enlist the harmony of metrical language, the ethereal combinations of the fancy, the rapid and subtle transitions of human passion, all those elements which essentially compose a poem, in the cause of a liberal and comprehensive morality'. It will be noted that 'all the elements which essentially compose a poem' are enlisted as subordinates in a moral cause that is separate from themselves. Writing to Peacock in January 1819, at the time of the composition of *Prometheus*, Shelley says quite bluntly, 'I consider poetry very subordinate to moral and political science'. In similar vein he confesses in the preface to *Prometheus* to 'a passion for reforming the world': yet adds 'it is a mistake to suppose that I dedicate my compositions solely to the direct enforcement of reform. . . . Didactic poetry is my abhorrence; nothing can be equally well expressed in prose that is not tedious and supererogatory in verse.' A contradiction is apparent, but it is reconciled in the passage that follows.

My purpose has hitherto been simply to familiarize the highly refined imagination of the more select classes of poetical readers with beautiful idealisms of moral excellence, aware that until the mind can love and admire and trust, and hope and endure, reasoned principles of moral conduct are seeds cast upon the highway of life which the unconscious passengers trample into dust, although they would bear the harvest of his happiness.

Poetry is to work by its own imaginative processes, but the aim is still to awaken and stimulate the moral sense. From this point of view Shelley never departed, and the *Defence of Poetry* is largely an expansion of it.

The *Defence of Poetry* appeared in 1821. It was originally intended to be a reply to a pamphlet by Peacock, *The Four Ages of Poetry*. This is a brilliant piece of work, satirical and only half serious, which maintains that in the current era of science and philosophy the poet is a relic of primitive barbarism 'wallowing in the rubbish of departed ignorance, and raking up the ashes of dead savages to find gewgaws and rattles for the grown babies of the age'. Shelley was indignant and resolved to break a lance with him. But what results is something different from a mere answer to Peacock; it is an exalted defence of the honours of poetry and the imagination, an extension of the tradition of Sidney and the Renaissance champions of the Muses, and the best statement in English of the early Romantic theory of poetry. Coleridge attempts to give his ideas a philosophical foundation which Shelley is content to assume; and he is more attractive to the speculative mind because it is never quite clear exactly what he is saying. Wordsworth's preface seems a more massive piece of polemic. But Shelley is a clearer expositor than either of these more celebrated theorists – and he remains a poet even in his prose. The *Defence* is itself a work of art – a claim which could not be made for the prose writings of Wordsworth or Coleridge.

He begins by stating as an axiom what Coleridge tries to prove – the power of the imagination to perceive, in some sense, essential reality with a directness impossible to the discursive faculties. His language here is partly Coleridgean; and since he had read *Biographia Literaria* in the year of its appearance, we need not doubt that this is the source of his theory of the imagination and its functions. Poetry is the expression of the imagination, and it has access, therefore, to this special kind of imaginative knowledge. All men have some imagination, so all are in some degree poets. But there is an absolute standard of beauty, to which every artistic representation approximates more or less closely. The poet is simply the man whose faculties for approximation to this standard are exceptionally great. Since he is able then to express essential truth in the form of beauty, from which all men of uncorrupted taste receive pleasure, the poet is not only the inventor of the arts, but the institutor of laws and the founder of civil society. Without him the beauty of order and the beauty of holiness would never have been perceived; and if their beauty had never been perceived, they would never have been desired. The poet is even a prophet, for by seeing the present as it really is he sees in it the seeds of the future.

A critical passage on the distinction between prose and poetry follows (Shelley does not equate poetry with verse; for him Plato and Bacon are poets); and there is a passage, Aristotelian in origin, but echoed by all the great Romantics, about the Universality of poetry. Then succeeds a long panoramic survey of poetry from Homer onwards, which occupies the bulk of the essay. Historical surveys of this kind are apt to date. Shelley's is remarkably fresh; and the whole passage is a testimony to the extent and sensitiveness of his reading. Its purpose is to show the effect of poetry on society, and to show that 'the presence or absence of poetry in its most perfect and universal form, has been found to be connected with good or evil in conduct or habit'. The reason for this is at the core of Shelley's belief.

The great secret of morals is love; or a going out of our own nature, and an identification of ourselves with the beautiful which exists in thought, action or person, not our own. A man, to be greatly good, must imagine intensely and comprehensively; he must put himself in the place of another, and of many others; the pains and pleasures of his species must become his own. The great instrument of moral good is the imagination; and poetry ministers to the effect by acting upon the cause.

An objection to many such lofty transcendental claims for poetry is that they fail to account for minor poetry and the lesser kinds. To this Shelley provides an admirable answer. Without interrupting the majestic sweep of his own theory, he does beautiful justice to the more modest kinds of imaginative writing. Such compositions, he says, may be read simply as fragments or isolated portions; but the more perceptive will 'recognize them as episodes to that great poem, which all poets, like the co-operating thoughts of one great mind, have built up since the beginning of the world'.

In modern times (and here the specific answer to Peacock begins) 'poets have been challenged to resign the civic crown to reasoners and mechanists' – on the plea of utility. Shelley opposes this, on hedonist and utilitarian grounds. Utility is whatever conduces to pleasure. But it has a narrow and a wider sense. The first is all that satisfies the mere animal needs, that conduces to transitory pleasure: the second is whatever strengthens and purifies the affections, enlarges the understanding, and conduces to durable and universal pleasure. It is to this second kind of utility that poetry contributes. We owe a debt of gratitude to the philosophers, to Locke, Hume, Gibbon, Voltaire and Rousseau: but if they had never lived

a little more nonsense would have been talked for a century or two; and perhaps a few more men, women and children burnt as heretics. We might not at this moment be congratulating ourselves on the abolition of the inquisition in Spain

– but without the poets and creative artists the moral condition of mankind would be inconceivably degraded; for the analytical reason can itself do nothing to arouse men's generous faculties. The passage which follows has even more relevance today than when it was written.

We have more moral, political and historical wisdom than we know how to reduce into practice: we have more scientific and economical knowledge than can be accommodated to the just distribution of the produce which it multiplies. . . . There is no want of knowledge respecting what is wisest and best in morals, government and political economy, or at least what is wiser and better than what men now practise and endure. But we want the creative faculty to imagine that which we know; we want the generous impulse to act on that which we imagine; we want the poetry of life. . . .

The cultivation of poetry is never more to be desired than at periods when, from an excess of the calculating principle, the accumulation of the materials of external life exceed the quantity of the power of assimilating them to the internal laws of human nature.

It is evident enough that by this time poetry has become something very different from making verses. It includes all the means by which the sympathetic and generous emotions are aroused. But of these the arts are the chief. Since imagination shows us the real nature of the world it inevitably takes us out of the small circle of self-regarding feeling. Since it sounds the depths of human nature it shows not only the goings on in the poet's mind, but in the mind of the age, and can see in them the germs of the future. Hence when Shelley in his final paragraph calls the poets 'the mirrors of the gigantic shadows which futurity casts upon the present', he is not merely using a rhetorical phrase, but expressing a real conviction — that the poet's intuitions often show him the direction in which the world is moving more clearly than the speculations of the political philosopher. And it would not be hard to find examples to substantiate this claim. But from this we pass to the final phrase: 'Poets are the unacknowledged legislators of the world'; we look forward into the succeeding century and observe that if the poets are legislators they have some very formidable competitors — soldiers, historians, economists, physicists. All that Shelley says about the gap between our natural science and our moral ability to use it is manifestly true — but is it really the business of poetry to bridge the gulf?

Many later nineteenth-century writers agreed that it was. Poetry, for Arnold, is to replace religion as the guide and teacher of mankind: for Pater and his successors, art itself is to become a sort of religion. Shelley's argument is more reasoned and his position stronger than theirs. It is a poor thing not to feel the purity and generosity of his enthusiasm; but there is, after all, a fallacy in the Romantic apology for poetry, as in all later attempts to save the world by literature; two senses of the word poetry are confused. Poetry as the whole imaginative and sympathetic life of man is one thing; poetry the work of art is another; and to transfer what is true of the first bodily to the second is only rhetorically effective. In Shelley's philosophical system there is always a gap between the wretched actuality and the radiant and possible ideal. In some of his expository prose writing, he is prepared to fill it laboriously by the methods of patient reformism. But his imagination was more impatient: the gap must be bridged by a spark, and the spark is to be poetry. Poetry becomes the instrument of redemption; it invades the territory of faith and sets up a succession of short-lived governments: while a horde of intrusive busybodies in the meantime invade its own domain. The generous confusion of the nineteenth century has begun.

SOURCE: extract from chapter 4 of *The Romantic Poets* (London, 1953; 2nd ed. 1957; reprinted 1970) pp. 150–5.

D. L. Clark

'IMAGINATION IN SHELLEY'S *DEFENCE OF POETRY*' (1954)

Shelley mainly insists on the moral value of poetry. Since poetry is fundamentally the product of the *creative imagination* and since a high state of civilization can be achieved only through insight into the moral problems facing men, and since sympathy and love are the very basis of moral life, and finally since love and sympathy can be awakened only by the active imagination, it follows that poetry, in the broad sense in which Shelley uses the word, is the *sine qua non* of the *Good Life*. Thus Shelley, in the main current of thought in his day, and particularly as seen in the philosophy of Adam Smith and David Hume, exalts imagination to the level of reason.

There is little or nothing of the mystic, the Platonist, or neo-Platonist in this essay. Shelley's position is a demonstrable fact, and the present chaotic condition of the world is ample proof of that. Our moral and social sciences have lagged behind the practical or natural sciences until we have more knowledge than we know how to use for achieving happiness! The creative imagination has been lulled to sleep to the persuasive hymns in praise of the active, the practical life. In a most eloquent portion of the essay, the author states his main theme: 'We have more moral, political, and historical wisdom than we know how to reduce into practice; we have more scientific and economic knowledge than can be accommodated to the just distribution of the produce which it multiplies. . . . We want the creative faculty to imagine that which we know; we want the generous impulse to act that which we imagine; we want the poetry of life; our calculations have outrun our conception; we have eaten more than we can digest. . . . Man having enslaved the elements remains himself a slave.' Or in other words in ferreting out the secret of the atom, man has made the achievement of the Good Life possible, but men lack the imaginative insight and moral courage to put the atom to work for the happiness of mankind. With 'mere reasoners' – as Shelley would say – as our leaders, we have only the insight of cavemen, preparing for another Dark Ages.

SOURCE: extract from *Shelley's Prose, or the Trumpet of a Prophecy* (Albuquerque, New Mexico, 1954; corrected edition 1966) p. 276.

J. E. Baker

IMAGINATION; *NOUS*; IMAGINATIVE REASON (1965)

'Plato was essentially a poet', says Shelley, because of 'the melody of his language', his ability 'to kindle a harmony in thoughts', and 'the truth and splendour of his imagery'. Thus 'the popular division into prose and verse is inadmissible', and 'the distinction between poets and prose writers is a vulgar error'.[1] We must keep this in mind when we find Shelley desiderating literary art as a *sine qua non* for our knowledge of the principles on which the social virtues are based. This may be illustrated by the very style in which Shelley says it: 'What were virtue, love, patriotism, friendship . . . if poetry did not ascend to bring light and fire from those eternal regions where the owl-winged faculty of calculation dare not soar?'[2]

Shelley's emphasis is in line with the 'neo-Platonic abandonment of Imitation, in favor of Imagination', referred to by Sikes:

Philostratus gave a new content to the term φαντασια: Pheidias and Praxiteles are not imitative but imaginative. . . . Plotinus settled the matter by his pronouncement that the arts 'go back to the reasons from which nature comes; and further they create much out of themselves and add to that which is defective, as being themselves in possession of beauty'. Plato's aesthetic was finally convicted by his own idealism.[3]

In 'On the Symposium', Shelley mentions both the rational and the imaginative aspects of his master's mind:

Plato exhibits the rare union of close and subtle logic with the Pythian enthusiasm of poetry, melted by the splendour and harmony of his periods into one irresistible stream of musical impressions, which hurry the persuasions onward, as in a breathless career. . . . His excellence consists especially in intuition, and it is this faculty which raises him above Aristotle. . . .[4]

– though the latter's genius is also 'vivid and various'.

Imagination does not merely create. What it perceives is real. Shelley carries this line of thought farther than most Platonists would. According to him, there is a *truth* of imagery. Even metaphor and rhythm are not arbitrary inventions; they discover something that was already there. (This view represents the opposite extreme from that which he sketched in his piece 'On Life', that 'Nothing exists but as it is perceived.')[5] Those in whom the

faculty of approximation to the beautiful . . . exists in excess are poets, in the most universal sense of the world. . . . Their language is vitally metaphorical; that is, it marks the before unapprehended relations of things. . . . These similitudes or relations are finely said by Lord Bacon to be 'the same footsteps of nature impressed upon the various subjects of the world' and he considers the faculty which perceives them as the storehouse of axioms common to all knowledge.[6]

And a few pages later Shelley recurs to this subject, designating three activities of poets: creative ('they are inventors'); metaphorical ('their words unveil the permanent analogy of things by images which participate in the life of truth'); and sensuous – and even in this third aspect poets are imitating something permanently real ('as their periods are harmonious and rhythmical, . . . being the echo of the eternal music'). In the very sentence from which these three passages have been quoted, Shelley is applying them to 'all the authors of revolutions in opinion' to show that they are 'necessarily poets'. For example, 'Lord Bacon was a poet'. And on the other hand 'Shakespeare, Dante, and Milton . . . are philosophers of the very loftiest power'.[7] Here the Platonic tradition comes full circle. Plato banished the poets. Now Bacon, whose rationalistic utilitarianism is more extreme than that of Plato, is praised as a poet, and admitted to the company of the great philosopher Milton!

To create literature requires not merely *phantasia*, fancy, but what Plato himself called *nous*, which we can now, following Coleridge's distinction, translate *reason*. But Shelley often used the word 'reason' for 'the owl-winged faculty of calculation' that

Coleridge labeled mere 'understanding'. Shelley was following eighteenth-century terminology, Coleridge reviving a Renaissance concept. Michael Roberts has shown that in some ways

the history of English and French philosophy in the eighteenth century is, in the main, the history of the gradual restriction of the concept of reason. And at the same time, because some name must be used for that which is felt to exist, it is the history of the growth and widening of the concept of 'imagination'.

Reason had been regarded as man's highest faculty at a time when it meant right judgment and the use of every kind of awareness. It was still regarded as man's highest faculty, though now its meaning had been narrowed down to the recognition of plain material facts and matter-of-fact logic. Something which had been necessary to make it worthy of such respect had evaporated. . . . The something which had evaporated, Coleridge proposed to call 'imagination'.[8]

– and so did Shelley. But 'to Coleridge, knowledge and truth and reason still meant a capacity for right judgment and for decisions involving the whole man'. The best solution of the terminological conflict was perhaps Matthew Arnold's fusion of the terms into the phrase 'imaginative reason'. That is the Platonic *nous*.

It is the mere Coleridgean 'understanding' Shelley means when, in the first paragraph of his *Defence*, he writes concerning the 'principle of analysis': 'Reason is the enumeration of quantities already known; imagination is the perception of the value of those quantities, both separately and as a whole. Reason respects the differences, and imagination the similitudes of things.' Noteworthy indeed is his assumption that the imagination, too, is cognitive, is a means of knowing.

And Shelley was not always willing to cede the word *reason* to the rationalists. With the Bodleian manuscript sources of *A Defence of Poetry*, Mr. A. H. Koszul found and printed fragments from a translation by Shelley of a passage from Plato's *Ion* that is used in the *Defence*. It is remarkable that in this translation Shelley manages to avoid saying what his fuller published translation of the *Ion* says, that the poets are like those 'who lose all control over their reason' and that the poet cannot compose 'whilst any reason remains in him'. E.g., for the latter he substitutes 'until understanding be no longer in him'.[9] And in an addition to his Proposed Letter to Ollier, the Editor of the *Literary Miscellany*, Shelley wrote of Peacock, 'He would extinguish Imagination which is the Sun of life, and grope his way by the cold and uncertain and borrowed light of that moon *which he calls* Reason, stumbling over the interlunar chasm of time where she deserts us. . . .' (Italics mine.) 'But let us *in true sense* place within the scan of reason an opinion so light. . . .'[10]

Nevertheless, when he came to write his *Defence* he allowed Peacock's eighteenth-century, or *philosophe*, meaning for the term *reason*, and thus planted in his essay a fruitful source of misinterpretation, tempting us to think it more romantic, less Platonic, than it really is.

SOURCE: extract from *Shelley's Platonic Answer to a Platonic Attack on Poetry* (Iowa City, 1965) pp. 26–9.

NOTES

1. Page references for the *Defence of Poetry* are to *Shelley: Selected Poems, Essays, and Letters*, ed. Ellsworth Barnard (New York, 1944). The present reference is to pp. 534–5.
2. Ibid., p. 561.
3. E. E. Sikes, *The Greek View of Poetry* (London, 1931) pp. 238–9.
4. *Shelley's Literary and Philosophical Criticism*, ed. J. Shawcross (London, 1909) pp. 41–2.
5. Ibid., p. 56, dated 1815 by Shawcross.
6. *Defence*, p. 532.
7. Ibid., p. 536.
8. Michael Roberts, *The Modern Mind* (London, 1937) pp. 123, 139.
9. *Shelley's Prose in the Bodleian Manuscripts*, ed. A. H. Koszul (London, 1910) p. 121; Shelley's translation of the *Ion* in *Essays, Letters from Abroad, Translations and Fragments*, ed. Mrs Shelley (London, 1840) vol. I, pp. 282–3.
10. Koszul, pp. 119–20.

SELECT BIBLIOGRAPHY

GENERAL AND BACKGROUND STUDIES

M. H. Abrams, *The Mirror and the Lamp: Romantic Theory and the Critical Tradition* (London and New York: O. U. P., 1953; New York: Norton, 1958; New York: O. U. P., 1971) esp. pp. 156–83.

W. J. Bate, *From Classic to Romantic: Premises of Taste in Eighteenth-Century England* (Cambridge, Mass.: Harvard U.P., 1946; London: Cumberlege, 1946; New York: Harper, 1961).

W. J. Bate and J. Bullitt, 'Distinctions between Fancy and Imagination in Eighteenth-Century Criticism', *Modern Language Notes*, LX (1945) 8–15.

R. L. Brett, *Fancy and Imagination* (Critical Idiom Series) (London: Methuen, 1969; New York: Harper & Row, 1969).

M. Kallich, 'The Association of Ideas and Critical Theory: Hobbes, Locke, and Addison', *Journal of English Literary History*, XII (1945) 290–315.

D. Perkins, *The Quest for Permanence: The Symbolism of Wordsworth, Shelley, and Keats* (Cambridge, Mass.: Harvard U.P., 1959; London: O. U. P., 1959).

H. W. Piper, *The Active Universe: Pantheism and the Concept of Imagination in the English Romantic Poets* (London: Athlone Press, 1962; New York: O. U. P., 1962).

E. L. Tuveson, *The Imagination as a Means of Grace: Locke and the Aesthetics of Romanticism* (Berkeley: California U.P., 1960; London: Cambridge U.P., 1960).

G. G. Watson, 'Contributions to a Dictionary of Critical Terms: Imagination and Fancy', *Essays in Criticism*, III (1953) 201–14.

WILLIAM BLAKE

P. F. Fisher, *The Valley of Vision: Blake as Prophet and Revolutionary* (Toronto: Univ. of Toronto Press, 1961 (repr. 1971); London: O. U. P., 1962).

N. Frye, *Fearful Symmetry: A Study of William Blake* (Princeton, N. J.: Princeton U.P., 1947; London: Cumberlege, 1947; Boston: Beacon Press, 1962).

R. F. Gleckner, 'Blake's Religion of the Imagination', *Journal of Aesthetics and Art Criticism*, x (1951) 35-42.

M. D. Paley, *Energy and the Imagination: A Study of the Development of Blake's Thought* (Oxford: Clarendon Press, 1970).

K. Raine, *Blake and Tradition*, 2 vols (London: Routledge & Kegan Paul, 1969; Princeton, N. J.: Princeton U.P., 1969).

W. B. Yeats, 'William Blake and the Imagination', *Academy*, 19 June 1897; in *Essays and Introductions* (London: Macmillan, 1924; repr. 1961.)

SAMUEL TAYLOR COLERIDGE

J. A. Appleyard, *Coleridge's Philosophy of Literature: The Development of a Concept of Poetry, 1791-1819* (Cambridge, Mass: Harvard U.P., 1965; London: O. U. P., 1965).

I. Babbitt, 'Coleridge and Imagination', *On Being Creative and Other Essays* (Boston and New York: Houghton Mifflin, 1932; London: Constable, 1932) pp. 97-133. Originally appeared in *The Nineteenth Century and After*, cvi (1929) 383-98.

J. V. Baker, *The Sacred River: Coleridge's Theory of the Imagination* (Baton Rouge: Louisiana State U.P., 1957; London: O. U. P., 1957; New York: Greenwood Press, 1969).

W. J. Bate, 'Coleridge on the Function of Art', in H. Levin (ed.), *Perspectives in Criticism* (Cambridge, Mass.: Harvard U.P., 1950; London: Cumberlege, 1950) pp. 125-59.

J. B. Beer, *Coleridge the Visionary* (London: Chatto & Windus, 1959; New York: Collier Books, 1962).

N. Brooke, 'Coleridge's "True and Original Realism"', *Durham University Journal*, new ser., xxii (1960) 58-69.

T. S. Eliot, *The Use of Poetry and the Use of Criticism* (London: Faber, 1933; Cambridge, Mass.: Harvard U.P., 1933; Faber reprints 1964, 1967, 1970, 1975).

R. H. Fogle, *The Idea of Coleridge's Criticism* (Berkeley: Univ. of California Press, 1962; London: C.U.P., 1962).

H. House, *Coleridge* (Clark Lectures 1951-2) (London: Hart-Davis, 1953; Toronto: Clarke, Irwin, 1953; repr. 1969).

P. Æ. Hutchings, 'Imagination: "as the Sun paints in the camera obscura"', *Journal of Aesthetics and Art Criticism*, xxix (1970-1) 63-76.

D. G. James, *Scepticism and Poetry: An Essay on the Poetic Imagination* (London: Allen & Unwin, 1937; repr. 1960).

F. R. Leavis, 'Coleridge in Criticism', *Scrutiny*, IX (1940) 57–69.

J. L. Lowes, *The Road to Xanadu: A Study in the Ways of the Imagination* (Boston: Houghton Mifflin, 1927; London: Constable, 1927; revised and enlarged ed. 1930; New York: Random House (Vintage Books), 1959; London: Constable, 1961, 1966).

T. McFarland, 'The Origin and Significance of Coleridge's Theory of Secondary Imagination', in G. Hartman (ed.), *New Perspectives on Coleridge and Wordsworth* (New York: Columbia U.P., 1972) pp. 195–246.

G. McKenzie, *Organic Unity in Coleridge* (Berkeley: California U.P., 1939).

S. Prickett, *Coleridge and Wordsworth: The Poetry of Growth* (Cambridge: C.U.P., 1970).

F. B. Rainsberry, 'Coleridge and the Paradox of the Poetic Imperative', *Journal of English Literary History*, XXI (1954) 114–45.

I. A. Richards, *Coleridge on Imagination* (London: Routledge, 1934; New York: Harcourt, 1934; 3rd ed. 1962).

Robert Penn Warren, 'A Poem of Pure Imagination' [*The Ancient Mariner*], *Kenyon Review*, VIII (1946) 391–427; repr. in Warren's *Selected Essays* (New York: Random House, 1958; London: Eyre & Spottiswoode, 1964) pp. 222–61.

WILLIAM WORDSWORTH

Matthew Arnold, 'Wordsworth', *Essays in Criticism: Second Series* (London, 1888).

S. K. Das, *Wordsworth on Imagination* (Calcutta: Pioneer Publications, 1973).

G. H. Hartman, *Wordsworth's Poetry, 1787–1814* (New Haven and London: Yale U.P., 1964).

R. D. Havens, *The Mind of a Poet*, 2 vols (Baltimore: Johns Hopkins, 1941; repr. 1967) esp. vol. I, pp. 203–65.

E. D. Hirsch, Jr, *Wordsworth and Schelling: A Typological Study of Romanticism* (New Haven: Yale U.P., 1960; London: O. U. P., 1960; New York: Archon Books, 1971) esp. pp. 98–146.

John Jones, *The Egotistical Sublime: A History of Wordsworth's Imagination* (London: Chatto & Windus, 1954; repr. 1964).

K. MacLean, 'Levels of Imagination in Wordsworth's *Prelude* (1805)', *Philological Quarterly*, XXXVIII (1959) 385–400.

W. J. B. Owen, *Wordsworth as Critic* (Toronto: Toronto U.P., 1969; London: O. U. P., 1969).

A. S. Pfeffer, 'Wordsworth on Imagination', *Publications of the Modern Language Association*, LXXXIV (1969) 141–4.

F. A. Pottle, 'The Eye and the Object in the Poetry of Wordsworth', in G. T. Dunklin (ed.), *Wordsworth: Centenary Studies Presented at Cornell and Princeton Universities* (Princeton: Princeton U.P., 1951; London: Cumberlege, 1951) pp. 23–42; repr. in H. Bloom (ed.), *Romanticism and Consciousness: Essays in Criticism* (New York: Norton, 1970) pp. 273–87.

Melvin Rader, *Wordsworth, A Philosophical Approach* (London: O. U. P., 1967; Oxford: Clarendon Press, 1967).

J. L. Scoggins, *Imagination and Fancy: Complementary Modes in the Poetry of Wordsworth* (Lincoln: Nebraska U.P., 1966).

N. P. Stallknecht, *Strange Seas of Thought: Studies in William Wordsworth's Philosophy of Man and Nature* (Bloomington: Indiana U.P., 1958; London: Mark Paterson, 1958; repr. 1966).

D. Stempel, 'Revelation on Mount Snowdon: Wordsworth, Coleridge, and the Fichtean Imagination', *Journal of Aesthetics and Art Criticism*, XXIX (1970–1) 371–84.

C. D. Thorpe, 'The Imagination: Coleridge *versus* Wordsworth', *Philological Quarterly*, XVIII (1939) 1–18.

M. Wildi, 'Wordsworth and the Simplon Pass', *English Studies*, XL (1959) 224–32.

WILLIAM HAZLITT

W. P. Albrecht, *Hazlitt and the Creative Imagination* (Lawrence: Kansas U.P., 1965).

H. Baker, *William Hazlitt* (Cambridge, Mass.: Harvard U.P., 1962; London: O. U. P., 1962).

J. Bullitt, 'Hazlitt and the Romantic Conception of the Imagination', *Philological Quarterly*, XXIV (1945) 343–61.

R. E. Cain, 'David Hume and Adam Smith as Sources of the Concept of Sympathy in Hazlitt', *Papers on Language and Literature*, I (1965) 133–40.

W. R. Niblett, 'Hazlitt's Contribution to Literary Criticism', *Durham University Journal*, new ser., II (1941) 211–22.

R. Park, *Hazlitt and the Spirit of the Age: Abstraction and Critical Theory* (Oxford: Clarendon Press, 1971).

E. Schneider, *The Æsthetics of William Hazlitt: A Study of the Philosophical Basis of his Criticism* (Philadelphia: Pennsylvania U.P., 1933; London: Milford, 1933).

JOHN KEATS

M. L. D'Avanzo, *Keats's Metaphors for the Poetic Imagination* (Durham, N. C.: Duke U.P., 1967).

C. L. Finney, *The Evolution of Keats's Poetry*, 2 vols (Cambridge, Mass.: Harvard U.P., 1936; London: Milford, 1936; New York: Russell & Russell, 1963).

N. F. Ford, *The Prefigurative Imagination of John Keats* (Stanford: Stanford U.P., 1952; London: O. U. P., 1952).

H. W. Garrod, *Keats* (Oxford: Clarendon Press, 1939).

P. W. Glenn, 'Keats's *Lamia*: The Imagination Brought Beyond its Proper Bound', *Proceedings of the Conference of College Teachers of English of Texas*, XXXVII (1972) 34−40.

K. Muir, 'Keats and Hazlitt', in K. Muir (ed.), *John Keats: A Reassessment* (Liverpool: Liverpool U.P., 1958; repr. 1969) pp. 139−58.

R. M. Ryan, 'Keats and the Truth of Imagination', *The Wordsworth Circle*, IV (1973) 259−66.

H. M. Sikes, 'The Poetic Theory and Practice of Keats: The Record of a Debt to Hazlitt', *Philological Quarterly*, XXXVIII (1959) 401−12.

S. M. Sperry, 'Keats and the Chemistry of Poetic Creation', *Publications of the Modern Language Association*, LXXXV (1970) 268−77.

S. M. Sperry, *Keats the Poet* (Princeton, N. J.: Princeton U.P., 1973).

C. D. Thorpe, 'Keats and Hazlitt: A Record of Personal Relationship and a Critical Estimate', *Publications of the Modern Language Association*, LXII (1947) 487−502.

PERCY BYSSHE SHELLEY

Fanny Delisle, *A Study of Shelley's 'A Defence of Poetry': A Textual and Critical Evaluation*, 2 vols (Salzburg: Institut für Englische Sprache und Literatur, 1974).

J. E. Jordan (ed.), *Shelley's 'A Defence of Poetry'; Peacock's 'Four Ages of Poetry'* (New York: Bobbs-Merrill, 1965).

J. A. Notopoulos, *The Platonism of Shelley: A Study of Platonism and the Poetic Mind* (Durham, N. C.: Duke U.P., 1949; New York: Octagon Books, 1969).

E. J. Schulze, *Shelley's Theory of Poetry: A Reappraisal* (The Hague and Paris: Mouton, 1967).

E. R. Wasserman, 'Shelley's Last Poetics: A Reconsideration', in F. W.

Hilles and H. Bloom (eds), *From Sensibility to Romanticism* (New York: O. U. P., 1965) pp. 487−511.

B. Weaver, 'Shelley: Values and Imagination', *American Scholar*, III (1934) 404−12.

NOTES ON CONTRIBUTORS

JOSEPH E. BAKER, Emeritus Professor of English at the University of Iowa, is the author of *The Novel and the Oxford Movement* (1932); he is also an editor of Browning and of other Victorian poets.

WALTER JACKSON BATE is Lowell Professor of Humanities at Harvard University. His major publications include *From Classic to Romantic* (1946), *The Achievement of Samuel Johnson* (1955), *John Keats* (1963), *Coleridge* (1968); he has also edited volumes II to V in the Yale edition of Samuel Johnson's works.

SIR MAURICE BOWRA (1898–1971) was Warden of Wadham College, Oxford. He served as Professor of Poetry (1946–51) and as Vice-Chancellor (1951–4) of Oxford University; in 1971 he was made a Companion of Honour for his services to literature. Best known for his studies in Classical literature, his publications include *Sophoclean Tragedy* (1944), *From Virgil to Milton* (1945), *Heroic Poetry* (1952), *Inspiration and Poetry* (1955), *In General and Particular* (1964), *Landmarks in Greek Literature* (1966).

DAVID LEE CLARK (1887–1956) was Professor of English in the University of Texas at Austin; he is the author of *Charles Brockden Brown: Pioneer Voice of America* (1952) and co-author of *The Voices of England and America* (1941).

BARBARA HARDY, Professor of English at Birkbeck College in the University of London, has written extensively on the Romantics and Victorians. Her publications include *The Novels of George Eliot* (1959), *The Appropriate Form* (1964), *The Moral Art of Dickens* (1970), and *Jane Austen* (1975).

J. A. W. HEFFERNAN is Associate Professor of English at Dartmouth College in Hanover, New Hampshire. He has published a number of important papers on Wordsworth's imagination in *Publications of the Modern Language Association*, *English Studies*, and *Studies in English Literature*.

GRAHAM HOUGH was, until his retirement (1975), Professor of English at Darwin College, Cambridge. His numerous publications include *The Last Romantics* (1949), *Image and Experience* (1960), *A Preface to the Faerie Queene* (1962), *Style and Stylistics* (1969) and *Selected Essays* (1978).

J. R. DE J. JACKSON, Professor of English at Victoria College in the University of Toronto, has written widely on Coleridge. He has also edited *Coleridge: The Critical Heritage* (1970) and is editing both the *Logic* and the shorter works and fragments for the *Collected Coleridge*, sponsored by the Bollingen Foundation.

JOHN SHAWCROSS (1871–1966) was a graduate of University College, Oxford where he took a First in Literis Graecis et Latinis in 1892. He edited *Shelley's Literary and Philosophical Criticism* (1909).

M. T. SOLVE is Emeritus Professor of English at the University of Arizona. He was for many years Associate Editor of the *Arizona Quarterly*.

CLARENCE DEWITT THORPE (1887–1959), Professor of English at the University of Michigan (Ann Arbor), wrote widely on the English Romantic poets. He is the author of *The Aesthetic Theory of Thomas Hobbes* (1940) and co-editor of *The Major English Romantic Poets: A Symposium in Reappraisal* (1957).

RENÉ WELLEK is Sterling Emeritus Professor of Comparative Literature at Yale University. His many publications include *Immanuel Kant in England* (1931), *The Rise of English Literary History* (1941), *Concepts of Criticism* (1963).

BASIL WILLEY (died 1978) taught for many years at Cambridge and held the Edward VII chair in English Literature. He wrote widely on English literature and his books include *The Seventeenth-Century Background* (1934), *The Eighteenth-Century Background* (1940), *More Nineteenth-Century Studies* (1956), *Darwin and Butler: Two Versions of Evolution* (1959), *Samuel Taylor Coleridge* (1972).

INDEX